A QUANTUM LEAP IN
THE WRONG DIRECTION?

What has development and democracy been for India in the last five years? The current Indian political discourse leaves the average citizen wedged between the intersection of wilful misinformation and bewildering statistics. Reliable data has been suppressed with deliberate intent. A clear, lucid, rational analysis is critical to understand our reality. The authors of this important collection show how reliable data, statistics, and sharp analysis can be genuinely used to show why the Modi years are, indeed, a 'quantum leap' backward, for India's democracy and development.

ARUNA ROY
Social and political activist

Dissection of government economic policies, and of their impact on people, is a much needed democratic exercise—particularly when elections are near. This collection of articles is such an attempt. It is to the credit of the authors that they have managed to arrive at what I think is a credible assessment, despite much difficulty in accessing reliable data because of delays and obfuscation that have become an unfortunate unprecedented feature of recent releases (or withholding) of official data. The authors' findings add considerable ballast to the argument that the impact of the present government's economic policies has largely been regressive. Although the other side in the debate is bound to contest this conclusion, the present collection definitely raises the bar to cross for those who would claim that promises of *Acche Din* have mostly been met.

ABHIJIT SEN
Former member, Planning Commission of India

The authors of this volume have done a great service to the Indian people who are about to participate in what is undoubtedly the most decisive election in our recent history. To choose wisely, the people need to be correctly informed about the state of the country. And information is precisely what is being denied to them. Even statistics from official sources which show the government's performance in a poor light are being suppressed. This undermines our democracy. It is in this context that this group of young scholars has sought to present in this book a true picture of the performance of the NDA-II government. Their courage and commitment to democracy is commendable.

PRABHAT PATNAIK
Professor Emeritus, Centre for Economic Studies and Planning, JNU

In times when state institutions, political power, and mass media are being used to mask the truth, this volume's insistence on laying bare plain, if inconvenient, facts about the record of Modi Raj is an act of patriotism. A must read for all citizens before they vote in the momentous election of 2019.

YOGENDRA YADAV
National President, Swaraj India

A QUANTUM LEAP IN THE WRONG DIRECTION?

Edited by

Rohit Azad
Shouvik Chakraborty
Srinivasan Ramani
Dipa Sinha

with a Foreword by

Jayati Ghosh

Orient BlackSwan

ORIENT BLACKSWAN PRIVATE LIMITED

Registered Office
3-6-752 Himayatnagar, Hyderabad 500 029 (Telangana), India
e-mail: centraloffice@orientblackswan.com

Other Offices
Bangaluru, Bhopal, Chennai, Guwahati, Hyderabad, Jaipur, Kolkata,
Lucknow, Mumbai, New Delhi, Noida, Patna, Visakhapatnam

© Orient BlackSwan, 2019
First published by Orient Blackswan Pvt. Ltd 2019

ISBN 978-93-5287-618-1

Typeset in
Adobe Garamond Pro 11/13.8
by Le Studio Graphique, Gurgaon 122 001

Printed in India at
Yash Printographics, Noida

Published by
Orient Blackswan Private Limited
3-6-752, Himayatnagar, Hyderabad 500 029
e-mail: info@orientblackswan.com

Contents

List of Tables and Figures — *vii*
List of Abbreviations — *xiii*
Foreword — *xxi*
Jayati Ghosh
Acknowledgements — *xxv*

Introduction — 1
Rohit Azad, Srinivasan Ramani,
Shouvik Chakraborty, and Dipa Sinha

Part I: The Economy

1. Modi Sarkar — 17
The Truth of *Sabka Saath, Sabka Vikas*
Rohit Azad

2. Breaking Bad — 41
India's Banking Distress
Prasenjit Bose and Zico Dasgupta

3. The NDA-II Regime and the Worsening Agrarian Crisis — 66
Arindam Banerjee and Ishan Anand

4. Employment Under the NDA-II Regime — 89
A Reality Check
Subhanil Chowdhury

PART II: SOCIO-ECONOMIC INDICATORS

5. School Education   109
  Denials and Delusions
  KIRAN BHATTY

6. The Price of Freedom   129
  The NDA-II Government's Report Card on Higher Education
  AYESHA KIDWAI

7. Painting a Picture of Ill-health   155
  INDRANIL MUKHOPADHYAY AND DIPA SINHA

8. Big-Bang Programmes for Women's Welfare   180
  An Evaluation
  SONA MITRA

9. *Samajik Nyay* and *Samajik Samrasata*?   200
  AMIT THORAT

10. Environmental Policies Delinked from *Aam Aadmi*   216
  Is the Mask of Environmentalism Falling?
  SHOUVIK CHAKRABORTY

PART III: GOVERNANCE

11. *Suit-Boot ki Sarkar* and its 'Battle' against Corruption   241
  ROSHAN KISHORE

12. *Aadhaa*(r) *Adhura* Welfare   256
  A Critical Assessment
  ANMOL SOMANCHI

13. The NDA-II Government's Foreign and Security Policy   277
  A Critical Assessment
  HAPPYMON JACOB

14. Damaging the Public Sphere   299
  A Toxic Legacy of the NDA-II Regime
  SRINIVASAN RAMANI

Notes on the Contributors   314

Tables and Figures

Tables

1.1 Economic Performance Pre- and
     Post-Demonetisation   34

2.1 NPA Recovery vs. Write-offs: 2004–05 to 2018–19   45

2.2 Bank Frauds in India: 2013–14 to 2018–19   47

2.3 Corporate Debt Resolution under IBC:
     Realisation of Financial Claims   48

2.4 Bank Credit Flow into the MSME Sector   55

3.1 Percentage of Indebted Rural Households by
     Source of Credit   69

4.1 Changes in Employment in Eight Selected
     Sectors (in lakhs)   94

4.2 Recruitment by Various Central Government
     Agencies (in lakhs)   96

4.3 Estimates of Employment and Unemployment
     from CMIE Data   97

6.1 Allocations for UGC (in crores)   136

6.2 Expenditure on Autonomous Bodies   140

6.3 Limited Intake Capacities of Colleges   143

7.1 Comparison of India with BRICS Countries,
     South Asian Countries, and Some Asian Nations
     in Key Health Indicators   159

8.1 Trends in the Allocations for Important
Employment-generating Programmes   187

8.2 Achievements and Funds Utilised under the PMUY   191

9.1 Crimes against SCs Total and those Registered
under the PoA Act in Major States, 2011–16   204

9.2 Percentage of Non-Dalit Hindus who say
they Practise Untouchability   211

9.3 Share of Population Admitted to Practising
Untouchability, 2011   212

14.1 Data for Parliamentary By-elections Held in
Two Time Periods: 2014–16 and 2017–18   311

Figures

1.1 Average GDP Growth Rate across Tenures   18

1.2 Growth in Per Capita GDP and Agricultural
Wage (in real terms)   20

1.3 Share of Taxpayers' Income (as % of GNI)   20

1.4 Income Distribution of Indian Taxpayers   21

1.5 Wealth Inequality in India since 2010   22

1.6 Credit-Deposit Ratio   23

1.7 Drivers of Growth   24

1.8 Important Components of the Budget   26

1.9a CPI Inflation and Crude Oil Price ($/barrel) 29

1.9b Oil Burden on the Consumer   29

1.10 Current Receipts/GDP, Foreign Investment/
GDP and Import Cover (in months)   30

1.11 The Indian Rupee had a Great Fall   32

1.12 Ill-effects of Demonetisation   35

2.1 India's Banking Profitability Indicators   43

2.2 Net Profit of Public-sector Banks: 2004–05 to
2017–18   45

2.3a Deposit Growth   51

2.3b Credit Growth   51

2.4 Credit-GDP Ratios   53

2.5 Sector-wise Deployment of Bank Credit:
Annual Growth Rates (%)   53

2.6a Newly Opened Branches of SCBs   60

2.6b Newly Opened Rural Branches of the SCBs   60

3.1 International Prices: Food Price Index, 2005 = 100   71

3.2 WPI for Food Articles (Y-o-Y percentage change)   72

3.3 Real MSP, Paddy and Wheat (rupees)   73

3.4 Real MSP, Gram, Tur, and Moong (rupees)   74

3.5 Groundnut   75

3.6 Arhar   75

3.7 Y-o-Y Growth in Real Rural Wages
(percentage change)   77

3.8 Y-o-Y Credit Growth Rate in Deployment of
Bank Credit for Agriculture and Allied Activities
(percentage change)   78

4.1 Employment and GDP Growth in India   92

4.2a Labour Force in India   93

4.2b Employment and Unemployment Rates in India   93

4.3 Employment in the Organised Manufacturing
Sector   95

4.4 Monthly Estimates of the Number of Employed   98

4.5 Net Response Rate for Current Employment
Situation   98

5.1 Annual Union Government Budget Allocations
for Education, from 2004–19   119

6.1 Gross Enrolment Ratio (GER, in %) in HEIs
from 2012–18   142

6.2 Growth in Number of HEIs by Type from 2012–18   143

6.3a Undergraduate Enrolment in HEIs by Type from 2012–18 144

6.3b Postgraduate Enrolment in HEIs by Type from 2012–18 145

6.4 Total MPhil Enrolment from 2012–18 146

6.5a MPhil Enrolment in HEIs by Type from 2012–18 147

6.5b PhD Enrolment in HEIs by Type from 2012–18 147

6.6 Number of Faculty Positions at Different Levels from 2012–18 148

7.1 Union Government Expenditure on Health as a Percentage of GDP 158

7.2 Annual Rate of Decline in Infant Mortality Rate (IMR) 160

7.3a Improvements in Key Health Indicators post-NRHM: Percentage of Child Deliveries in Health Facilities 161

7.3b Improvements in Key Health Indicators post-NRHM: Percentage of Children who Received Full Vaccination by 12–23 Months of Age 161

7.4 Comparison of Growth in Allocations for NHM by Union Governments, at Constant (2004–05) Prices 162

7.5 Allocations for NHM by Union Governments, and Expenditure Including State Contribution (in crores), at Constant (2004–05) Prices 163

7.6 Union Government Budgetary Allocations for ICDS at Constant (2004–05) Prices 165

7.7 CAGR of Allocations for ICDS by Union Governments versus Tenure, at Constant (2004–05) Prices 165

7.8 A Comparison of General Prices with Medicine Prices from 2013–18 174

8.1 Funds Allocated and Utilised under BBBP
(in Rs Crore) 184

8.2 Share of Expenditure for Schemes Exclusively
for Women to Total Budgetary Expenditures (%) 196

8.3 Allocations to MWCD as Proportion of Total
Expenditure (%) 197

9.1 Households Practising Untouchability (%),
Social Groups, All India 209

9.2 Gender and Regional Divide on Practising
Untouchability 210

10.1a Global Levelised Cost of Electricity from
Utility-scale Renewable Power-generation
Technologies in 2010 224

10.1b Global Levelised Cost of Electricity from
Utility-scale Renewable Power-generation
Technologies in 2017 224

10.2 Additions in Installed Solar Capacity (2014–17) 225

10.3a Additions to Installed Renewable Energy Capacity 226

10.3b Installed Renewable Energy Capacity (GW) 227

10.4 Consumption of LPG 229

10.5a Year-wise Villages Electrified 231

10.5b Annual Average Number of Villages Electrified,
2004–18 231

10.6 The Number of Polluted River Stretches in India,
2015 and 2018 233

11.1 BJP's Income Surges Ahead of Others 251

12.1 How ABBA in PDS Works 264

14.1 Deaths Due to Vigilantism Across India 301

14.2 When Voters Did Not Come Out: Srinagar's
Voter Turnout is its Lowest Ever in Lok Sabha Polls 306

14.3 Deaths Due to Violence in the Valley 307

Abbreviations

AAP	Aam Aadmi Party
ABBA	Aadhaar-based Biometric Authentication
AePS	Aadhaar-enabled Payments System
AIBOC	All India Bank Officers' Confederation
AICTE	All India Council for Technical Education
AISHE	All India Survey On Higher Education
ANI	Asian News International
AQR	Asset Quality Review
ASHA	accredited social health activist
ASI	Annual Survey of Industries
BARC	Bhabha Atomic Research Centre
BBBP	Beti Bachao Beti Padhao
BC	Business Correspondent
BE	Budget Estimates
BECA	Basic Exchange and Cooperation Agreement for Geo-spatial Cooperation
BJP	Bharatiya Janata Party
BPL	below poverty line
BRICS (countries)	Brazil, Russia, India, China and South Africa
BSBDAs	Basic Savings Bank Deposit Accounts
BSF	Border Security Force
CAATSA	Countering America's Adversaries Through Sanctions Act
CABE	Central Advisory Board of Education
CAG	Comptroller and Auditor General

CAGR	compound annual growth rate
CBCS	choice based credit system
CBGA	Centre for Budget and Governance Accountability
CBI	Central Bureau of Investigation
CCE	Continuous and Comprehensive Evaluation
CCS	Cabinet Committee on Security
CCS	consumer confidence survey
CCTV	closed circuit television
CEPI	Comprehensive Environmental Pollution Index
CET1	Common Equity Tier 1 ratio
CFVs	Ceasefire Violations
CMIE	Centre for Monitoring the Indian Economy
COMCASA	Communications Compatibility and Security Agreement
CPA	Critically Polluted Area
CPCB	Central Pollution Control Board
CPEC	China–Pakistan Economic Corridor
CPI	consumer price index
CPSE	Central Public Sector Enterprise
CRAR	Capital to Risk Weighted Assets ratio
CSE	Centre for Sustainable Employment
CSO	Central Statistical Organisation (now Central Statistics Office)
CSR	child sex ratio
CSR	corporate social responsibility
CSS	Centrally Sponsored Schemes
CUs	Central universities
DBT	Direct Benefit Transfers
DeMon	Demonetisation
DFIs	Development Financial Institutions
DIRI	Digital Identity Research Initiative
DISE	District Information System for Education
DPC	Defence Planning Committee
DPCO	Drug Price Control Order

EIA	Environmental Impact Assessment
EPFO	Employees Provident Fund Organisation
EPI	Environment Performance Index
EUMA	End-Use Monitoring Agreement
EUS	employment and unemployment survey
FDCs	fixed drug combinations
FRBM	Fiscal Responsibility and Budget Management Act 2003
FRDI	Financial Resolution and Deposit Insurance Bill, 2017
FY	financial year
GBS	gender budget statement
GDP	Gross Domestic Product
GER	Gross Enrolment Ratio
GFHI	government funded health insurance
GGHE-D	domestic general government health expenditure
GoM	Group of Ministers
GRB	Gender Responsive Budgeting
GST	Goods and Services Tax
GSTN	Goods and Services Tax Network
GW	gigawatt
HDI	Human Development Index
HECI	Higher Education Commission of India
HEFA	Higher Education Financing Agency
HEI	higher educational institution
HLEG	High Level Expert Group
HSS	Hindu Swayamsevak Sangh
IAS	Indian Administrative Service
IB	Intelligence Bureau
IBBI	Insolvency and Bankruptcy Board of India
IBC	Insolvency and Bankruptcy Code
ICDS	Integrated Child Development Services
ICRIER	Indian Council for Research on International Economic Relations

ICT	information and communications technology
ID	Identity (This abbreviation has a specific usage in Chapter 12; this chapter makes use of varied terms such as 'identity', 'identification document', signifying the identification of individuals in the context of Aadhaar. For the purpose of standardisation, with due permission from the author, 'ID' has been provided as a common abbreviation of these variations.)
IHDS	India Human Development Survey
IIIT	Indian Institute of Information Technology
IIM	Indian Institute of Management
IISc	Indian Institute of Science
IISER	Indian Institute of Science, Education and Research
IIT	Indian Institute of Technology
IL&FS	Infrastructure Leasing and Financial Services Limited
IMF	International Monetary Fund
IMR	infant mortality rate
INIs	institutes of national importance
ISB	Indian School of Business
JCPOA	Joint Comprehensive Plan of Action
JDU	Janata Dal (United)
JNU	Jawaharlal Nehru University
J-PAL	Jameel Poverty Action Lab
KYC	Know-Your-Customer
LAC	Line of Actual Control
LB	Labour Bureau
LEMOA	Logistics Exchange Memorandum of Agreement
LFPR	labour force participation rate
LoC	Line of Control
LPG	liquefied petroleum gas
MEA	Ministry of External Affairs

MGNREGA	Mahatma Gandhi National Rural Employment Guarantee Act (now NREGA)
MGNREGS	Mahatma Gandhi National Rural Employment Guarantee Scheme
MHRD	Ministry of Human Resource Development
MNC	multinational corporation
MoEFCC	Ministry of Environment, Forestry and Climate Change
MOOCs	massive open online courses
MoSPI	Ministry of Statistics and Programme Implementation
MoU	memorandum of understanding
MSDE	Ministry of Skill Development and Entrepreneurship
MSME	Micro, Small and Medium Enterprises
MSP	Minimum Support Price
MWCD	Ministry of Women and Child Development
NAAC	National Assessment and Accreditation Council
NAPS	National Apprenticeship Promotion Scheme
NATGRID	National Intelligence Grid
NBFC	Non-Banking Financial Companies
NCF	National Curriculum Framework
NCLT	National Company Law Tribunal
NCRB	National Crime Records Bureau
NDA	National Democratic Alliance
NEFT	National Electronic Fund Transfer
NEP	National Education Policy
NFSA	National Food Security Act
NHM	National Health Mission
NITI Aayog	National Institution for Transforming India
NPAs	Non-performing Assets
NRC	National Register of Citizens
NRHM	National Rural Health Mission
NSA	National Security Advisor
NSAB	National Security Advisory Board

NSAP	National Social Assistance Programme
NSC	National Security Council
NSC	National Statistics Commission
NSCS	National Security Council Secretariat
NSDC	National Skill Development Corporation
NSSO	National Sample Survey Office
OBC	Other Backward Class
OBOR	One Belt One Road
OFBJP	Overseas Friends of BJP
OOPS	*out-of-pocket* spending
OTP	One-Time Password
PAN	Permanent Account Number
PAT	primary assistant teacher
PC&PNDT	Pre-Conception and Pre-Natal Diagnostic Techniques
PCA	Prompt Corrective Action (framework)
PDP	Peoples Democratic Party
PDS	Public Distribution System
PE	physical education
PLFS	Periodic Labour Force Survey
PMFBY	Pradhan Mantri Fasal Bima Yojana
PMJAY	Pradhan Mantri Jan Arogya Yojana
PMJDY	Pradhan Mantri/Prime Minister Jan Dhan Yojna
PMMMNMTT	Pandit Madan Mohan Malviya National Mission for Teachers and Teaching
PMMVY	Pradhan Mantri Matritva Vandana Yojana
PMMY	Prime Minister Mudra Yojana
PMO	Prime Minister's Office
PMPRY	Pradhan Mantri Rojgar Protsahan Yojana
PMUY	Pradhan Mantri Ujjwala Yojana
PNB	Punjab National Bank
PoA	Prevention of Atrocities
PoS	Point of Sale
PPP	public–private partnership

PSBs	Public-sector Banks
PV	photovoltaic
PvBs	Private-sector Banks
PVTG	Particularly Vulnerable Tribal Group
Quad	Quadrilateral Security Dialogue
RAW	Research and Analysis Wing
RBI	Reserve Bank of India
RCT	Randomised Controlled Trial
RE	revised estimate
RJD	Rashtriya Janata Dal
RLD	Rashtriya Lok Dal
RoAs	Return on Assets
RRB	Railway Recruitment Board
RRBs	Regional Rural Banks
RSBY	Rashtriya Swasthya Bima Yojana
RSS	Rashtriya Swayamsevak Sangh
RTE	Right of Children to Free and Compulsory Education (Act)
RTI	Right to Information
RUSA	Rashtriya Uchchatar Shiksha Abhiyan
SAARC	South Asian Association for Regional Cooperation
SARI	Social Attitudes Research for India
SC	Scheduled Caste
SCBs	Scheduled Commercial Banks
SECC	Socio-Economic Caste Census
SHG	self-help group
SIM	Subscriber Identification Module
SOAR	State of Aadhaar Report
SPA	Severely Polluted Area
SPG	Strategic Policy Group
SSA	Sarva Shiksha Abhiyan
SSBN	nuclear-powered ballistic missile submarine
SSC	Staff Selection Commission
ST	Scheduled Tribe

SWI	State of Working India 2018 (report)
UAE	United Arab Emirates
U-DISE	Unified District Information System for Education
UGC	University Grants Commission
UIDAI	Unique Identification Authority of India
UN	United Nations
UP	Uttar Pradesh
UPA	United Progressive Alliance
UPSC	Union Public Service Commission
UTs	union territories
WGFE	Working Group of Feminist Economists
WHO	World Health Organization
WPI	Wholesale Price Index
WRRI	Wage Rates in Rural India
WTO	World Trade Organization
ZPT	zilla parishad teacher

Foreword

The tenure of the Modi government has been nothing if not controversial. The resounding victory of the Bharatiya Janata Party (BJP) in 2014 was in many ways a turning point for an electoral democracy that had been based for three decades on coalition governments of varying degrees of stability. It created hope in the minds of many Indians (who longed for strong and decisive leadership) and fear in the minds of others (who worried about majoritarian and centralising tendencies).

The optimism amongst large sections of the public in that period was based on several expectations: that a decisive leader could rid the country of corruption and bring in reforms that would put the economic growth trajectory on a solid and more inclusive footing; that the country would benefit from the window of the 'demographic dividend' as more young people entered the labour force and reduced dependency ratios; that a stable government without any need for the ruling party to placate various allies to stay in power would be able to plan for a full term and thereby develop policies fit for the medium term. The fact that the Indian economy was then in what the Chief Economic Advisor of the time, Arvind Subramaniam, characterised as 'a sweet spot' because of the demographic dividend, as well as India's ability to benefit from the expansion in global trade and low global oil prices that reduce import bills, also added to the optimism.

Nearly five years later, many of those hopes have been belied, and the public mood—at least with respect to the economy—has turned much more despondent. Despite seemingly high GDP growth, other material indicators have been stubbornly resistant to improvement. The investment rate has continued to fall; inequality of assets and incomes has increased; major sectors like agriculture are experiencing crisis while others like manufacturing languish; and most significantly, employment has simply not taken off and instead appears to have declined in absolute numbers. The government, by contrast, claims success in many indicators such as low inflation and high rates of foreign capital inflow, even though recent moves towards providing budget handouts before the elections suggest that it implicitly recognises the limits of its economic successes.

Meanwhile, these same economic processes have given rise to forces that have justified some of the earlier fears, as inequalities and insecurities have combined with the majoritarian thrust of the ruling party to create unpleasant socio-political tendencies expressed in extreme form in aggressive vigilantism and attacks on minorities, riots, assassinations of free-thinking rationalists, motivated yet unwarranted arrests of human rights activists, and the encroachment of the State and of vigilante groups into areas of personal space and choice, like whom to marry, how to dress, and what to eat.

How does the average citizen make sense of all this? What exactly has happened to the economy, and why? How much of this was because of the government's policies? The answers to these questions are often lost in a fog of partisan debate that does not really provide answers or enable people to make up their own minds on the basis of the data. *A Quantum Leap in the Wrong Direction?* fills that gap, shedding light on the actual policies, mechanisms, and processes that affected the economy over this five-year period, by identifying the context of the existing structures and patterns when the Modi government came to power and then considering various aspects of its economic performance relative to its electoral and other promises. Relying entirely on a sober assessment of available official data and other reputable information, the analysis probes different sectors, aspects, and tendencies in the Indian economy under the Modi government.

Two major undercurrents provide a leitmotif in terms of economic impact: the unprecedented and still shocking demonetisation move; and the hasty attempt to implement an overly complicated Goods and Services Tax (GST). But the various chapters in the volume are not confined to assessing the impact of these policies, significant as they were: they focus on a wide range of economic policies and encompass both internal and external trends and formal and informal activities across all sectors.

This is a critically important exercise, because the essence of a democracy is that citizens must be informed about those whom they vote to power. All too often, economic trends and patterns are presented in such a way as to obfuscate the reality and mislead people about the actual impact of policies. By contrast, this volume seeks to present the policies and the available data on the outcomes in a clear and approachable manner. So this is not just a useful volume, but a truly significant one, which provides a basis for a better informed citizenry at a crucial period in the country's history.

Jayati Ghosh
Professor of Economics,
Centre for Economic Studies and Planning,
School of Social Sciences,
Jawaharlal Nehru University, New Delhi

Acknowledgements

First and foremost, we thank the publishers, Orient BlackSwan, for taking on this project and reposing their faith in us. We would especially like to acknowledge Nilanjana Majumdar at Orient BlackSwan, whose encouragement and diligence made the publication of this volume possible.

We thank all the authors who committed and contributed to this project and put up with the constant queries of demanding editors.

We are grateful to Professor Jayati Ghosh for her valuable advice, piercing comments, and her encouragement throughout this project. Comments by her and by the anonymous referee helped us immensely in streamlining the chapters.

A special thanks to Siddhartha Chatterjee for designing the book cover for us, and to Vignesh Radhakrishnan and Varun B. Krishnan for help with the data visualisation despite their busy schedules.

The editors would like to thank their families and friends, who supported this book in many different ways. Anubhuti Maurya helped with comments, mostly critical, on some of the chapters, and loads of moral support.

Introduction

Rohit Azad, Shouvik Chakraborty,
Srinivasan Ramani, and Dipa Sinha

When the Narendra Modi-led government came to power in 2014, the Bharatiya Janata Party (BJP) attained an absolute majority in terms of seats, even though they fell short of a popular majority in vote share terms. This reversed a trend that had been prevalent in Indian politics for more than two decades—the need for post-electoral coalitions to retain a majority in the Indian Parliament. This was made possible by the BJP's domination of the western and northern states in seat terms.

The party used the persona of its former Gujarat Chief Minister Narendra Modi to promise decisive leadership and a change from the Congress-led United Progressive Alliance (UPA) government in its second term. The latter was perceived by many in the electorate as wracked with corruption, incohesion, and indecision while inflicting high inflation on them, even as the economic growth faltered in its second term between 2009 and 2014. Since 2014, the BJP has governed in the image of Modi—every programme launched (or relaunched with a different name), every initiative, every campaign for votes in Assembly elections was headlined by the prime minister and his visage.

Before the elections in 2014, two supposedly contrasting images of Modi were projected by the media: Modi, 'the man of development' and Modi, the Hindutva champion. Post-election analyses stated that the BJP had managed to sell the former image to people who were not traditional adherents of the party, while the BJP's core support base was happy to endorse the Hindutva crusader. The 'Gujarat model of development' was projected as a huge success that had brought growth and prosperity to the state, and a similar experience was promised for the entire country. The election campaign highlighted the plank of *vikas* (development), to be delivered along with weeding out corruption and improving governance. The key slogans therefore were '*Sabka Saath, Sabka Vikas*' (with everyone, everyone's development) and 'Maximum Governance, Minimum Government'. So did the Modi government deliver on its promise of development? Or did India take a 'quantum leap in the wrong direction', as Nobel-laureate Professor Amartya Sen has recently asserted? This is the question that this volume seeks to address.

A Quantum Leap 'Forwards' or 'Backwards'?

A fair evaluation of this government requires that the outcomes be compared against the promises it made in the run-up to the elections. The BJP's 2014 manifesto had poll promises that ran into 42 pages! It will, of course, be unfair to hold them accountable for all of those 42 pages, but one could still choose certain basic promises they made and carefully evaluate them.

The 2014 BJP manifesto is divided under subsections such as 'issues of imminence', 'strengthening the policy framework', 'reforming the political system', 'widening the platform', and most importantly, 'leaping forward'. In this volume, we analyse the performance of the government along three broad themes that emerge from the BJP's election manifesto.

First, on the issue of the economy, the BJP promised to revive a flagging economy, while focusing on agriculture and employment generation (100 crore jobs were to be generated). Second, on the issue of social welfare, it promised '*sabka vikas*' (development for all) through access to quality healthcare, inclusive education, environmentally sustainable development, social as well as economic justice, with political empowerment for both the socially disadvantaged and women in the society. Third, on the issues of governance, it swore by 'minimum government with maximum governance', thereby moving away from the State's role as a provider to that of a regulator.

DOWNTURN IN FORTUNES?

The BJP has become the central pole of Indian politics, and by the time the government at the Centre completed four years, it was enjoying power in more than two-thirds of the Indian states while growing in new areas such as the Northeast. But perhaps something has changed in the past year. The BJP steadily lost seats in parliamentary by-elections, which brought it below the absolute majority even as it alienated its coalition partners. In late 2018, the BJP lost to the otherwise down-and-out Congress in places where it had been in power for long—Madhya Pradesh, Rajasthan, and Chhattisgarh. Just as the government was completing its full five-year term, the ruling party's electoral fortunes were no longer as certain.

What explains this slow downturn in the BJP's fortunes? Was it a galvanised Opposition posing an unusual electoral challenge? Or is it the case that the government's failure to deliver on its promise of development for all is beginning to dampen public support for it? The recent spate of protests, especially by farmers, highlighting issues of rural distress, and the increasing concern about the unemployment situation in the country have dented the pro-development image of this government.

This edited volume, with contributions from academics and journalists, attempts to look at the National Democratic Alliance-II (NDA-II) government's performance on multiple fronts, with each chapter focusing on one issue in detail. The chapters also consider where the current government stands in terms of its priorities, performance, and philosophy, and whether the advances made by independent India on various parameters—economic, democratic, and governance—have progressed, stalled, or regressed.

Lately, public debate has been hijacked by the Opposition and the partisans of the government throwing 'facts' at each other. It is when partisan ideology trumps objectivity that propaganda is rolled out. But Indians clearly deserve better; they should be allowed to evaluate their own government and arrive at an informed decision while exercising their mandate. This volume seeks to let the facts speak for themselves, helped by substantiation through data.

THE RISE OF THE BJP AND MODI

Unlike much of the developed as well as the developing world, the global financial crisis of 2008 did not affect India all that much. After impressive economic income growth between 2003 and 2011, there has been a decline in its growth, although it is still nowhere close to a recession. What is, however, remarkable about its growth is that it was premised on exclusion. A popular term used in India for this phase is 'jobless growth'—which, in its very definition, is inequality-enhancing because a large part of the population is left untouched by this growth. This is what probably lay at the heart of the disenchantment with the UPA and the rise of the BJP.

During the tenure of the United Progressive Alliance-I (UPA-I), largely because of the political pressures from different social movements as well as the Left parties that were providing the government with outside support, this inequality was sought to be addressed through attempts at redistributive measures. The most popular, and perhaps the only one of its kind in the world, was a guarantee of jobs for 100 days in rural India, which came to be known as the Mahatma Gandhi National Rural Employment Guarantee Scheme (MGNREGS). Other significant legislations, such as the Forest Rights Act, the Right to Education Act, and the Right to Information Act, were also passed during the tenure of

UPA-I. These left-of-centre social and economic policies contributed to bringing the UPA back to power in 2009. However, UPA-II charted a trajectory different from its previous avatar by jettisoning this politics. Added to that were two parallel developments—growing inflation and the exposure of big-ticket corruption cases, a heady combination, as they are among the top issues that determine voter choice.

Voters had the sense that while working people and the poor were trying to make ends meet, corruption had enriched the rich and the politically powerful. Large-scale corruption was seen as a way to transfer resources meant for the poor and the working people to the rich and the connected. The civil society movements for a Lokpal blamed the UPA for the rampant corruption and gave voice to this growing frustration amongst the electorate. The UPA-II was also beginning to appear as a lame-duck government unable to make any economic decisions, seeming less committed to its welfare policies and finding it difficult to keep its coalition partners together. All of this led to the decline of the Congress and the ascendance of the BJP led by Modi, which was projected as the clean and refreshing alternative.

In a vast, democratic, and parliamentary system of representative government such as India, it is indeed problematic to reduce governance to a machine led by one individual. But it is precisely to this that the BJP made its electoral pitch during the 2014 elections, and to which it has since managed to reduce its regime. Modi was projected as an outsider to the entrenched power centres in Delhi, as the leader of a 'strong and efficient' government in Gujarat that was not beholden to special interests like the UPA, and was therefore 'incorruptible'.

STATE AS A 'BROKER' OF BIG CAPITAL

While the UPA, particularly in its second avatar, and the NDA-II government both stood for a State which had 'no business to be in business', we believe there has been a paradigmatic shift in the nature of the State during the present government's rule.

Under UPA-I, in particular, the philosophy of social welfare was premised on public provisioning, reflected in measures such as the MGNREGA, the Integrated Child Development Services (ICDS), etc., and on developing a regime of rights. These policies were implemented unevenly and there were failures and successes, but the intent was clear. From a rights-based and the 'State as a provider' approach of the UPA-I, there was a shift to the State playing a more transactional role during UPA-II, with emphasis on the Public-Private Partnership (PPP) model of delivery, in which the State primarily plays the role of a regulator.

Under the NDA-II government, however, as seen in the chapters in this volume, the nature of the State has changed fundamentally. Its primary agenda across sectors seems to be to create avenues for the expansion of profits for big business through privatisation and commercialisation, while withdrawing from public provisioning or its 'social' role. In this sense, the State is increasingly becoming a 'broker' for big business.

Moving away from its role as a regulator of the excesses of the private corporate sector, it has become a conduit through which public resources are being transferred to finance the profligacies of big business houses in this country. Getting public-sector banks to write off loans to wealthy corporates that have become bad assets because of non-repayment is one example of such brokerage.

In the social sector as well, the State is moving away from a model of direct provisioning of services towards insurance-based schemes, such as in healthcare services or compensation for crop failures. The role of the State is now limited to just making a partial payment towards the insurance premium, with the rest being paid by the recipients themselves, to the private insurance companies. This, as the chapters here show, results in these companies making windfall profits since the total premium amount is much greater than the claims paid, and claim settlement rates tend to be much lower than they are for public-sector providers. In the absence of adequate checks and balances on profit-seeking insurance companies and missing grievance redressal mechanisms, recipients end up getting the short end of the stick, even as profits for the corporations soar. This is another way in which the State is making *ex-gratia* transfer of public resources to the private corporate sector, while claiming to be working for the welfare of the people.

The NDA-II government has therefore taken forward the process of reorienting the State from public provisioning to 'marketable goods and services' and towards an 'insurance-based' approach, where the private corporate sector acts as a conduit for their delivery. Examples of this shift can be found across the chapters of this volume—be it in banking, in higher education, or in agriculture.

The NDA-II government also sought to reform the State itself—bringing about a centralising emphasis on financial matters (the GST), and expanding its governmental nature through projects such as Aadhaar and policies such as demonetisation.

In other words, there has been a philosophical shift away from the Scandinavian model of social welfare towards an American model. Perhaps this constitutes one part of the 'quantum leap' that Amartya Sen was referring to.

The Problem of Missing Data

Statisticians would perhaps agree that there has certainly been a leap backwards when it comes to data under this government. While evaluating the NDA-II government's tenure, some of the authors here, too, have faced the same problem. In quite a few instances, either the data source based on which one analyses a particular aspect of the economy has gone missing or, if the data is to be found, it is difficult to compare with previous versions. While a revision of methodology is quite normal with time, a basic principle of such a process is that it should be performed in a transparent manner and should not end up creating disjointed datasets. Unfortunately, for example, in the case of the new GDP series, the process of revision has not been entirely transparent, nor has the joining of the two series been without its share of controversy.

A more significant problem, however, is that of 'missing data'. It is ironical for a government promising jobs to discontinue the statistical measure of how it is doing on this count. The government has stopped the annual surveys of the Labour Bureau, and delayed and then suppressed the results of the large employment surveys conducted by the National Sample Survey Office (NSSO). It is an alarming state of affairs when a country, whose statistical system was once known to be among the best in the world, has to learn about its rising open unemployment rates through a 'leak' to the press because the government did not release the data which had already been vetted by the statistical authorities. And if we are to believe the leak, the unemployment rate in 2017–18 under this government was the highest in the last 45 years, and the primary contributors to this were the twin decisions of demonetisation and GST on the economy.

Two Economic Experiments: Demonetisation and GST

After four-and-a-half years, the record of the NDA-II government has been found wanting in the delivery of its promises, even as its flawed economic policies have had their own deleterious implications for the Indian economy. Two glaring examples of flawed economic decisions were demonetisation and a haphazard and hasty implementation of the Goods and Services Tax (GST). Since these policies have had a wide-ranging impact across different sectors of the economy, this volume discusses them across different chapters instead of focusing separately on them.

Never before has an economic experiment of such mammoth proportions—demonetisation—been attempted in the history of this country, or perhaps globally. The evidence clearly suggests that none of the three stated objectives—unearthing black money, controlling terrorism, and stopping the use of fake currencies—were met. The failure of this policy can be gauged from the fact that the government kept putting forward new arguments to defend the policy when the data proved its previous claims to be wrong. The most extreme change in the policy was the U-turn in its basic objective. From the belief that much of the 'black money' would not return to the banking system, the government later claiming that all of it returning was proof of the success of demonetisation. However, as a result of this ill-judged policy, not only did the economy suffer a decline in employment and growth, but it also pushed the already precarious unorganised sector and the poorer sections of the population towards unimagined economic hardship, including deaths.

Similarly, the hasty implementation of the GST disrupted the pace of economic growth, with effects like increasing unemployment. At a more fundamental level, GST eroded the decision-making powers of state governments, while centralising such powers in the hands of the Central government. It had a particularly adverse impact on small businesses, both because of a lack of technical infrastructure and stringent compliance measures that significantly added to their costs.

Modi, the Champion of Hindutva

While this volume's primary focus is on whether Modi has lived up to his reputation as the 'man of development', this is not to argue that the two personas associated with him are two 'contrasting' images, or that his pro-Hindutva plank should be given less importance. On the contrary, we believe that these two 'contrasting' images are inextricably linked.

Let us take the example of one of his government's programmes—Make in India. The project, which aimed at overseas enterprises setting up manufacturing facilities in India, was based on a model that would out-compete international competitors by cutting costs. This project had little to do with other comparative advantages in India and required a suppression of wages and the transfer of natural resources to big businesses for it to work. This was not very different from other policies that sought economic growth using globalisation, but 'Make in India's' inherent contradictions were much more stark, tilted clearly in favour of capital with little by way of benefits to workers, who lose both in terms of wages and employment since export industries are generally more capital-intensive.

Such a development by encroachment on the resources of the working people, by its very intent creates fertile political grounds for a discourse of 'us (the "have-nots") vs. them ("haves")', which has the potential of challenging the unjust nature of this growth path. But what is transformative for the working people, for the same reason, is also disruptive for the rich and the elite. Parties like the BJP, backed by corporate power, look for an alternative category of 'us vs. them' based on religion, caste, region, and ethnicity, which can be employed to deflect attention and divide the working people. The creation of a Hindutva crusader is, therefore, *essential* for the 'man of (such) development'.

The BJP's use of identity fault-lines to win elections—the attacks on Muslims and dalits, communal polarisation through the reinvigoration of the issue of the Ram Mandir in Ayodhya, or the national register of citizens (NRC) and upper-caste consolidation against the forces of 'Mandal politics'—is therefore not divorced from its policies in government that emphasise 'development'.

While the volume tangentially touches upon the 'Hindutva' agenda of the BJP, it *deliberately* steers clear of focusing on it because our primary purpose is to evaluate this government on the promises of development and inclusion that brought it to power.

Organisation of the Volume

This volume is divided into three sections.

Section I, 'The Economy', begins with Rohit Azad's evaluation of the macro-economic performance and policies of the NDA-II government. Prasenjit Bose and Zico Dasgupta discuss the Indian banking crisis while evaluating schemes aimed at financial inclusion, such as MUDRA and Jan Dhan Yojana. Arindam Banerjee and Ishan Anand study the impact of some of the major policy initiatives of the government, such as the hike in minimum support prices, the crop insurance scheme, and demonetisation, on Indian agriculture. Subhanil Chowdhury examines the far-reaching claims made about employment generation put forward by the government, the use of controversial methodologies to make these claims, and the pervasive problem of joblessness. This section finds that while there is stagnation in growth on the one hand, the employment potential of growth continues to decline on the other. Despite this, the focus of this government has been on supply-side initiatives such as skill development or loans for entrepreneurship, in complete denial of the problem of depressed demand, especially in the rural areas. Agriculture is in crisis, public-sector banks are being allowed to die a slow death, and no new jobs are being created.

Section II, 'Socio-economic Indicators', looks at the government's performance in education, healthcare, environment, and the impact of the government on the marginalised and the vulnerable. The chapters on education and health find a similar trend here as well. Primary and higher education reforms are aimed at providing a 'skilled workforce' for the market, while ignoring the equity considerations that must be central to the education system in a country like India. So Kiran Bhatty finds that the government's initiatives have focused on leveraging the education sector more for public-private partnerships and edu-business rather than on strengthening government schools by improving access, infrastructure, and quality, even as there has been a lag in implementing the Right to Education Act. Ayesha Kidwai also finds a similar trend in higher education, with a growth in private universities and reduced funding for State-funded higher education institutions. In the health sector, too, Indranil Mukhopadhyay and Dipa Sinha find that the approach of the NDA-II government towards health has been one that has focused on insurance-based schemes whose potential to reduce the burden of health expenditure on the common person is in doubt, even as it opens doors for the expansion of the private sector in health.

In her chapter on women's empowerment schemes, Sona Mitra argues that a number of schemes, such as Beti Bachao Beti Padhao, Ujjwala Yojana, and the Mudra scheme targeting women's empowerment, were only a repackaging of older programmes without commensurate fund allocations, while the newly launched schemes were also not effective. Amit Thorat focuses on the policy decisions of the government related to social justice, where he argues that these policies and actions by BJP leaders have resulted in violence against, and the abuse and harassment of, members of the minority communities and dalits. Shouvik Chakraborty argues that the environmental policies were skewed in favour of the private corporate sector and large business houses, not only in terms of further relaxing regulations to ease their growth, but also to facilitate greater capital accumulation under the guise of environmental governance.

Section III, 'Governance', delves deeper into issues of governance. Roshan Kishore examines whether the government addressed one of the chief failings of its predecessor—corruption—and whether it managed to arrest this feature of Indian democracy as it had promised to do. Anmol Somanchi assesses Aadhaar to see if it truly brought about substantive inclusion and reduction in corruption, as the government claims. Happymon Jacob looks at the regime's foreign policy and its personalisation by the prime minister, and how this has had an impact on India's interests. In the final chapter, Srinivasan Ramani focuses on the public sphere in India: What has been the impact of the regime on the country's secular fabric, and on sensitive issues related to the conflicts in border states such as Kashmir and Assam?

This volume is by no means an exhaustive account of every single economic and social policy of this government. Some prominent politico-economic issues, such as housing, failures in federalism, and the Swachh Bharat mission, which deserve attention, have unfortunately not been touched upon.

The title of the volume ends with a question mark. The reason for this is that we would like the reader to draw her/his own conclusions based on the arguments made here, instead of us passing a verdict on this government without giving it a fair trial. We hope that the trial has indeed been fair.

Part I

The Economy

one

Modi Sarkar

The Truth of Sabka Saath, Sabka Vikas

Rohit Azad

Prime Minister Narendra Modi came riding high on a wave of discontent as well as aspirations of a young India. If there is one slogan that became synonymous with Modi, it was '*Sabka Saath, Sabka Vikas*' (with everyone, everyone's development), a promise of high growth which was inclusive. He promised social welfare for the poor, financial inclusion, to stamp out corruption, and above all, high growth with jobs. But how many promises has his government fulfilled? This chapter examines the macro-economic outcomes of government policies since 2014.

Since 2003–04, the Indian economy has grown at rates unprecedented since Independence. I have divided the period since the turn of this century into periods coinciding with the four governments in power: the National Democratic Alliance (NDA-I) (1999–2004), UPA-I (2004–09), UPA-II (2009–14), and the NDA-II government (2014–present).

Na Saath, Na Vikas

My Growth is Greater than Yours!

We have been hearing about inclusive growth for a while now. Before Modi, Manmohan Singh had made a promise of 'inclusive growth' somewhere towards the end of his first term, that is, UPA-I. In that period, despite a high rate of growth in the economy, there was no commensurate growth in employment. Moreover, there was a significant increase in income as well as wealth inequality. That Manmohan Singh had to emphasise 'inclusivity' was an acknowledgement of the fact that growth in India has been exclusionary in nature, and appropriate policies are required to address that. Did Modi achieve what remained elusive to Singh during most of his tenure? Did the economy outperform the two terms of the UPA in terms of *vikas* and inclusion?

Such a comparison, however, is not straightforward since the underlying methodology of measuring national income was changed[1] under NDA-II. However, in the absence of a reliable common measure[2] between the two periods, I compare growth rates *within* the two available series, using the old series for the first three governments and the new series for the period from 2014 (Figure 1.1).

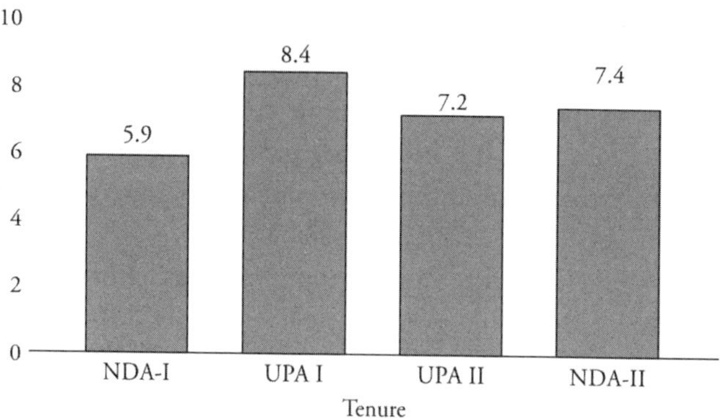

FIGURE 1.1: Average GDP Growth Rate across Tenures

Source: RBI, *Handbook of Statistics on the Indian Economy* (accessed December 2018).

The data shows that the economy grew the fastest during UPA-I, which was 2.5 percentage points higher than the NDA-I. The growth rate declined during UPA-II and recovered only marginally under NDA-II. An economy grows as a result of a rise in the demand for its goods and services. Such a source of demand can come from domestic as well as international markets. During UPA-I, both these markets played a critical role in pushing the growth rate up, whereas during the Modi government, both declined in comparison. I will discuss this issue in detail later.

Growth and Inequality

Let us now consider the *sabka saath* aspect of what was perhaps lower *vikas* under Modi. Has the expansion in total GDP been shared equally by the different income groups of the population? Unfortunately, there is no reliable data on income distribution available for India to draw a robust conclusion. The time-series estimates of inequality of the most recent study[3] end in 2015. Nor is there a sample survey by the NSS covering the years under the NDA-II government to assess how the consumption of different classes has changed. So let us consider some approximations that could indicate the extent of inequality: the wages of workers in agriculture, which employs close to half of all Indian workers; the government's tax collection data (which, of course, covers a small section of the population); and data on wealth inequality.

It is well-known that there has been a very sharp rise in inequality since 1990–91, but the pace of this rise has picked up particularly since the high growth phase post 2003–04. Let us compare the real wages of agricultural workers with the average (or per capita) rise of income in India (Figure 1.2).

I find that except for the UPA-II period, agricultural wages rose at a slower rate than that of the average national income. So, most of the 48 per cent Indians employed in agriculture got a worse deal in comparison to others. This was true during both the NDA-I and the UPA-I governments, but things improved dramatically during UPA-II, only to be reversed under NDA-II. In fact, the agriculture sector as a whole showed rapidly declining shares of national income, particularly since the economic reforms, even though it continues to account for around half of the workforce.

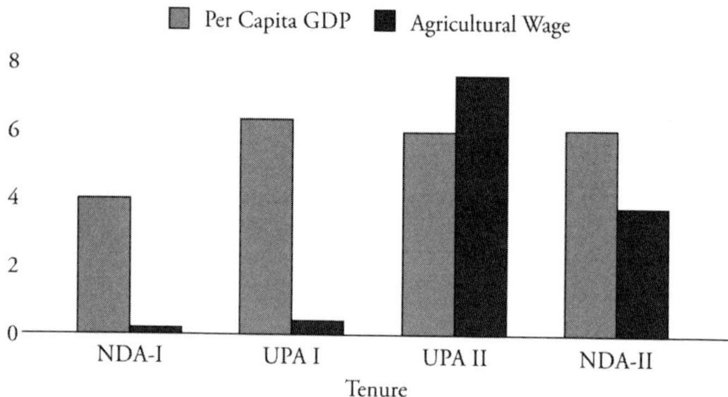

FIGURE 1.2: Growth in Per Capita GDP and Agricultural Wage
(in real terms)

Source: RBI, *Handbook of Statistics on the Indian Economy* (accessed December 2018).

A similar picture of worsening income distribution emerges if we look at the tax data for Modi's tenure. While the share of the richest taxpayers has increased, that of the lowest-income taxpayers has declined[4] (Figure 1.3). At a more comprehensive level, if we divide the taxpaying population into three income categories of top 10,

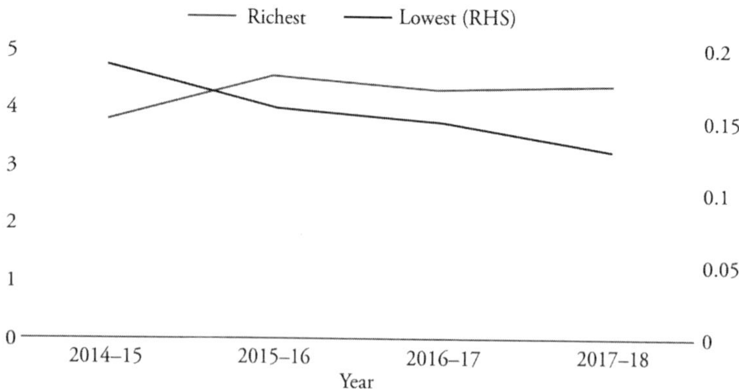

FIGURE 1.3: Share of Taxpayers' Income (as % of GNI)

Source: Central Board of Direct Taxation, Income Tax Department of India (accessed December 2018).

middle 40, and bottom 50 per cent, the share of the top 10 has increased at the cost of the bottom 50, with the middle remaining constant, by and large (Figure 1.4). These figures could perhaps help to explain the continuing acceptance of the NDA-II government among sections of the middle class, whose gains have been commensurate with the growth in the economy. One could argue that this rise in the share of the richest could purely be on account of higher income disclosures under Modi as a result of demonetisation, but, as Figure 1.4 shows, the share of the richest did not change much in 2017–18 as compared to 2016–17, when demonetisation was announced.

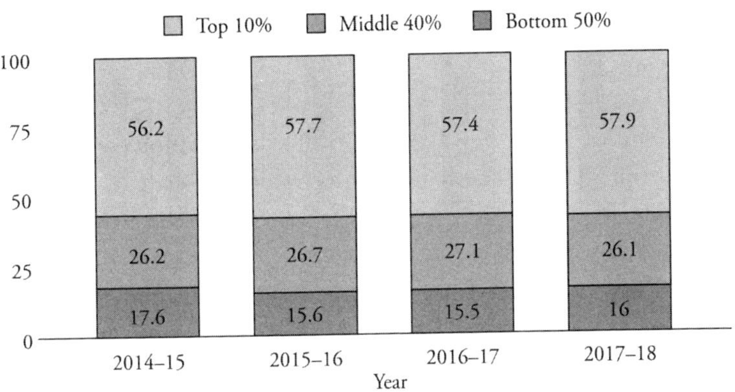

FIGURE 1.4: Income Distribution of Indian Taxpayers

Source: Central Board of Direct Taxation, Income Tax Department of India (accessed December 2018).

As far as wealth inequality is concerned, for the first time under NDA-II, the wealthiest 1 per cent crossed the threshold of owning half the total wealth of the country, while the top 10 per cent owned more than three-fourths of the total (Figure 1.5). A marginal decline in 2017, as the Credit Suisse reports, is on account of the depreciation of the Indian rupee.

It is not very difficult to understand why inequality in India has risen during this period. While the economy was growing at an average of 7 per cent, job growth was less than 1 per cent. Even those who managed to find employment in organised manufacturing clocked wages which were only 1.5 times higher than before, while contributing six times more to the output.[5] A low-employment, low-wage share kind of growth path is, *by its very nature*, not inclusive. It appears that the slogan of 'sabka saath, sabka vikas' or 'inclusive growth', under the current growth trajectory/regime, is a contradiction in terms.

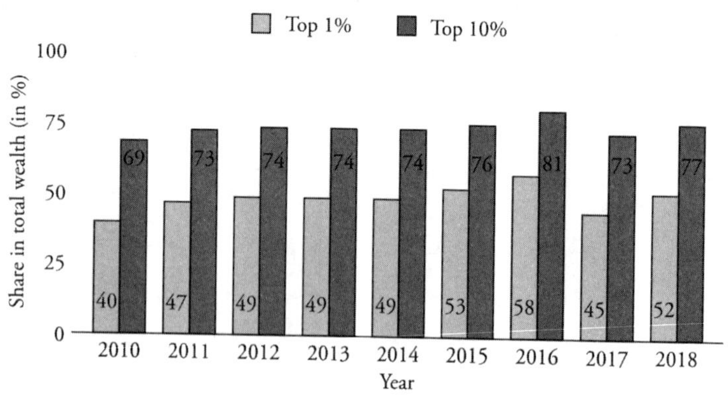

FIGURE 1.5: Wealth Inequality in India since 2010

Source: Credit Swisse Global Wealth Database.

ACCESS TO CREDIT: PANACEA FOR INEQUALITY?

The government has made the claim that greater access to credit, through schemes like the Prime Minister Jan Dhan Yojana (PMJDY), the MUDRA scheme, or the recent 59-minute loan scheme, can compensate for the initial lack of income and/or wealth, and that once the virtuous cycle of income generation starts, such a process can enable families to emerge from this low-income trap. However, did the poor in India receive greater access to credit under the NDA-II government? Since Chapter 2 (this volume) deals with PMJDY, it will suffice here to present just one figure to see whether access to formal credit in the rural areas has improved.

Since deposits generate potential credit, a good metric for access to credit is how much loan one gets for the deposits made, what economists call the credit-deposit ratio. Figure 1.6 shows that the credit-deposit ratio for the rural population increased under UPA-I and has been declining ever since (Figure 1.6). The only section that saw an improvement in credit during the term of the NDA-II was the metropolitan areas.

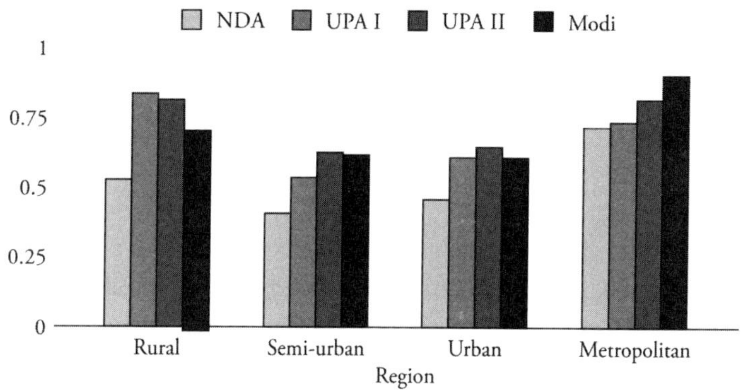

FIGURE 1.6: Credit-Deposit Ratio

Source: RBI, *Handbook of Statistics on the Indian Economy* (accessed December 2018).

WHY WAS THE *VIKAS PURUSH* UNABLE TO DELIVER ON *VIKAS*?

An immediate question to ask would be: Why was vikas elusive to Modi, despite his image as a *vikas purush*? Growth in any economy means a rise in investment, but for that to increase, the investors have to be convinced that there is a potential market for their products. There are only two markets possible—domestic and international; the former depends on the purchasing power of the citizens and the latter, on the international/transnational markets. Contrary to popular belief, government expenditure, like any other form of spending, means higher domestic demand.

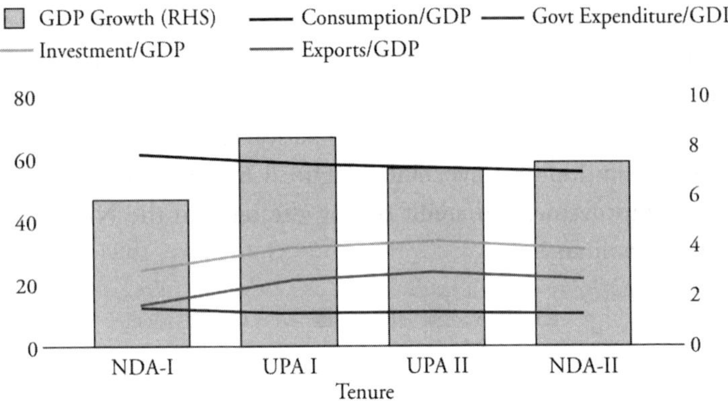

FIGURE 1.7: Drivers of Growth

Source: RBI, *Handbook of Statistics on the Indian Economy* (accessed December 2018).

The NDA-II government has espoused an ideological adherence to 'fiscal consolidation', where the government expenditure does not rise as a proportion of the GDP (Figure 1.7), which in turn limits the scope for investment for domestic markets. But what does fiscal consolidation signify? Governments spend on social-sector schemes, infrastructure, national security, etc., while they levy taxes which constitute their receipts. Fiscal consolidation means that the difference between the expenditure and the taxes, what is called the fiscal deficit, needs to be kept under check because, arguably, the indebtedness of the government rises as a result of this. I will return to the point of fiscal consolidation later. Let us now look at the other source of demand, the external markets.

Exports under NDA-II fell in proportion to the GDP in comparison to both the UPA governments (Figure 1.7). As a result of both domestic and external factors, investment fell, although it had been rising through the two UPA governments. Further, domestic consumption (as a proportion of GDP) also fell during Modi's tenure. This had a lot to do with the rising income and wealth inequality in the economy, as the rich consume a relatively smaller part of their income in contrast to the poor.

Inequality is often seen as being driven by market forces, but if that is the case, how can governments be held responsible for it? The issue is that governments have the tools to address inequality, even if they did not contribute to it in the first place. What is more, the goal of 'fiscal consolidation' itself could have been used for this purpose. The readers can immediately see that even if every other source of demand was falling, by addressing inequality and thus expanding the domestic consumption, Modi could have bolstered his image as a man committed to development.

PITFALLS OF FISCAL CONSERVATISM

The gap between the government's expenditure and taxes, that is, fiscal consolidation, can be brought down either by increasing taxes or decreasing expenditure, or by increasing taxes more than the increase in expenditure. In this subsection, I am deliberately taking 'fiscal consolidation' as given without questioning its legitimacy.[6] A 'progressive' fiscal consolidation, which counteracts inequality, would entail a rise in direct taxes (on corporate profits, wealth and inheritance tax). A part of these taxes could then be spent on employment generation such as the MGNREGA and/ or on redistributive programmes providing accessible healthcare and education to the have-nots. As opposed to this, a 'regressive' fiscal consolidation would entail a rise in indirect taxes, even as the expenditure on social welfare falls. But between the two taxes, why is a rise in direct taxes considered 'progressive', while that in indirect taxes is taken as 'regressive'?

Direct taxes are levied 'progressively' on income and wealth, that is, the tax slabs rise as you move up the income scale, as a result of which the rich have to pay a higher proportion of their income as compared to the poorest, who do not have to pay any income tax. In sharp contrast, however, indirect taxes burden the poor more since they have to pay *a greater proportion* of their income to buy the same product.

There is an added benefit of a progressive fiscal consolidation. A rise in direct taxes helps to plug the 'leakage' of domestic income on international products in demand by the wealthy and the rich, which brings the imports down, even as the redistribution in favour of the poor increases domestic demand.

Unfortunately, however, the NDA-II government has relied on a model of 'regressive' fiscal consolidation, even as the option of progressive consolidation was open to them. While the government expenditure on social welfare has fallen (as argued extensively in later chapters), the share of indirect to direct taxes, which exacerbates inequality, has risen during Modi's tenure. This reverses a falling trend which had started with the UPA governments (Figure 1.8). Moreover, the NDA-II government has actively reduced its spending on capital expenditure, which helps to build infrastructure and other long-term capital assets for the nation and even on defence, despite its repeated exhortations in the name of the *jawans* standing on the country's borders.

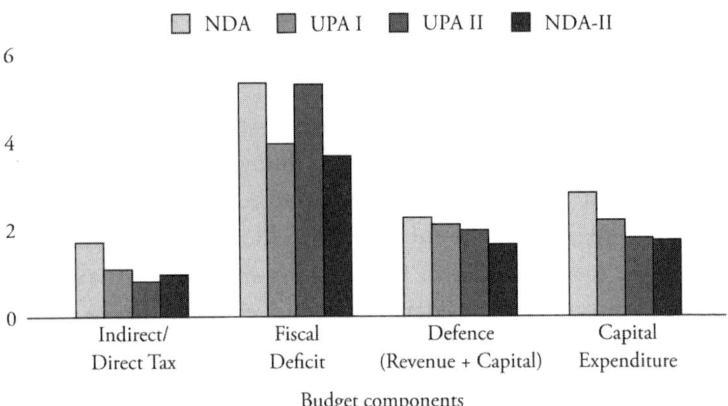

Figure 1.8: Important Components of the Budget

Source: RBI, *Handbook of Statistics on the Indian Economy* (accessed December 2018).

Why, then, did this government, with an espoused claim of *sabka saath*, choose the route of indirect as opposed to direct taxes? No government that comes to power financed by the wealthy corporates, while gaining political legitimacy articulated by the middle class, can afford to anger these sections by increasing their taxes. As opposed to this, a rise in indirect taxes is, in the popular imagination, seen as 'class-neutral'. You will always see a rise in income tax slabs, capital gains tax, and inheritance tax leading to upheavals in the stock markets and abuse for the government from pundits on TV channels, even as the rise in excise and customs duties do not necessarily elicit a similar violent opposition.

INFLATION UNDER CHECK; WAS IT LUCK?

The NDA-II government has managed to deliver on low inflation, which affects the poorer sections the most since their incomes, unlike those of the salaried middle classes or the rich, are not indexed to inflation. Perhaps this is one of the reasons why there is no visible anti-Modi wave such as there was against the UPA-II, which saw the highest level of inflation. It will not be an exaggeration to say that price rise in general, and of oil in particular, was one of the reasons for the anger against the UPA government. An interesting factor, however, is that low inflation during the NDA-II government's tenure is also perhaps just simply good fortune, since the international oil prices have been quite low during this period, even though they have partially recovered towards the end of his tenure (Figure 1.9a). Modi acknowledged this in one of his speeches. 'Do you want a lucky person or someone who is less lucky?' he asked the audience.[7]

Nonetheless, the point remains that low inflation may not have much to do with his policies, and instead was an outcome of international factors over which governments have little control. While it is true that the Modi government has not seen the levels of inflation of the UPA-II years, an upswing in crude oil prices, as was witnessed recently, can reverse the fortunes of this government too. This will become more likely if the government insists on mobilising tax revenue in the form of high customs and excise duties on oil.

It is important to ask if Modi's good fortune has been shared equally with the citizens of this country. By way of comparison, while the crude oil prices were quite high during UPA-II (USD 106.85 per barrel in May 2014, before the UPA demitted office), they have fallen dramatically during the better part of the Modi government (in the range of USD 30s), and yet we find the trend of retail prices to have *increased*. Why has this occurred? Was it because the fall in the value of the rupee more than compensated for the fall in the dollar price of crude oil? To cancel this opposite movement of the value of the rupee and the dollar price of oil, I calculate the crude oil component in *rupee terms* per litre of petrol. The difference between the retail price and the crude oil price comprises the taxes levied by the government, refining charges, and the profit margins of the oil retailers in India. I call this difference a burden on the ordinary citizens of this country, since it measures which part of the fall in the international prices is being appropriated by the government or the oil oligarchs of the country, instead of being passed on to the consumers.

Figures 1.9a and 1.9b show that this burden is currently about 50 per cent higher than it was when Modi took office in May 2014 (Rs 46.6/litre now, as opposed to Rs 31.6/litre earlier). It is easy to understand that this is because of an inbuilt asymmetry in retail pricing. While a rise in crude oil prices is passed on to the consumers, a fall is not, or is only marginally, passed on to the consumers. Between May 2014 and December 2015, the cost of crude oil fell by Rs 25 per litre, whereas the retail prices fell only by Rs 11 per litre. At the same time, an increase in crude oil prices has been matched by an equivalent rise in retail prices. The result is a paradoxical situation where, instead of reducing the role of the government in interfering with the prices of petrol and diesel, deregulation of oil prices in India has resulted in the exact opposite. But who has gained from this gap? The Indian Oil Corporation's latest data on the breakup of retail prices shows that close to half of what we pay goes as taxes to the government (Central and state combined).

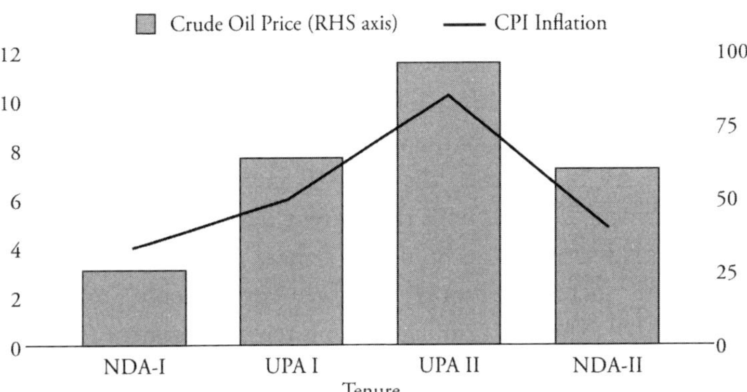

FIGURE 1.9A: CPI Inflation and Crude Oil Price ($/barrel)

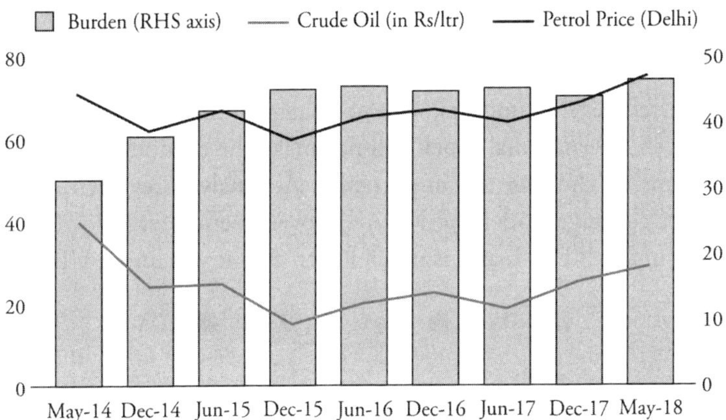

FIGURE 1.9B: Oil Burden on the Consumer

Source: RBI, *Handbook of Statistics on the Indian Economy*; Petroleum Planning and Analysis Cell (accessed December 2018).

MAKE IN INDIA

One of Modi's pet industrial policy projects has been 'Make in India', which entailed the substitution of imported manufactured products with domestically produced ones, for both the domestic and the international markets. It was meant to be a push for an export-oriented growth, perhaps at a sectoral level. It is inspired by what the Chinese have achieved over the past three to four decades. Has the policy delivered in terms of India gaining in the exports market vis-à-vis the rest of the world?

At a very broad level, the NDA-II government falls short of its predecessor, UPA-II, with the current receipts (from the export of goods and services) declining (as a share of GDP), after having consistently increased through the three governments preceding it (Figure 1.10). There is a similar fall in foreign investment (portfolio and direct), contrary to all the hype around the capital inflows during this government and India's rise in the international ranking of ease of doing business. What has surely increased during Modi's term is the magnitude of foreign exchange reserves. However, the absolute amount does not tell you much. A better yardstick for gauging foreign reserves is how many months of cushion it can provide for the current level of imports, with no change in the status quo, so that a sudden international shock will not make the economy vulnerable in terms of choking the importables. An analysis reveals that the import coverage under the NDA-II government is even lower that it was under NDA-I, and is much lower than it was under UPDA-I.

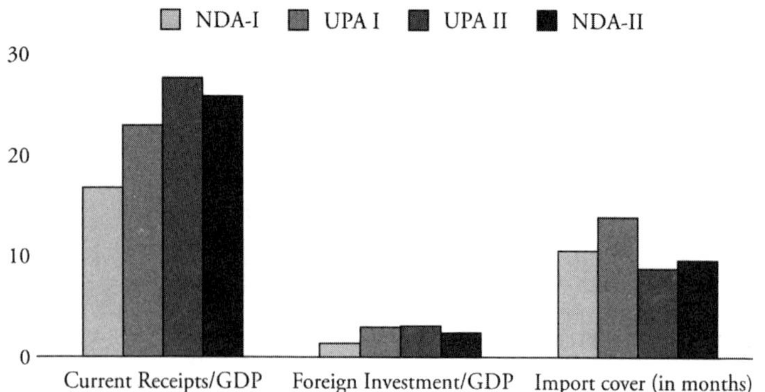

FIGURE 1.10: Current Receipts/GDP, Foreign Investment/GDP and Import Cover (in months)

Source: RBI, *Handbook of Statistics on the Indian Economy* (accessed December 2018).

I believe that there are multiple reasons for why Make in India has not delivered, at least in terms of creating international markets.

One, it relies heavily on the public-private partnership (PPP) model instead of a State-led development model, even though the PPPs spectacularly failed to deliver under the UPA. The failure of this model leads to failed infrastructure development, a condition critical for a policy take-off of this magnitude. Apart from this, the financial model of PPP carries with it the potential to destabilise the capital base of the public-sector banks, thereby limiting credit to non-infra sectors. Rising non-performing assets of the public-sector banks (discussed in detail later in Chapter 2, this volume), particularly in the infrastructural sector both during the UPA and the NDA-II governments, is just one indicator of the failed PPP model. As far as infrastructural development by the government is concerned, the report card of the Modi government speaks for itself. The status of implementation of such projects shows[8] that the share of the Central-sector projects stalled/delayed stands at an average of 100 per cent for the atomic energy sector, 50 per cent for civil aviation, and 45 per cent for the coal sector. Compare this to the figure of the oft-lampooned policy-paralysed UPA-II, where the respective figures were lower at 71 per cent, 45 per cent, and 44 per cent.

Two, this strategy is, by its very nature, in conflict with a domestic demand-driven approach. This is because it requires a *continuous* decline in the cost of production, a significant proportion of which is the wage cost, to outcompete the rivals. Two ways in which it is possible to keep the relative wage costs down is by depressing the wages and/or increasing the productivity of labour relative to the competitors. Both involve a fall in the share of wages in the economy (as has been the case with the Chinese, or other such experiments). This squeezes the domestic demand in the economy in the long run, either through a fall in income (wage fall) or unemployment (through labour displacing technological expansion).

Three, even if we assume that growth is delivered, it will be inequitable for the working masses in general. Modi appears to equate the interests of the corporates, who surely benefit from such a strategy, with those of the majority of the population.

Four, the other part of the cost—raw materials—requires that the corporates be given a free hand in terms of exploiting natural resources. This has resulted in massive corporate scams. The extent of environmental degradation domestically, coupled with the exploitation of the resource-rich-but-politically-weak countries abroad should surely be a matter of concern, even for the export enthusiasts.

Last, but not the least, this growth, if delivered, would still be beholden to the importing nations. If, for some reason, they hit a roadblock in terms of providing a market, as is happening today, it will have a cascading effect on the export-oriented sectors, which would have lost the fallback options in the very process.

India has failed to create an international niche market as promised under the Make in India campaign. It has also lost its position as a destination for portfolio capital. As a result of a net outflow in recent times, the rupee has come under severe strain. Modi had promised to 'bring the pride back' to the Indian rupee. Instead, the currency is now valued at its lowest ever in Indian history (Figure 1.11).

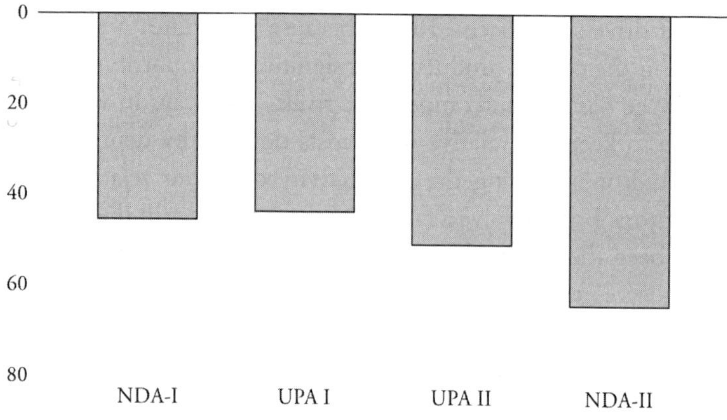

FIGURE 1.11: The Indian Rupee had a Great Fall

Source: RBI, *Handbook of Statistics on the Indian Economy* (accessed December 2018).

One could perhaps argue that the increased net outflow of capital from India has more to do with the increasing returns in the home countries from where this capital had initially come. So it is more a pull factor from the global North than a push factor from India that has resulted in this outflow. But Modi's promise was that the Indian economy would create pull factors of its own. To add insult to injury, the fall in the value of the rupee, which lowers the dollar price of Indian goods in the international market, has not improved its exports prospects. This is because the purchasing power of international buyers influences the volume of trade between countries, more than the price of an exporting country's commodity.

DEMONETISATION AND THE GOODS AND SERVICES TAX

Demonetisation

No piece on the macro policy of the Modi government can be complete without discussing what has been touted as perhaps the biggest macro-economic experiment in recent times, anywhere in the world, that is, the decision to demonetise high-denomination old currency notes in November 2016. The policy has been in the eye of a storm, both domestically and internationally. There may not be a foolproof way of measuring the impact of any such shock since a counterfactual of what would have happened had demonetisation not taken place cannot be created. Recently, the former Chief Economic Advisor to Modi, Arvind Subramanian, has publicly stated that this exercise was a 'massive, draconian, monetary shock'. Another prominent figure, Raghuram Rajan, who resigned from the post of RBI Governor before demonetisation was announced, has said that even as the growth rate of the world economy was picking up (Table 1.1), India slowed down as a result of demonetisation and the introduction of the Goods and Services Tax (GST).

One way of ascertaining, at least partially, the effect of this policy is to look at how the economy behaved before and after this shock. The picture is quite telling (see Table 1.1 and Figure 1.12).

TABLE 1.1: Economic Performance Pre- and Post-Demonetisation

Period	World GDP	India GDP	Government Expenditure	Indirect/Direct Share
Pre-Demonetisation	2.6	7.8	7.8	90.5
Post-Demonetisation	3.1	6.8	12.5	96.9

Source: RBI, *Handbook of Statistics on the Indian Economy* and World Bank Data (accessed December 2018).

The shock was delivered in the third quarter of 2016–17, so we divide the Modi government's tenure between the quarters before this and the ones after it. The break is quite palpable (Figure 1.12). There was a significant 1 percentage point drop in the growth rates from 7.8 to 6.8 between these two periods, even as there was a recovery in the world economy from 2.6 to 3.1 per cent (see Table 1.1). But what is interesting is that the post-demonetisation phase witnessed an almost 5 percentage point rise in government expenditure, which goes contrary to an otherwise fiscally hawkish government (Table 1.1). There are two issues here. One, in the absence of such expenditure, which partially mitigated the contractionary effects of demonetisation, the economy would have grown even slower than 6.8 per cent (more on this below) and would have perhaps further exposed an ill-thought-out policy. Two, given its fiscal hawkishness, how did the government propose to compensate for this rise on the revenue side? And the result is, as expected, through a dramatic rise in indirect taxes.

This 'draconian' measure doubly squeezed the poorer sections of the society. On the one hand, they lost jobs and incomes, or at times even their lives standing in day-long queues to get their meagre, hard-earned money converted to the new currency notes. On the other hand, they also 'paid for' this ill-conceived policy in sweat and blood, through higher taxes on the goods they had to purchase with an already diminished income.

To see how the economy would have fared under a 'pure' demonetisation policy, that is, without the mitigating effect of the injection of demand through government expenditure, I make a simplifying assumption. The question I pose is: What would have happened to the economy if the government had continued to spend at its pre-demonetisation rates? It would have brought the rate of growth further down in the post-demonetisation period to 6.4 per cent from 7.8 per cent in the pre-demonetisation phase (Figure 1.12).

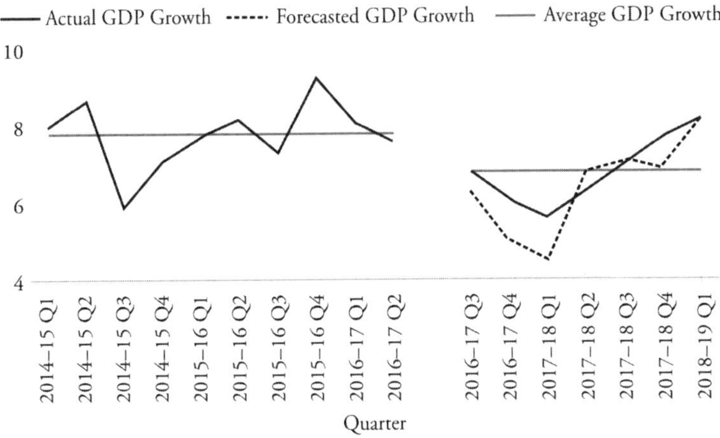

FIGURE 1.12: Ill-effects of Demonetisation

Source: RBI, *Handbook of Statistics on the Indian Economy* (accessed December 2018).

Goods and Services Tax

The other macro-economic experiment that this government had introduced is the GST. Much like demonetisation, there are many problems with the GST. Taxes decided at the levels of the states used to give them relative freedom in terms of policy priorities, but a common national tax policy dismantles the federal nature of the Indian economy. The state governments are, in any case, bound by the limits set on state deficits by the targets set by the Fiscal Responsibility and Budget Management (FRBM) Act 2003. In such a situation, the autonomy of state governments vis-à-vis taxing possibilities is of central importance. If the Central government fixes their deficit targets and then takes away their influence on generating revenue, then it effectively also determines their expenditure policy. Consequently, the state governments, even if they are of a different political affiliation, are forced to align their policy to that of the Centre.

In a recently televised interview to the Asian News International (ANI), PM Modi made three major claims in defence of demonetisation and GST—that it resulted in an increase in the tax net and better collection of indirect taxes; formalisation of the economy; and a fall in the currency-GDP ratio. Let us look at these three claims in some detail.

With regard to his first claim, since the taxes rise in tandem with the GDP, a more appropriate variable than the *number* of tax filings would be whether tax collections grew faster than the GDP in the post-policy phase as compared to the pre-policy phase, what the economists call tax buoyancy.[9] Data on direct tax suggests that this buoyancy had indeed increased in the year after demonetisation. But this was on account of corporate taxes. Meanwhile, the buoyancy of personal income tax *declined* (recall that the target of demonetisation was the black income generated by tax-evading households). As far as indirect taxes are concerned, data[10] suggests that the post-GST indirect tax buoyancy has actually *declined*.

On his second claim, the formalisation of the economy, the jury is still out. But a more fundamental question is whether formalisation through this route was desirable in the first place. When PM Modi links demonetisation and GST with his 'crusade' against the existing informalisation of the Indian economy, there is an explicit assumption of conflating the informal sector with the black economy. What is the difference between the formal and the informal economy? Formal sectors are ones where workers have social protection and economic security, while those belonging to informal sectors do not have such rights. The informal economy, therefore, is by no means synonymous with corruption or black economy. What differentiates white from black income is surely not the usage of cash, since cash in itself is not black or white. Instead, it is the income, in the form of cash or otherwise, escaping the tax net that makes it black. Nothing stops the formal sector from being more or less corrupt than its informal counterpart. After all, the massive corporate scams the world over involve companies in the formal sector. Under-reporting profits, over-invoicing costs (particularly of imports), the round-tripping of profits to tax havens abroad are all done by big sharks in the profession, and not the poor *rediwala* or a contract worker engaged in the informal sector.

What Modi has turned a blind eye to is that a higher level of informalisation in India is *not* out of choice, but one of compulsion since the formal sector does not generate enough jobs. And some of these jobless people are engaged in petty production to somehow make their ends meet. After all, in the absence of a social security net, how would the have-nots survive? And for the relatively better-off within the have-nots, who own small informal businesses, it is precisely because of their low capital base that such distress-driven small operating businesses cannot compete with big firms and have to stay in the informal sector to stay afloat. *Forcing* formalisation, say, through GST, on such producers and on the people working for them without providing a sustainable model of job creation and development in the formal sector worsens the condition of the informal-sector workers.

The third claim, of movement towards a more cashless economy as a result of both these policies, is also not entirely correct since the data on the cash-GDP ratio suggests that while there was a dip in this ratio right after demonetisation, with time the use of cash in transactions has gone up. Even here, there is nothing wrong with the use of cash *per se*. If the cash circulating is obtained through legal means, it is as good as any other form of transaction. Moreover, in the rural economy, non-cash-based transactions are limited due to a lack of technology or familiarity.

In conclusion, I would say that not only has the NDA-II government failed to deliver on Modi's '*vikas purush*' image, but it has also further inflicted hardship on the dispossessed through demonetisation and put the brakes on the aspirations of small businesses through the implementation of the GST.

As for what can be done, to begin with, there needs to be a fundamental shift away from a focus exclusively on growth. While growth may be a means to an end—that of human development—it is definitely not the only means. Hence, the obsession with growth at the cost of everything else is quite misplaced. After all, what good would come out of the rising income of a poor dalit woman if there are no schools, hospitals, water, sanitation, and other basic facilities over and above what she suffers at the bottom of the caste and patriarchal hierarchy? A simple statistic may help to explain this contradiction between growth and development. Take for example India, which is currently ranked first at the global level in growth rate among the large economies and sixth in GDP. India is also ranked 130th in the human development index (HDI), a comprehensive statistic capturing life expectancy and level of education, along with other per capita indicators.

I believe that a revival of the Indian economy requires a radical shift in the policy focus—from looking at the elusive external markets to looking inwards and for opportunities in the domestic markets, thereby creating decent employment for the youth in this country. It requires giving priority to equity over growth; developing the capabilities of the Indian people by ensuring quality healthcare and education; providing equal opportunities to people irrespective of their caste, gender, region, or religion; environmental sustainability; and building South–South relationships. As we will see in the rest of this volume, unfortunately Modi did not seem to be convinced about this basic shift in focus required to face the challenges that lie ahead.

Notes and References

1. This may not, in fact, be a fair comparison since the methodologies for the two series are entirely different, and the jury is still out on the new methodology, its transparency, and limitations. In fact, economists from across the entire political spectrum were sceptical when it was first introduced. Reservations about the new methodology have been raised since the new Gross Domestic Product (GDP) numbers do not match with other economic parameters, such as growth in bank credit, investment, and tax collections, which normally move in tandem with the GDP.

2. While the Central Statistical Organisation (CSO) has recently released data going back to 2004–05 using the new methodology, it has been controversial. To make matters worse, there were two contradictory figures calculated by bodies under this government, with the 'unofficial' one showing the UPA governments in an even better light compared to the NDA-II government and the 'official' one downgrading them! It is no wodner that it resulted in a political storm. This divergence itself makes *both* these estimates suspect. This means that neither should really be taken at face value.

3. Lucas Chancel and Thomas Piketty, 'Indian Income Inequality, 1922–2015: From British Raj to Billionaire Raj?', CEPR Discussion Papers 12409, 2018. Available at https://wid.world/document/chancelpiketty2017widworld/ (accessed February 2019).

4. The richest taxpayers here are those with incomes greater than Rs 500 crore annually, while the lowest-income taxpayers have an income less than Rs 1.5 lakh annually.

5. Centre for Sustainable Employment, 'State of Working India', Azim Premji University, 2018. Available at https://cse.azimpremjiuniversity.edu.in/state-of-working-india/ (accessed February 2019).

6. A more fundamental issue to raise here is whether fiscal consolidation itself is correct. And the answer is no, particularly in an economy suffering from low demand. The usual arguments against fiscal deficit—of eating up the savings of the private enterprise, fuelling inflation, scaring foreign investors—are often either misplaced or downright wrong. Higher expenditure by the government without a commensurate taxation means a net increase in demand, which generates profits for enterprises. Since this increases the production and supply of commodities, this higher demand

does *not* lead to inflation. As for international rankings, why it is extremely risky for a sovereign country to be governed by footloose international capital, which is notoriously whimsical and has the potential to wreak havoc.

7. As reported in *The Hindu*, 1 February 2015.

8. Figures from the implementation of end-March status of Central-sector projects, *Handbook of Statistics on the Indian Economy*, RBI (accessed December 2018).

9. Tax buoyancy measures the ratio of the growth of tax collection and GDP (both in nominal terms). But instead of complicated terms like buoyancy, it would be simpler to look at the tax-GDP ratio. Suppose the tax-GDP ratio has been rising in the past prior to a policy, then it is difficult to say whether the post-policy rise is indeed as a result of the policy—something that tax buoyancy can clearly expose. A policy targeted at changing the trend in tax collection should be able to show that there is a *structural* break in the growth of the variable targeted (say, direct taxes in the case of demonetisation and indirect taxes in the case of GST).

10. Indirect taxes here are exclusive of customs and excise duties, since these have nothing to do with the GST policy.

two

Breaking Bad

India's Banking Distress

PRASENJIT BOSE AND ZICO DASGUPTA

The year 2017–18 was a good year for the global banking industry.[1] In the same year, however, India's banking sector recorded its worst financial performance in decades. *The Financial Times*' 'The Banker'[2] reported:

> There is one glaring exception to the glowing returns reported in the 2018 ranking: India. Only half of its banks managed a profit and the sector collectively posted a $9.2 billion loss. The country is home to 48% of the Top 1000's loss-makers and dominates the table of biggest losses .... Among the 25 banks with the highest NPL (non-performing loans) ratios are 11 Indian banks and 11 from the Eurozone, plus one from Bulgaria and two from Africa.

A little over 10 years ago, the picture was the exact opposite. While the global banking industry was collapsing during the global financial crisis, the Indian banking system seemed resilient and largely insulated. What lies behind this severe deterioration in the profitability of the Indian banks?

The United Progressive Alliance (UPA) regime (2004–14) had presided over a period of unprecedented bank credit growth, which had also involved reckless lending to the private sector and PPP infrastructure projects, alongside lax regulation, which allowed delinquent corporates and pliant banks to collude and conceal big ticket loan defaults through corporate debt restructuring. The Modi government claims to have brought such crony capitalism to an end. While the inescapable recognition of the non-performing assets (NPAs) have led to the humongous losses by banks in recent times, we are being told by the finance ministry and the Reserve Bank of India (RBI) that the policy changes introduced under the present regime have already started turning things around.

Is a banking recovery around the corner? Do those crony capitalist forces still remain, which have resulted in corporate delinquency and the accumulation of bad loans, thereby severely impairing the banking sector? What has been the impact on the banking industry, and what are the implications for the millions of ordinary bank customers, who depend on the banking system as both debtors and depositors? These are the issues that we address in the rest of the chapter.

Bad Loans Crisis: NPAs, Bank Frauds

Economic growth witnessed an acceleration in India under the UPA-I and II regimes, driven by increasing levels of private corporate investment.[3] The bulk of this private corporate investment was financed by credit extended by the public-sector banks (PSBs), which had assumed the lead role in industrial financing, replacing the erstwhile development financial institutions (DFIs) like ICICI, IDBI, and UTI, which were converted into commercial banks in the post-liberalisation period.[4]

Bank credit to various industrial sectors, including infrastructure sectors like power, roads, telecommunications, aviation, etc., had reached unprecedented levels during the high-growth phase, alongside sharp declines in the interest rates. While the private-sector banks withdrew from such lending after the global financial crisis and recession in 2008–09, the PSBs—prodded by the Central government—continued to finance risky industrial projects, in order to prolong the investment boom. The credit-driven investment bubble eventually burst in 2011–12, causing economic slowdown. With declining corporate profitability, loan defaults became the norm, leading to the private corporates offloading their losses onto the PSBs. It was this phenomenon that was termed 'riskless capitalism' by the then Governor of the RBI.[5]

The Indian banking sector was rendered weaker following this credit boom. As can be seen from Figure 2.1, which provides a time-series of the financial profitability indicators for the Indian banking sector, the NPA ratio (non-performing assets to total gross loans) shot up significantly between 2015 and 2018. Besides, the profitability of the Indian banking sector has declined every year from 2013 onwards, and has turned negative in 2018. The severity of the crisis can be understood from the fact that there are only two countries in the world, crisis-stricken Greece and San Marino, whose banking sectors have performed worse than India's in 2018.[6]

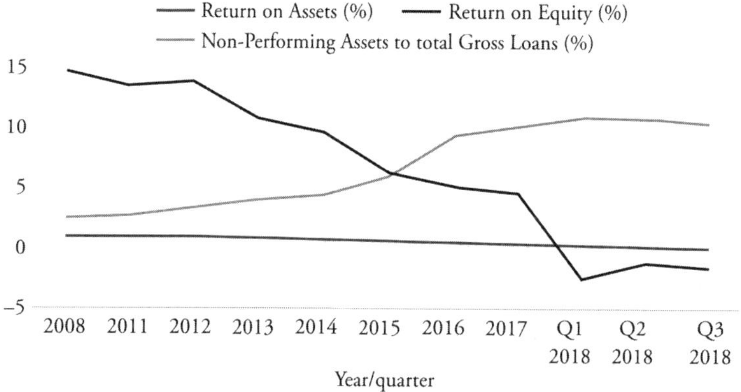

FIGURE 2.1: India's Banking Profitability Indicators

Source: Financial Soundness Indicators (FSIs) Database, IMF.

The RBI had encouraged the reckless lending practices of the UPA era. Once corporate profitability started declining and defaults rose, the RBI had initially allowed the banks to window-dress their balance sheets and conceal the severity of the problem.[7] The expectation perhaps was that an economic recovery would occur soon, reviving corporate profitability and relieving the debt distress. Having realised that no such recovery was in sight in the near future, the RBI conducted an Asset Quality Review (AQR) in 2015–16, compelling banks to stop concealing loan defaults and gradually start recognising NPAs in a transparent manner. As a result, the total stock of NPAs of the scheduled commercial banks (SCBs) nearly doubled in a single financial year.

The Modi government has often claimed credit for this transparent recognition of the NPAs by the banks. RBI data shows that Rs 16 trillion worth of fresh NPAs were added in the past four years (2014–15 to 2017–18) by the SCBs, in contrast to Rs 5.7 trillion during the previous five years (2009–10 to 2013–14) (see Table 2.1). However, a closer look at the data reveals that the banking distress has, for reasons other than the mere recognition of the NPAs, actually worsened under the present regime.

NPA Write-offs

Rising bad debts chokes the banking system because it limits its capacity to extend credit for new investments, which creates a vicious cycle. Therefore, reduction of the NPAs should have been the top priority of this government. Reduction in NPAs can happen either by recovering the due amount through various channels or by writing them off. Writing off bad corporate debts is the extreme form of 'riskless capitalism', where the loss in business is borne entirely by the banks instead of the delinquent borrowers. If the bank losses are then compensated by the government, it amounts to an ex-gratia transfer from the State to the private corporate sector.

Under the NDA-II regime, NPA write-offs have been almost eight times as high as that of the UPA-II (Table 2.1). These write-offs have in turn been reflected in higher NPA provisioning for the banks. Despite making positive operating profits, rising NPA provisioning has led to the banks making net financial losses. The situation vis-à-vis the PSBs is particularly grim, with the 21 PSBs taken together making net losses over the past three financial years (2015–16 to 2017–18) (Figure 2.2).[8]

TABLE 2.1: NPA Recovery vs. Write-offs: 2004–05 to 2018–19

(in Rs Billion)

		2004–05 to 2008–09	2009–10 to 2013–14	2014–15 to 2017–18
All SCBs	Fresh NPAs	1,553.2	5,758.3	16,709.1
	NPA Recoveries	1,394.5	3,241.9	4,252.8
	NPA Write-offs	85.0	550.0	4,032.5
PSBs	Fresh NPAs	1,078.9	4,799.2	13,795.9
	NPA Recoveries	1,119.0	2,642.6	3,237.7
	NPA Write-offs	21.6	321.1	3,219.2
PVBs	Fresh NPAs	325.2	670.0	2,639.7
	NPA Recoveries	195.8	396.2	878.6
	NPA Write-offs	34.4	194.2	705.7

Source: Statistical Tables Relating to Banks in India, RBI.
Available at https://dbie.rbi.org.in.

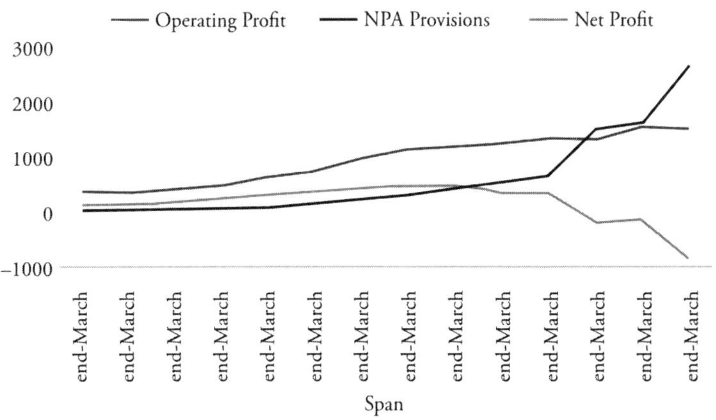

FIGURE 2.2: Net Profit of Public-sector Banks: 2004–05 to 2017–18

Source: Basic Statistical Returns of SCBs in India, RBI.

Even after such massive NPA write-offs worth Rs 4 trillion in four years, the total stock of NPAs stood at Rs 10.4 trillion in end-March 2018, out of which the PSBs accounted for Rs 9 trillion. One-fifth of these bad loans are against the top 100 defaulters and more than four-fifth against large borrowers, whose credit exposure exceeds Rs 5 crore.[9] So, it is the wealthy big corporates and not the small businesses or the farmers who hold the bulk of these bad loans. Going by the latest *Financial Stability Report*, the total stock of NPAs is not going to come down significantly in the foreseeable future.[10]

Bank Frauds

Bank frauds are the other major contributors to the mounting losses of the banks. The fact that the number of bank frauds in various banking operations has increased under the present government was acknowledged in the latest Annual Report of the RBI (2017–18).[11] The fraud committed by Nirav Modi and Mehul Choksey on the Punjab National Bank (PNB) contributed to a jump in the total amount involved in bank frauds from Rs 239 billion in 2016–17 to Rs 411 billion in 2017–18.[12] The RBI's latest *Financial Stability Report* (December 2018) provides data on total bank frauds and loan frauds, each above Rs 10 lakh in value (Table 2.2).

Overall, Rs 1.33 trillion have been ripped off the banking system by the fraudsters under the present government's rule, with around Rs 1.2 trillion belonging to the PSBs.[13] The amount lost by the PSBs in bank frauds is more than the cumulative net loss of Rs 1.14 trillion made by the PSBs in the past three years. These reflect the impunity with which bank frauds have been perpetrated, and also expose the complacency (if not complicity) of the bank managements, policymakers, and the regulators.

Despite the slight improvement in the NPA ratio of the SCBs in September 2018 over March 2018, the disturbing increase in bank frauds in 2018–19 do not provide confidence in the restoration of the financial health of the PSBs. Moreover, there is no transparency

TABLE 2.2: Bank Frauds in India: 2013–14 to 2018–19

(amount involved larger than Rs 10 lakh)

	Cases of Bank Frauds		Amount Involved (in Rs Billion)		Average Size (in Rs Crore)	
	Total Number	Number of Credit-related Frauds	Total Bank Frauds	Credit-related Frauds	Bank Frauds	Credit-related Frauds
2013–14	4,306	1,990	101.7	84.1	2.4	4.2
2014–15	4,639	2,251	194.6	171.2	4.2	7.6
2015–16	4,693	2,125	187	173.7	4	8.2
2016–17	5,076	2,322	239.3	205.6	4.7	8.9
2017–18	5,917	2,526	411.7	225.6	7	8.9
H1: 2018–19	3,416	1,792	304.2	287.5	8.9	16
Total under NDA-II	23,741	11,016	1,336.8	1,063.6	5.6	9.7

Source: December 2018 *Financial Stability Report*, RBI.

regarding the NPA write-offs since, beyond reporting bank group-wise aggregate NPA data, neither individual banks nor the RBI discloses the details of these write-offs. Even the names of wilful defaulters and fraudsters are not disclosed, citing non-disclosure norms regarding credit information.[14]

No End in Sight

The NDA-II government's claim, that mechanisms put in place under its rule—like the Insolvency and Bankruptcy Code (IBC) and the RBI's revised Prompt Corrective Action (PCA) framework—is gradually resolving the bad loans problem is also questionable.[15]

Under the IBC, only Rs 1.25 trillion worth of NPA cases have been resolved so far.[16] The average recovery rate of bad debt by the banks stood at around 45 per cent only (see Table 2.3). Going by this rate of recovery and given the current stock of NPAs worth over Rs 10 trillion, the banks will have to bear a loss of over Rs 5 trillion in the next few years.

TABLE 2.3: Corporate Debt Resolution under IBC: Realisation of Financial Claims

(Cases involving Claims over Rs 50 Billion up to September 2018)

Name of Corporate Debtor	Admitted Claims of Financial Creditors	Realisation by Financial Creditors	% of Claims Realised (Right axis)
Bhushan Steel Ltd.	560.2	355.7	63.5
Electro Steels Steel Ltd.	131.8	53.2	40.4
Amtek Auto Ltd.	126.1	43.3	34.4
Monnet Ispat and Energy Ltd.	110.1	28.9	26.3
Orissa Manganese & Minerals Ltd.	53.9	3.1	5.8
Adhunik Metaliks Ltd.	53.7	4.1	7.6
Zion Steel Ltd.	53.7	0.2	0.3
Total	1,089.4	488.5	44.8

Source: The Quarterly Newsletter of the Insolvency and Bankruptcy Board of India, Various Issues.

As far as the RBI's revised PCA framework is concerned, 11 of the 21 PSBs have so far been brought under it since April 2017, with stringent restrictions imposed on their lending, branch and staff expansion, capital expenditure, etc. While the stated objective of the PCA framework is to restore the financial health of these banks, the outcome so far has been the opposite. RBI's latest *Report on Trend and Progress of Banking in India 2017–18* provides a comparative analysis of the 11 PCA-PSBs with that of others which are not facing these restrictions. The results show that by further restricting the core operations of the already stressed PSBs, the PCA framework has been pushing them further into the red.[17]

The PCA framework appears quite counter-productive, especially when seen in the context of the bank recapitalisation that has been undertaken by the Modi government. On the one hand, Rs 1.4 trillion has already been spent by the government in the past two years to infuse capital into the PSBs to improve their financial positions, the bulk of which has gone into the PCA-PSBs.[18] On the other hand, the restrictions on lending and branch expansion have further eroded the profitability of the PCA-PSBs and contributed to their capital erosion. Such a capital infusion has thus only inflicted fiscal costs, without restoring the financial health of these PSBs.[19]

Bank recapitalisation in the absence of effective NPA recovery is nothing but a taxpayer-funded bailout of the delinquent corporate defaulters and fraudsters, as well as the inefficient decision-makers of the finance ministry and PSB Boards, who appear to be presiding over a surreal self-destruction. With the PCA-PSBs caught in a vicious cycle of bad loans accumulation, NPA write-offs, loan loss provisioning, financial losses and capital erosion, the government and the RBI—both of which are responsible for bringing matters to this pass—are only blaming each other. Urjit Patel's resignation from RBI's Governorship in December 2018 was a result of this imbroglio.

Those advocating the utilisation of the 'excess reserves' of the RBI to recapitalise the PSBs are missing the larger context in which capital infusion is being undertaken by the government.[20] Even if such RBI capital-funded recapitalisation occurs for the PCA-PSBs while their financial losses keep mounting because of NPA provisioning, it would nonetheless amount to a bailout with public funds, although the immediate burden will not have been borne by the taxpayers. The point is to arrest the source of capital erosion of the PSBs, rather than keep throwing money into a bottomless pit.

The government has come up with another non-solution to the bad loans problem, in the form of PSB mergers. The move to amalgamate the Bank of Baroda, Dena Bank, and Vijaya Bank, while being officially justified in terms of elusive potential synergies, is quite clearly an exercise in financial engineering. By amalgamating the balance sheet of the Dena Bank, a PCA-PSB, with those of the Vijaya Bank, a profitable PSB, and the much larger Bank of Baroda, the government expects the capital and NPA ratios of the merged entity to reflect an improvement. However, such an exercise would not help in the process of actual NPA recovery. Rather, organisational disruption caused in these PSBs through the merger, along with staff and branch rationalisation, may actually lead to a deterioration of financial performance, as has been the case after the merger of the parent SBI with its subsidiaries in April 2017.[21]

Deleterious Economic Impact

The worsening bad loans crisis in the Indian banking sector has also resulted in a slowdown in bank credit and deposit growth, which has adversely affected economic activity over the past four years. Growth in bank deposits during UPA-I, preceding the global financial crisis, had already started falling during UPA-II, but instead of a revival in deposits, the declining trend continued during the Modi government's tenure (see Figure 2.3a). This was despite the spike in bank deposits witnessed in 2016–17 after the sudden decision to demonetise 86 per cent of the economy's currency in circulation in November 2016, which had forced people to deposit and exchange the proscribed high-value currency notes in the banks. Once the supply of currency notes normalised, bank deposit growth for all SCBs fell further in 2017–18, with the PSBs' deposit growth plummeting to its lowest annual growth rate in decades.

In contrast to the PSBs, the private-sector banks (PvBs) registered a higher deposit growth in 2017–18 (Figure 2.3a), which reflects that the decline in the PSB deposit growth rate is also a manifestation of the eroding confidence of bank customers in the PSBs. A reverse trend was witnessed in the aftermath of the global financial crisis, when the deposit growth rates of private banks had fallen sharply in the two years, 2008–09 and 2009–10, while PSB deposit growth had surged.

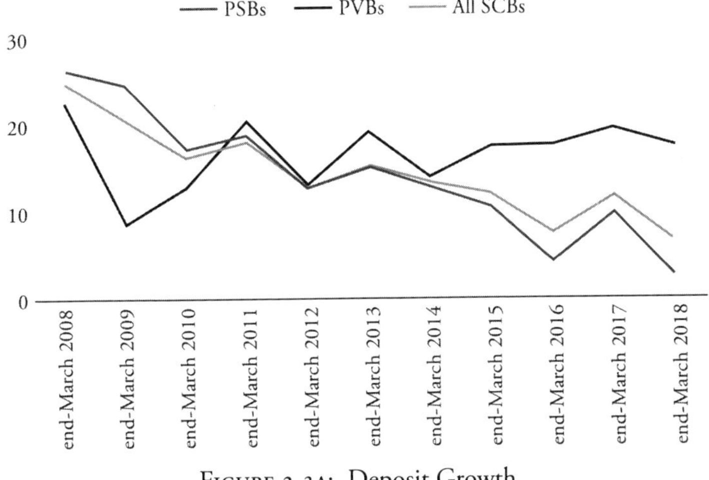

FIGURE 2.3A: Deposit Growth

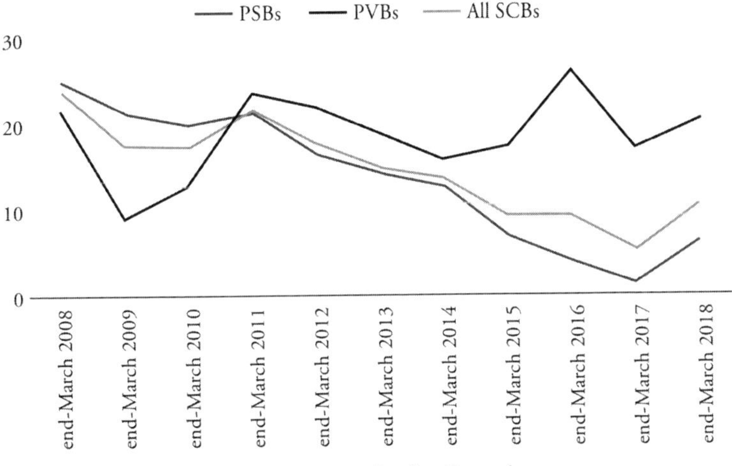

FIGURE 2.3B: Credit Growth

Source: Basic Statistical Returns of SCBs in India, RBI.

In the backdrop of the deteriorating financials of the PSBs in the recent period, the attempt made by the Modi government to pass the Financial Resolution and Deposit Insurance Bill (FRDI), 2017 in Parliament played a role in scaring depositors away from the PSBs.

The main objective of the FRDI Bill was to dilute the sovereign guarantee, which insulates the PSBs from bank failures, and introduce a 'bail-in' provision, which would enable the use of bank deposits to fund bailouts in case of bank failures.[22] This controversial move created widespread anxiety and discontent amongst depositors across the country, which eventually forced the government to backtrack and shelve the bill; but the episode has certainly sent wrong public signals about the PSBs.

The divergence between the performance of the private banks and the PSBs is also seen in credit growth (Figure 2.3b). The overall trend in credit growth followed a more or less similar pattern as that of deposits. While the PSBs still account for a much larger share of credit and deposits in the banking system than the private and foreign banks, the PSBs' shares in deposits and credit have consistently declined between UPA-II and NDA-II.

After declining for six consecutive years, from 2011–12 to 2016–17, growth in overall bank credit has shown a modest revival in 2017–18, which has been cited in official circles as an indication of banking recovery. However, the outstanding credit-GDP ratio, as well as the incremental credit-GDP ratio (which measures the flow of fresh credit), have fallen during the Modi government's tenure (see Figure 2.4).[23] It is clear that the very large lending space being vacated by the PSBs owing to their deteriorating financials is not being occupied fully by the PvBs, despite aggressive lending on their part. Given the 63 per cent share of the PSBs in outstanding credit, there cannot be any credit revival in the economy without reviving the PSBs.

A closer look at the sectoral credit data also reveals the lopsided nature of this so-called credit revival (see Figure 2.5). Even as the industrial sector has seen a collapse in bank credit, agriculture and priority sectors have witnessed sharp declines. The only sectors to beat this trend were services and the personal loans segment. This broadly mirrors the real growth trajectory of the economy from 2014–15 till now, although a rosier-than-reality picture has been painted through official manoeuvring over the GDP statistics.

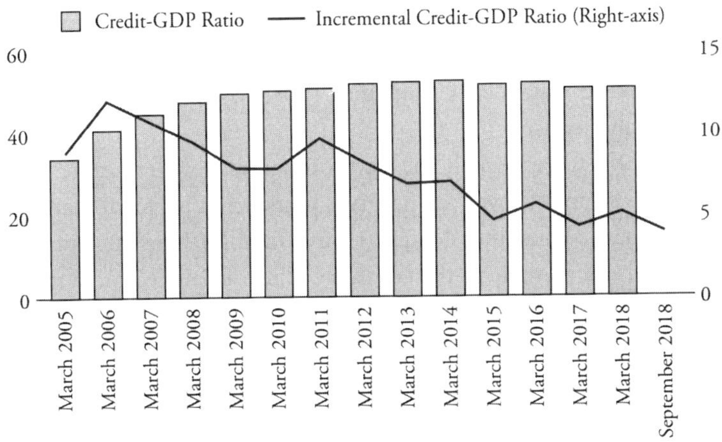

FIGURE 2.4: Credit-GDP Ratios

Source: Basic Statistical Returns of the SCBs, RBI; Monthly Bulletin, RBI; and National Account Statistics, CSO, MoSPI.

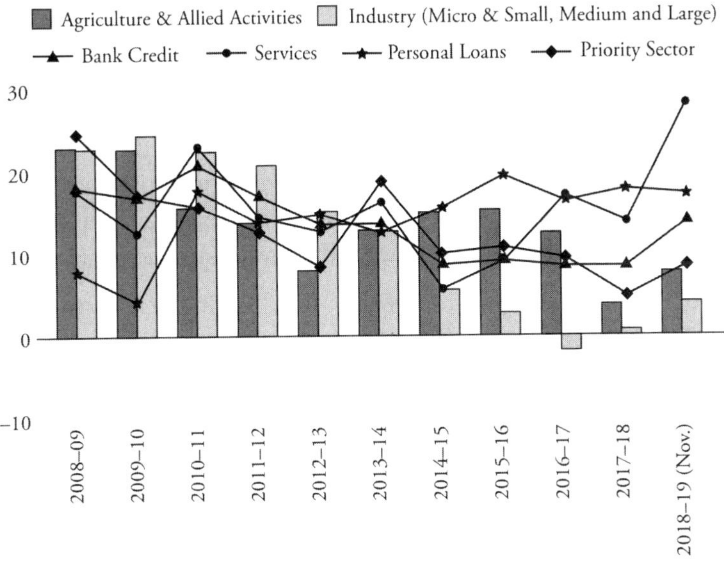

FIGURE 2.5: Sector-wise Deployment of Bank Credit: Annual Growth Rates (%)

Source: Basic Statistical Returns of SCBs in India, RBI.

What is remarkable is that the sharp rise in services-sector credit and personal loans in 2018–19 has been driven by bank lending to Non-Banking Financial Companies (NBFCs), other than services and housing loans.

The NBFCs, especially the loan companies, have lent aggressively to various segments over the past two years; from personal loans like vehicle loans, consumer loans to buy durables like smartphones, etc., to advances made to the commercial real-estate sector. With the slowdown in PSB credit, the NBFCs have sought to increase their market share in the lending space by borrowing from the banks and mutual funds. An analysis carried out in the RBI's latest *Report on Trend and Progress of Banking* suggests that the sharper decline in the NBFCs' lending rates compared to the banks have helped in their gaining a market share, and confirms the vulnerability of the NBFCs to liquidity risks, given their strategy of borrowing short and lending long.[24]

The possibility of a borrowing and lending bubble in the NBFC sector came into focus after the takeover of the Infrastructure Leasing and Financial Services Limited (IL&FS) by the government in October 2018, following successive defaults on repayments. The exposure of the banks and mutual funds to the NBFC sector, whose aggregate asset size stood at $26 trillion in September 2018, remains high. The bursting of this credit bubble can have serious consequences, adding to the woes of the already stressed banking and financial sector.[25]

THE CHIMERA OF FINANCIAL INCLUSION

The NDA-II government's unwillingness to address the worsening distress in the banking sector has been accompanied by the announcing of two financial inclusion initiatives, the Pradhan Mantri Mudra Yojana (PMMY) and the Pradhan Mantri Jan Dhan Yojana (PMJDY). How effective have these schemes been in enhancing financial inclusion?

MUDRA and PMMY

Our calculations, based on RBI data on bank credit to the MSMEs in the industrial sector, show that aggregate credit flow to them in the past three years has actually been *negative*, in keeping with the general trend in the industrial sector (see Table 2.4).[26] For the MSMEs in the services sector, the aggregate net credit flow in the past three years has increased in comparison to the two years before the introduction of the MUDRA scheme. Being unable to revive bank credit to the MSME industrial sector, bank credit growth seems to have been channelled into the MSME services sector. Yet, even if we combine the two, the net aggregate bank credit flow to the total

TABLE 2.4: Bank Credit Flow into the MSME Sector

(in Rs Billion)

Parameters	2013–14	2014–15	2015–16	2016–17	2017–18
Micro and Small Enterprises, Industry	638.46	318.34	−85.61	−17.36	32.68
Medium Industry	−6.35	4.67	−97.15	−100.15	−11.26
Micro and Small Enterprises, Services	816.71	606.96	558.06	561.21	911.25
Total MSME (Right axis)	1,448.82	929.97	375.3	443.7	932.67

Parameters	Before MUDRA	After MUDRA
Micro and Small Enterprises, Industry	956.8	−70.29
Medium Industry	−1.68	−208.56
Micro and Small Enterprises Services	1,423.67	2,030.52
Total MSME	2,378.79	1,751.67

Source: Calculated from Sectoral Deployment of Non-Food Gross Bank Credit, RBI. Available at https://dbie.rbi.org.in

MSME sector in the post-MUDRA period is actually *lower* than the previous two years.

What could not be achieved through bank credit, however, has been somewhat compensated by non-bank (NBFC) credit. The December 2018 issue of the *MSME Pulse* reported that the NBFCs' share in fresh sanctions of MSME loans has gone up from 13 per cent in December 2015 to 17 per cent in September 2018.[27] Against the backdrop of the increasing share of NBFC lending to the MSMEs, disturbing signals have already started emanating. The December 2018 issue of *MSME Pulse* has expressed concern over 'loan stacking behaviour', that is, borrowers taking multiple loans from multiple lenders within a period of 60 days. While such borrowers have much higher default rates, it has been observed that NBFCs have contributed to almost half of loan sanctions under loan stacking. These symptoms do not reflect a sustainable trajectory of MSME loans advanced by the NBFCs.

Moreover, the June 2018 issue of *MSME Pulse* reported that out of all the first-time borrowers who availed of the sub-Rs 10 lakh loan during January–June 2016 (numbering around 2.7 lakhs), 28 per cent have subsequently exited formal lending, 16 per cent have turned into NPA, and around 55 per cent borrowers have sustained or grown their level of credit activity in two years. From January 2016–June 2018, the total number of first-time MSME borrowers was below 18 lakhs, which was less than 3 per cent of the total number of MSMEs in the country.[28] If we consider the fact that only 60 per cent of first-time borrowers continue to borrow the next year, the number of MSME borrowers under MUDRA does not appear to be very insignificant.

Moreover, 91 per cent of the total accounts under the PMMY had an average loan disbursal amount of only Rs 22,435.[29] It would be difficult to set up even a *pakoda*-selling unit with such an amount! These micro-loans to individuals, much like personal consumption loans, have comparatively lower NPA rates. But such micro-loans are too small for individual entrepreneurs to utilise for augmenting capital expenditure. Hence, such credit has a very limited impact on asset creation and employment generation.

Only around 9 per cent of the total PMMY loan accounts had an average size of Rs 1.86 lakh and above. This is closer to the total share of the larger GST-registered MSMEs, which shows the limited extent of financial inclusion achieved under the PMMY.

The PMMY remains vulnerable to an increase in NPA rates in the NBFC sector, which has seen a 396 per cent rise in credit flow from 2016–17 to 2017–18. The very quantum of this increase points towards a bubble. The attempt to replace the DFIs with NBFCs in providing debt-finance for the MSMEs, far from offering any durable solution, may actually end up spreading the bad loans crisis into new areas.

PMJDY

While zero balance accounts or Basic Savings Bank Deposit Accounts (BSBDAs) were introduced under RBI's financial inclusion plan under the previous regime, the NDA-II government repackaged and accelerated the scheme implementation under the PMJDY from 2014. This has led to a rapid rise in account ownership, with around 340 million accounts opened till end-December 2018 with aggregate deposits worth Rs 870 billion.

As per the World Bank's Global Findex Database, the share of adults with a bank account has more than doubled since 2011 to 80 per cent in 2017. However, the same database also showed that the share of inactive accounts in India, without any withdrawal or deposit in the past one year, was 48 per cent, which was the highest in the world. The figure has subsequently been revised to 38.5 per cent.[30] Moreover, the Findex also estimates that while 19.6 per cent of the adult population in India saved money in any financial institution in the past one year, only 8 per cent borrowed money from an institution or used a credit card. The PMJDY has therefore expanded financial inclusion in a very limited sense.

It is difficult to assess the efficacy of the additional benefits announced by the government for JDY account holders, such as the overdraft facility, debit card, and insurance coverage, in the absence of data availability vis-à-vis their beneficiaries. Only 23 per cent of the JDY accounts received direct benefit transfers (DBT) from the government till August 2018.[31] While the average amount per JDY account has been around Rs 2,580 only by end-December 2018, the number of inoperative accounts, where there have been no transaction in the previous two years, has grown between 2017 and 2018.[32] The initial spurt in bank deposit growth under the JDY till 2016–17 had tapered off in 2017–18, but has seen a rising trend in 2018–19.

The most important debate regarding the JDY, however, does not relate to its impact on financial inclusion, but to the trends in the deposits and withdrawals in a large number of these accounts in the aftermath of the decision to withdraw the high-value currency notes in November 2016. Deposits in JDY accounts had shot up by 41 per cent in the first week after demonetisation and continued rising over the next few months. By end-March 2017, however, the deposits fell sharply, but started rising subsequently.[33]

Such movements in JDY deposits have raised suspicions since November–December 2016 that the accounts are being used for money laundering after demonetisation. The RBI had imposed restrictions on withdrawals from JDY accounts in November 2016, based on the same suspicion. The finance minister and other ministry officials have on occasion mentioned ongoing investigations by the Income Tax department into suspicious account holders, but the outcomes of such investigations are still unknown, even after the passage of two years. It is indeed ironic that a financial inclusion scheme launched with much fanfare by the NDA-II government has turned out to be controversial for having become a conduit for large-scale money muling.

Bank Branch Retrenchment

Even as the efficacy of the financial inclusion initiatives of the NDA-II government remain suspect, the deteriorating financial health of the PSBs and the loss in their market shares have already led to a decline in their bank branches and staff recruitment. While the total employee strength of the PSBs (including officers and clerical and subordinate staff) came down between 2014–15 and 2017–18, that of the private-sector banks increased in the same period. The significant increase in recruitment by the private banks suggests an aggressive push on their part to occupy the lending space being vacated by the PSBs. However, given their smaller size in comparison to the PSBs and the differences in their business models, the shift towards private-sector banking, which the present government has actively encouraged, can only result in deteriorating financial inclusion in the Indian context.

This can be clearly seen from the declining rate of bank branch expansion over the past few years (Figure 2.6a). The number of new branches opened per year has declined for the PSBs and Regional Rural Banks (RRBs), and the expansion rate of the private-sector banks has also fallen. Despite the newly licensed Small Finance Banks and Payments Banks opening branches, the overall number of new bank branches in 2017–18 was way below its numbers in 2013–14 or 2015–16. This declining rate of branch expansion is more pronounced in the rural areas (Figure 2.6b). This happened mainly because of the decline in the number of new branches opened by the PSBs and RRBs, as well as the historical reluctance of the private banks to open rural branches, which do not offer quick or high business returns.

The net branch expansion, which takes into account the closure of branches, has actually turned negative for the PSBs in 2017–18. Here, the SBI accounted for 1,206 branch closures following the merger of the parent bank with its subsidiaries. The contraction in the number of PSB bank branches, which has continued in 2018–19, will have an adverse impact on economic activities, particularly in the rural areas. The RBI has already reported a decline in the total number of bank branches in rural areas in 2017–18, both brick-and-mortar branches and branches in the business correspondent (BC) mode, as a result of branch closures and 'non-performance' by the BCs.[34] Continuation of this trend can turn all attempts to enhance financial inclusion on its head.

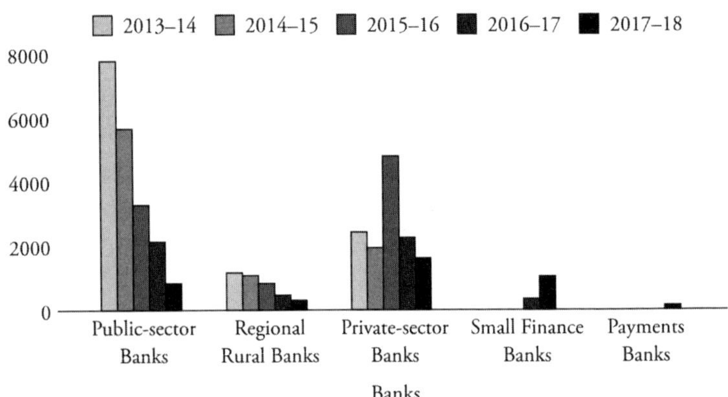

FIGURE 2.6A: Newly Opened Branches of SCBs

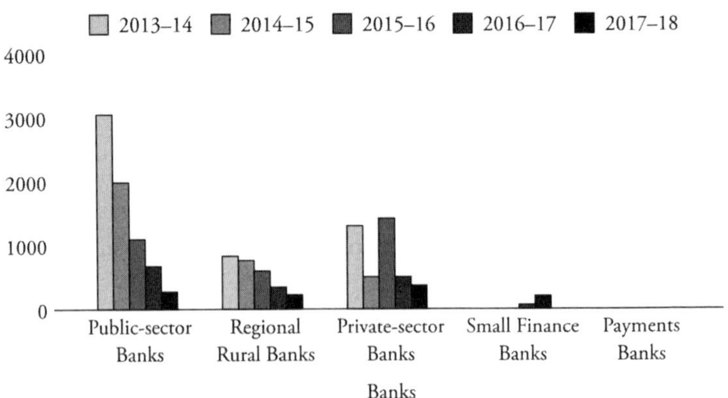

FIGURE 2.6B: Newly Opened Rural Branches of the SCBs

Source: Basic Statistical Returns of SCBs in India, RBI.

Conclusion

The way out of the mess in India's banking sector can only be found when both the Central government and the RBI finally recognise that the existing institutional framework in the form of the IBC and the PCA is grossly inadequate to meet the enormity of the bad loans crisis. The National Company Law Tribunal (NCLT) mechanism under the IBBI needs to be overhauled, giving more teeth to the financial creditors to speed up bad loans resolution and enhance the realisation rates. The PCA framework as well as the regulatory capital norms fixed by the RBI need to be reviewed and further revised, in order to relax the restrictions on credit and restore the normal operations of the PSBs. In sum, the entire policy focus needs to shift to speedy and effective NPA recovery from the delinquent corporate defaulters and to a serious crackdown on bank frauds, which are bleeding the PSBs to death.

Dealing with crony capitalism requires the political will to take on entrenched vested interests and the courage to dismantle the extant nexus between delinquent corporates and financial decision-makers. This is where the real governance deficit lies. The inaction of the Modi government vis-à-vis Vijay Mallya, Nirav Modi, Mehul Choksey, and hundreds of other serious economic offenders, in the backdrop of the worsening bad loans crisis and rising bank frauds, is proof enough of its becoming a part of the status quo ante.

The NDA-II regime has been unable to revive the PSBs and has squandered fiscal resources in corporate bailouts, masked under NPA write-offs and PSB recapitalisation. The expansions seen in the private-sector banks and NBFCs have not been to the extent that could compensate for the shrinkage of the PSBs. As a result, while credit to the productive sectors of the economy has got squeezed, a borrowing and lending bubble has emerged through the NBFCs, which can cause defaults and distress in the future. Despite the official claims of enhanced financial inclusion, the failure of the NDA-II government on that score is also manifested starkly in the grim reality of bank branch closures, particularly in the rural areas.

Notes and References

1. *The Financial Times'* 'The Banker' reported double-digit growth in capital and pre-tax profits for the top 1,000 banks from across the world, hailing it as a sign of all-round revival 10 years after the beginning of the global financial crisis.

2. D. Myles, 'Top 1000 World Banks 2018', 'The Banker', 2 July 2018. Available at https://www.thebanker.com/Top-1000-World-Banks/Top-1000-World-Banks-2018.

3. Mahesh Vyas, 'Subdued Animal Spirits', *Economic Outlook*, Centre for Monitoring Indian Economy, 18 January 2019.

4. For a detailed analysis of this phase of credit-driven economic expansion, see R. Azad, P. Bose, and Z. Dasgupta, '"Riskless Capitalism" in India: Bank Credit and Economic Activity', *Economic and Political Weekly* LII (31), 2017.

5. Raghuram Rajan, 'Saving Credit', Speech by RBI Governor at the third Dr Verghese Kurien Memorial Lecture at Institute of Rural Management Anand, 25 November 2014.

6. Comparison with other economies is based on the International Monetary Fund's (IMF) Financial Soundness Indicators database.

7. The RBI had shown considerable regulatory forbearance towards corporate debt defaults through successive debt restructuring schemes. Put simply, such restructuring entailed concealing these bad assets by extending the period of repayment, lowering interest rates, and granting more loans to pay off the bad loans, amongst other such measures.

8. NPA provisioning for corporate debt write-offs in each of these years has surpassed their operating profits.

9. See RBI, *Financial Stability Report*, December 2018.

10. The baseline projections of the latest *Financial Stability Report* expect the NPA ratio of the PSBs to decline only marginally, from 14.8 per cent in September 2018 to 14.6 per cent in March 2019 and 14.3 per cent in September 2019.

11. The Annual Report of the RBI (2017–18) states: 'The number of cases on frauds reported by banks were generally hovering at around 4500 in the last 10 years before their increase to 5835 in 2017–18. Similarly, the amount involved in frauds was increasing gradually, followed by a significant increase in 2017–18 to ₹410 billion. The quantum jump in the

amount involved in frauds during 2017–18 was on account of a large value fraud committed in gems and jewellery sector, mainly affecting one public sector bank.'

12. While this particular fraud related to off-balance sheet exposures involving credit guarantees issued by the PNB (letters of credit), loan frauds (frauds related to actual credit) have emerged as the dominant category of bank frauds over the years.

13. The annual number of bank frauds as well as the amounts involved in them have increased every year since 2013–14. The average sizes of each bank fraud and loan fraud have also doubled between 2013–14 and 2017–18.

14. In a recent note presented by a former Governor of the RBI to the Parliament Estimates Committee (dated 6 September 2018) on NPAs, he mentioned that a list of high-profile loan fraud cases was sent to the Prime Minister's Office (PMO) on 4 February 2015, urging coordinated action against them. The PMO and the RBI have refused to disclose this list in response to Right to Information (RTI) applications, including one made by one of the present authors, citing Section 45E of the RBI Act, 1934.

15. The IBC was passed by Parliament in May 2016, under which the Insolvency and Bankruptcy Board of India (IBBI) was established on 1 October 2016. The RBI introduced the revised PCA framework with effect from 1 April 2017.

16. Under the IBC, the National Company Law Tribunals have been able to resolve only around 50-odd NPA cases till September 2018, involving admitted claims of Rs 1.25 trillion, as reported in the latest *Financial Stability Report*. Data provided in the IBBI quarterly newsletter shows that seven high-value cases out of the 52 resolved cases till September 2018 involved total claims of over Rs 1 trillion.

17. The analysis reveals that while Return on Assets (RoAs) and regulatory capital position (CRAR and CET1 ratios) have deteriorated for the PCA-PSBs till September 2018, credit and deposit growth have also lagged behind the non-PCA-PSBs, leading to a rise in the NPA ratios (see *Report on Trend and Progress of Banking in India 2017–18*, Ch. IV, Figure IV.21). (CRAR stands for Capital to Risk Weighted Assets ratio while CET1 refers to Common Equity Tier 1 ratio.)

18. Capital infusion into the PSBs by the government was to the tune of Rs 900 billion in 2017–18 and over Rs 515 billion in 2018–19

(end-December), as reported by the Finance Minister in Parliament (Lok Sabha starred question # 342, answered on 4 January 2019).

19. The latest *Financial Stability Report* has projected that as many as eight of the 11 PCA-PSBs may have CRAR below 9 per cent by March 2019, 'without taking into account any further planned recapitalisation by the government'.

20. Abhishek Anand, Josh Felman, Navneeraj Sharma, and Arvind Subramanian, 'How Much Capital is Enough for the RBI? Paranoia or Prudence?', *Economic and Political Weekly* 53 (48), 8 December 2018. The suggestion to use the RBI's excess capital to finance bank recapitalisation has been made by the former Chief Economic Advisor.

21. Prasenjit Bose, 'A merger that will not pay off', *The Hindu Business Line*, 25 September 2018. The proposed amalgamation has been legally challenged in the Delhi High Court by the All India Bank Officers' Confederation (AIBOC). For a critique of the proposal to amalgamate the Bank of Baroda, Dena Bank, and Vijaya Bank, see Bose, 'A merger that will not pay off'.

22. Prasenjit Bose, 'FRDI Bill, 2017: Inducing Financial Instability', *Economic and Political Weekly* 53 (3), 20 January 2018.

23. The incremental credit-GDP ratio, which measures the annual flow of credit, fell from an average 8 per cent of GDP during the UPA-II phase to around 5 per cent of GDP in the past four years. In the first half of 2018–19, incremental credit-GDP was only 4 per cent.

24. See RBI, *Report on Trend and Progress of Banking in India 2017–18*, Box VI.I, 'What Explains the Robust Credit Growth of NBFCs?'

25. C. P. Chandrashekhar, 'Forbearance over Default: Dangers of Misuse', *Economic and Political Weekly* 54 (2), 12 January 2019. The recent move by the RBI to relax the norms of micro, small and medium enterprises (MSME) debt restructuring for the banks and NBFCs has been critiqued on the grounds that it will once again pave the way for concealment of NPAs, only to be bailed out by taxpayers' funds in the future.

26. As per SIDBI-TransUnion CIBIL's MSME Pulse, which provides MSME credit data on a quarterly basis, the outstanding credit of the MSMEs stood at Rs 14.3 trillion as of September 2018, out of which Rs 6.9 trillion was advanced by the PSBs (48 per cent), Rs 4.7 trillion by the private banks (32.6 per cent), and Rs 1.6 trillion by the NBFCs (11.6 per cent). In September 2018, the MSME segment registered year-on-year credit growth of 19 per cent, which was significantly higher than the credit

growth of the mid-sized and large corporates. However, estimates of MSME credit provided in the RBI database on Deployment of Gross Bank Credit shows that outstanding bank credit to the MSME sector in the three years after the launch of the refinance agency MUDRA in 2015–16 has stagnated at around Rs 11 trillion in 2017–18.

27. See December 2018 issue of the MSME Pulse report.

28. NSS, 73rd Round, 2015–16, estimates the number of MSMEs at 63.4 million. GST-registered MSMEs (with turnover below Rs 5 crore) numbered 12.3 million as of October 2018.

29. Data on PMMY has been sourced from MUDRA Annual Report, 2017–18.

30. See World Bank, *The Little Data Book on Financial Inclusion* (Washington, D.C.: The World Bank, 2018).

31. Data provided in RBI, *Report on Trend and Progress of Banking in India 2017–18*, para IV.90.

32. 'Nearly 23.3% of total Jan Dhan accounts lay inoperative in 2018, shows data', *Business Standard*, 3 January 2019.

33. The outstanding deposit amount in the Jan Dhan accounts increased from Rs 456 billion to Rs 642 billion, and further to Rs 746 billion by the end of the first week of December 2016. See Somesh Jha, '60% of money deposited in Jan-Dhan accounts after note ban under lens', *Business Standard*, 5 September 2018.

34. See RBI, *Report on Trend and Progress of Banking in India 2017–18*, Table IV.25.

three

The NDA-II Regime and the Worsening Agrarian Crisis

ARINDAM BANERJEE AND ISHAN ANAND

National Crime Records Bureau (NCRB) data shows that the number of protests by farmers in India has increased exponentially, jumping from 628 in 2014 to 4,837 in 2016. Over the past two years, farmers' protests have made headlines a number of times, with protests erupting across Maharashtra, Haryana, Madhya Pradesh, Uttar Pradesh, and Rajasthan—all of which are BJP-ruled states. The first two years of the NDA-II government (2014–15 and 2015–16) were drought years, and this had an obvious impact on agriculture. Economic growth also slowed down in the initial years of the NDA-II government. Just as both the economy and agricultural production started to recover, the woes of rural India were compounded by measures like demonetisation and Goods and Services Tax (GST), brewing anger and despair amongst the peasantry. The Central and state governments have responded by delegitimising the protests and preventing demonstrations. And whenever these governments have come up with a policy response, it has largely been palliative and short-sighted.

The present crisis is not one of agricultural production, as foodgrains production crossed 280 million tonnes in 2017–18. Record production also occurred for pulses, vegetables, and sugarcane in the past year. Peasants are agitated despite the high production levels and new schemes, and claims. The farmers' demands are centred around farm loan waivers, assured reasonable output prices in a timely manner, and a check on rising input prices. The farmers' anger has to be understood in the context of the failure of the BJP to address the structural neglect of the peasantry—issues that it had promised to address when asking for the people's mandate.

Agricultural growth in the first four years of the NDA-II government has been a modest 2.5 per cent,[1] which is a significant decline from the close to 4 per cent growth rate achieved during the UPA regime. This decline has also been accompanied by a decline in the growth of the construction sector, which had emerged as the main source of non-farm employment in the recent period.[2] Despite this slowdown, the NDA-II government has claimed to be working towards doubling farm incomes by 2022.[3] The main interventions targeted towards achieving this were the declaration that the Minimum Support Price (MSP) would be fixed at a pre-determined level of cost plus 50 per cent, and the support from the crop insurance scheme, Pradhan Mantri Fasal Bima Yojana (PMFBY).

Despite these measures announced by the government, the unrest continues. We therefore look at empirical evidence to explain why the peasantry, which voted for the NDA-II government just four years ago, is up in arms against it. While there has been an intensification in the past few years, the persistent agrarian crisis is something that rural India has grappled with since the late 1990s. We discuss below how solutions to the problem that do not address the structural roots can only provide temporary relief.

THE CURRENT AGRARIAN CRISIS: AN OUTCOME OF LIBERALISATION

What constitutes the agrarian crisis we are referring to, and what brought this about? There are two connected issues here—dwindling output prices and the growing indebtedness of farmers in India.

The first resulted from a deleterious combination of price and non-price factors that emerged in the context of economic reforms and India's conformation to the World Trade Organization (WTO) regime of trade liberalisation in the 1990s. As a result, more than three lakh farmers have committed suicide across the country over the past two decades, a tragic indicator of the persistent distress in the rural economy. The export-oriented agricultural strategy that India and many other developing countries embarked upon in 1995, primarily under the pressure of advanced capitalist countries led by the US, proved disastrous for various sections of Indian farmers. The collapse of global crop prices in the late 1990s, driven by a glut in world agricultural commodity markets, meant that farmers already specialising or newly investing in commercial crop cultivation aimed at exports were saddled with major losses repeatedly.[4] On the other hand, escalating costs of farming, with big multinationals entering the Indian agricultural upstream and downstream markets for seeds, fertilisers, and pesticides, and uncertain fluctuating prices caused a 'scissors crisis'[5] or an effective income squeeze. This initial shock to the rural economy was soon transformed into a more systemic crisis due to several other policies that emerged as part of the economic reforms package.[6]

The second was the effect of the banking reforms which, by relaxing the priority-sector lending norms, skewed the provision of formal credit in favour of large farmers and corporations engaged in agri-business.[7] This withdrawal of institutional credit from rural areas between the early 1990s to the mid-2000s undermined the goal of 'social banking', leading, in turn, to farmers' greater dependence on non-institutional credit sources like private moneylenders and traders, who offered credit at much higher interest rates.[8]

The high levels of indebtedness amongst farmer households, which has been one of the primary causes behind the farmer suicides, can be attributed to a combination of the above factors.[9] The incidence of accumulating indebtedness began with commercial farmers growing export crops with volatile prices, but it also spread to other farmers, given the systemic policy bias against petty production in agriculture. Even when agricultural credit expanded in the late 2000s and thereafter, it barely addressed the question of credit access for large sections of farmers. Much of the agricultural credit expansion was directed towards large corporate entities and disbursed increasingly in urban metropolises where these corporations were located.[10]

As a result of these policies, there has been an increase in overall rural indebtedness between 1991 and 2012, of which an increasing proportion came from non-institutional sources of credit such as landlords, moneylenders, and suppliers (Table 3.1). Further, formal credit was disproportionately cornered by large farmers. Among the marginal and small farmers,[11] only about 27 per cent had access to institutional credit, whereas about 72 per cent of large landowners[12] reported taking loans from formal sources. It is this rise in indebtedness that is reflected in the demands for farm loan waivers across the country.

TABLE 3.1: Percentage of Indebted Rural Households by Source of Credit

Year	Institutional (as % of total)	Non-Institutional (as % of total)	Total
1991	66.7	41.9	23.4
2002	50.6	58.5	26.5
2012	54.8	60.5	31.4

Source: All-India Debt and Investment Survey, National Sample Survey Office (NSSO).

Starting from the mid-1990s, the crisis of farming transformed into an agrarian crisis by stagnating or depressing the wages of agricultural labour, while also contracting the demand for non-agricultural goods and services in rural areas, because of the deflation of income within agriculture. The targeting of food subsidy through the public distribution system (PDS) based on erroneous poverty lines, which grossly underestimated the nutrition insecurity in rural areas, further compounded the rural distress.[13] In recognition of the agrarian crisis, the UPA-I government, which was elected to power in 2004, introduced measures like the Mahatma Gandhi National Rural Employment Guarantee Act (MGNREGA; now NREGA) in 2005 and the debt relief in 2008. Both policies, while providing some relief to farmers and rural labourers, were inadequate to address the structural challenges of the agrarian crisis.

While the NREGA represented a clear break from neoliberal ideas in its conception, the implementation, constrained by fiscal conservatism, reduced it from a 'right' to more of a 'relief'. The NREGA provided some non-agricultural jobs to rural labourers, but it was well short of the 100 days per year target, generating not more than 50 days per household annually on average.[14] Apart from poor budgetary allocations for NREGA, various bureaucratic barriers restrained the implementation of the job guarantee programme. The debt relief programme, on the other hand, entirely excluded informal credit from its ambit, thereby bypassing the challenge of rising usurious indebtedness. Also, a limit of 5 acres of landholding for eligibility meant that commercial farmers in dryland areas with larger land sizes, although poor and indebted, were ineligible for any relief. While the debt waiver of 2008 was undoubtedly a crucial intervention for sustaining Indian agriculture, much of the structural causes of the agrarian crisis was left unaddressed.

The high overall economic growth spanning the years 2004–09 led to significant rural-urban migration due to a demand for labour in urban growth sectors like real estate-driven construction and associated occupations. A substantial portion of agricultural labour also shifted to rural construction activities. Real wages exhibited an increase after 2007, after a very long period of stagnation. Crop prices, including food prices, were high and rose over that period (in tandem with the high international prices caused, among other factors, primarily by the global food crisis),[15] which meant that escalating cultivation costs for farmers were temporarily absorbed. However, one must note that it was largely the thin class of the big farmers, the *net food sellers*, who benefited during this regime of high food prices.

This apparently favourable economic situation until 2012 allowed the government to gloss over the more fundamental issues of ensuring remunerative agricultural output prices, increasing costs of cultivation, and provision of cheap formal credit to farmers. These contradictions started intensifying with the downturn in the economic situation after 2012. While this created anxiety amongst the farming population, which was politically channelised behind the Opposition, it also meant that the task for the newly elected NDA-II government was clearly defined in terms of addressing the question of farmers' income and indebtedness. A 'price stabilisation' policy as recommended by the Swaminathan Commission found its way back into the discourse on agricultural policy, along with other promises of 'doubling farmers' income' and providing debt relief.

DWINDLING OUTPUT PRICES

The lack of remunerative output prices has emerged as a major source of distress for a large segment of the peasant population under the NDA-II government. Reversing a long-term stagnation, international food prices rose sharply in the mid-2000s, and remained high between 2011 and 2014 (Figure 3.1). However, the appointment of Modi as the prime minister coincided with falling

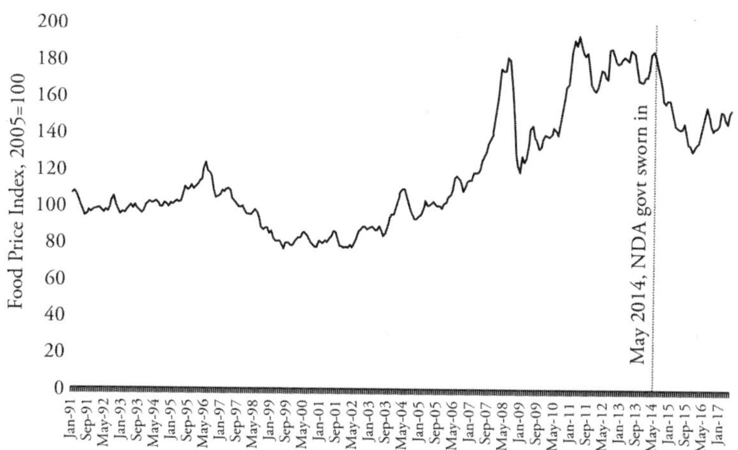

FIGURE 3.1: International Prices: Food Price Index, 2005 = 100

Source: International Monetary Fund Primary Commodity Prices.

international prices, putting downward pressure on domestic prices. Figure 3.2 shows the year-on-year change in the wholesale price index (WPI) for food articles. A sharp decline in the growth of WPI for food articles was visible from mid-2014. The terms of trade for agriculture started to deteriorate and the agrarian crisis intensified. Terms of trade reflect the relative price movement of agricultural and non-agricultural goods. This is worsening, and when the farmers sell agricultural output at a lower price but buy non-agricultural goods at a higher cost, it affects them adversely.

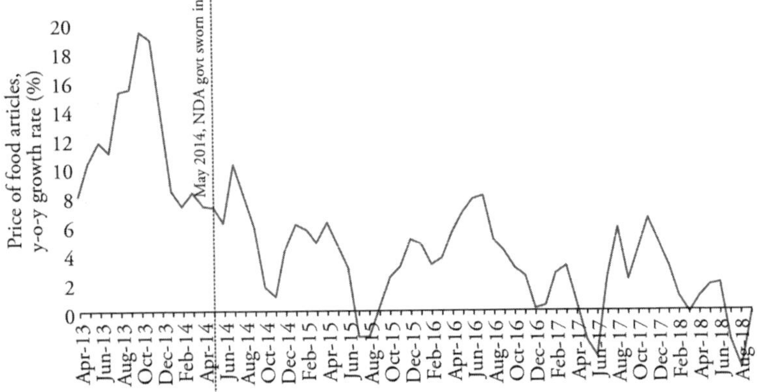

FIGURE 3.2: WPI for Food Articles (Y-o-Y percentage change)

Source: Office of the Economic Advisor, Ministry of Commerce and Industry, Government of India. Taken from *Database on Indian Economy*, RBI's Data Warehouse.

Minimum Support Price

The BJP had promised to increase the MSP to cost plus 50 per cent in its election manifesto in 2014. Soon after coming to power, however, the BJP government changed track and argued in the Supreme Court that prescribing MSP at 50 per cent over cost would be counter-productive and distort the markets.[16] Later, when put under massive pressure from the peasantry and with an eye on the upcoming elections, a hike in MSP was announced in Budget 2018. The MSP hike was implemented for the kharif marketing season 2018–19 and the rabi marketing season 2019–20.

Contrary to the statements made about the MSP hike being historic, the rise in the MSP is much lower than the hikes seen in the previous regimes. The MSP for paddy has been increased by 13 per cent in 2018–19, which is significantly lower than the previous hikes of 28 per cent in 2007–08, 20 per cent in 2008–09, 17 per cent in 2009–10, and 16 per cent in 2012–13. Moreover, the increase in the MSP in the first few years under the NDA-II government was modest. The real MSP declined in the first two years of the NDA-II government, and the hike could increase it only marginally (Figures 3.3 and 3.4).[17] While the long-awaited hike will come as a partial relief to a section of the peasantry, it is far from adequate in addressing the agrarian crisis.

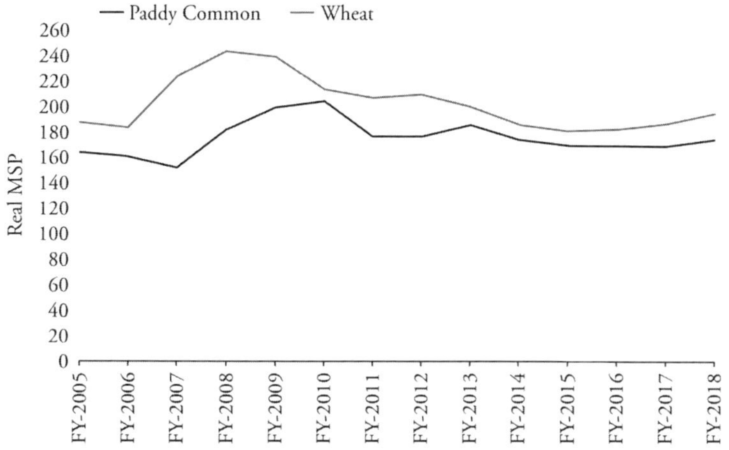

FIGURE 3.3: Real MSP, Paddy and Wheat (rupees)

Note: Nominal MSP values deflated using CPI AL (1986–87 = 100).

Source: *RBI Handbook of Statistics on the Indian Economy, 2017–18.*

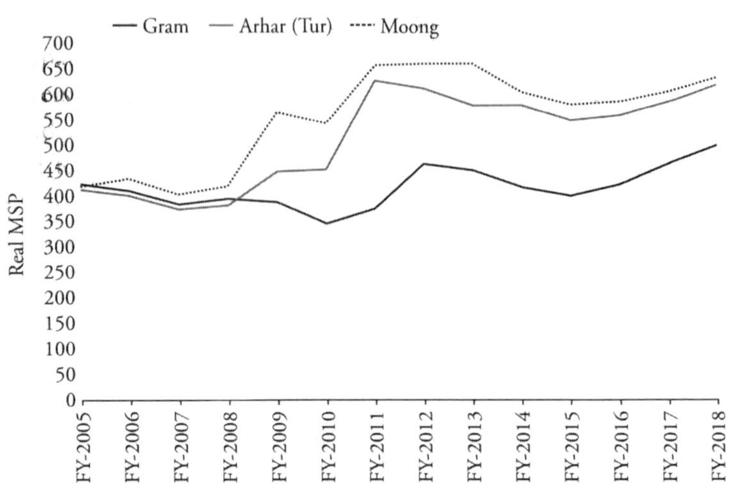

FIGURE 3.4: Real MSP, Gram, Tur, and Moong (rupees)

Note: Nominal MSP values deflated using CPI AL (1986–87 = 100).

Source: *RBI Handbook of Statistics on the Indian Economy*, 2017–18.

Procurement

For the MSP hike to be effective, the government has to back it up with procurement of all these crops. Procurement, however, is effective only for a few crops, and that too in a few regions. In 2016, only about 35 per cent of the paddy produced at the all-India level was procured by government agencies. While paddy procurement functions relatively well in Punjab, Haryana, Andhra Pradesh, and Chhattisgarh, it is negligible in states such as Assam and Uttar Pradesh. Due to ineffective procurement, prices in major rice-producing states tend to fall below the MSP from time to time.[18] Other than paddy, MSP is effective only for wheat and cotton, in regions where it is backed by procurement. For other crops, MSP is unable to provide a cushion when prices crash.

A good example of this is the domestic prices crash for oilseeds and pulses in 2016 (Figures 3.5 and 3.6). The MSP was unable to provide a price floor as the domestic prices of arhar and groundnut nosedived. Along with the fact that MSP is effective only for select

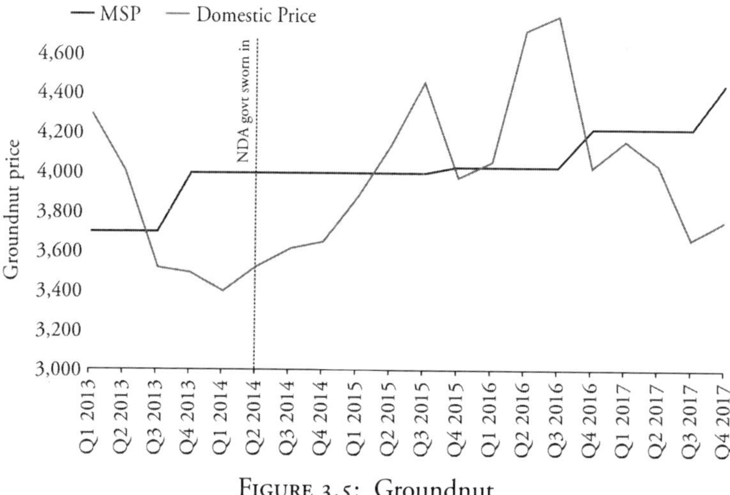

FIGURE 3.5: Groundnut

Source: Price Policy for Kharif Crops: The Marketing Season 2018–19, CACP.

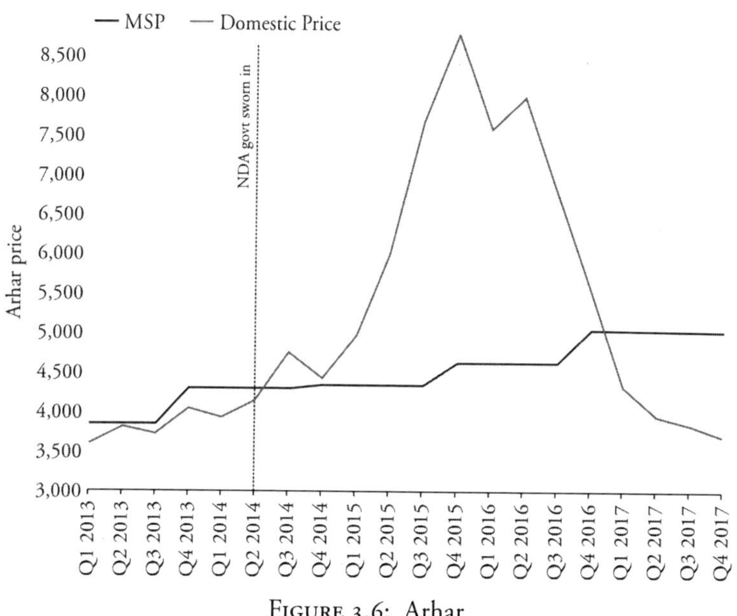

FIGURE 3.6: Arhar

Source: Price Policy for Kharif Crops: The Marketing Season 2018–19, CACP.

crops and regions, it is also biased towards the large landholders. The NSS Situation Assessment Survey for Agricultural Households data for 2013 reveals that only about 22 per cent of marginal and small farmers are aware of the existence of a procuring agency, as opposed to 60 per cent of the large farmers. The data also shows an increase in the share of horticulture crops in area cultivated and value of output. Horticulture crops such as fruits and vegetables, which are more prone to volatile prices, are outside the ambit of the MSP. In a nutshell, for the MSP to be effective, much more needs to be done along with the hike to ensure procurement across crops, regions, and size-class of cultivators.

Trade Policy

Even as the Union Cabinet approved an agricultural export policy with a stated goal of increasing exports to USD 60 billion by 2022, trade measures under this government have hurt farmers at a time when output continues to rise. In August 2018, the NDA-II government imposed an indefinite ban on exports of live cattle from all ports. The ban was a setback to the livestock sector, which has performed well in terms of exports in recent years. The erratic trade policy of the government has adversely affected the interests of farmers. For instance, even with high domestic production, the government continued with duty-free imports of pulses in 2016–17, resulting in a price crash. Potato and onion farmers also suffered in the initial years of the NDA-II government, as export restrictions prevented the gains from higher international prices. A pattern can be seen in the modus operandi of the government on the trade front. The response to any upward movement in prices is to impose restrictions on exports, allow duty-free imports, and put a limit on stock holdings. These policies, however, continue even when production recovers, resulting in a price crash. The policy response to the dynamics of global and domestic supplies has been woefully inadequate.

Declining Real Wage Growth

The NSS Situation Assessment Survey data shows that wage earnings are a major source of income for a large majority of marginal and small cultivators. They are even more important for the landless agricultural and non-agricultural rural labourers. In the early to mid-2000s, the real wages remained stagnant even in the midst of high economic growth.[19] After recovering from a long period of stagnation, real rural wages started to rise from 2007–08 and grew at an unprecedented rate between 2010 and 2014. Figure 3.7 shows the three-year moving average for year-on-year growth rates for general agricultural labourers and non-agricultural labourers.[20] Growth in real wages started to collapse after 2014 and declined sharply till mid-2016. This sharp decline in wages added to the woes of the rural labour (including poor farmers, who hire out their labour) already suffering from back-to-back drought years. The downward trend was reversed in August–September 2016, but the uptick was short-lived, and the declining pattern was visible again from June–July 2017. Wage growth has remained negative or close to zero for all the months in 2018 for which data is available.

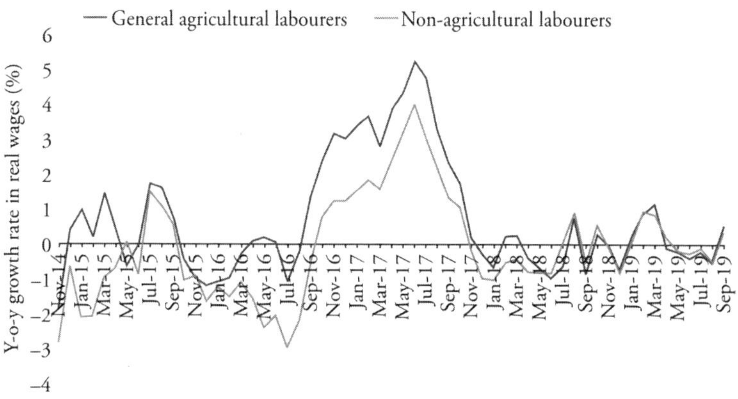

Figure 3.7: Y-o-Y Growth in Real Rural Wages (percentage change)

Note: Nominal values deflated using CPI-Rural (2012 = 100).

Source: Labour Bureau data obtained from Database on Indian Economy, RBI.

Continuing Apathy towards the Farm Sector

While the rural economy was reeling under the impact of back-to-back droughts, falling output prices, and the collapse of wage rate growth, the NDA-II government did little to provide relief to the farm sector. Deployment of bank credit to agricultural and allied activities slowed down considerably under this regime. Bank credit to agriculture had increased by over 20 per cent during 2004–05 and 2014–15. Credit growth collapsed post 2014–15 and was less than 6 per cent for the latest period (Figure 3.8). This decline in the provision of formal credit adds to the increasing burden of usurious credit.

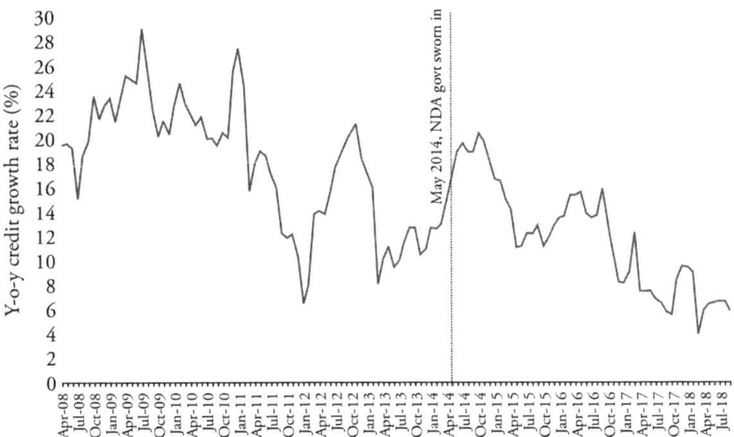

Figure 3.8: Y-o-Y Credit Growth Rate in Deployment of Bank Credit for Agriculture and Allied Activities (percentage change)

Source: Reserve Bank of India, Database on Indian Economy, RBI's Data Warehouse.

Budgetary Allocations for Agriculture

The gap between intention and rhetoric on the part of the government is stark. This divergence is evident when we study the budget documents of this government for various years. The announcement to double farm incomes by 2022 was first made in Budget 2016.

In the first NDA-II budget in 2014, the government's budgetary allocation for agriculture was only 7 per cent higher than that of the previous budget in nominal terms. Even this amount was not spent, and the actual expenditure was a meagre 1.8 per cent higher than that in Budget 2013 in nominal terms, signifying a reduction in budgetary spending in real terms. The next budget of the NDA-II government turned out to be worse. The actual spending in 2015–16 was 15 per cent less than the previous years in nominal terms. Budget cuts for agriculture in a country where millions of poor people depend on it are harsh on their own, but are even more so when they coincide with droughts, falling wages, and declining output prices.

The budgetary allocation for agriculture has increased since 2016, but a major part of this increase is due to the inclusion of the allocation on interest subsidy for short-term credit to farmers, which earlier used to be included in the finance ministry's outlay. If this head is excluded, the rise in budgetary allocation is seen to have only been nominal, given the serious fund cuts in the previous two budgets. The budgets of the NDA-II government also reveal another disturbing trend—the government is failing to spend even the meagre increases in the budget allocation. There was a drastic cut in the Centre's transfer to the states for the Centrally Sponsored Schemes (CSS), such as the Pradhan Mantri Krishi Sinchayee Yojna, Rashtriya Krishi Vikas Yojana, and National Food Security Mission in 2017–18. The last full budget of this government also saw a reduction in the share of agriculture in proportion to the total budgetary allocation. In 2017–18, the agricultural budget as a per cent of the total budgetary outlay was only 2.4 per cent, which came down even further to 2.3 per cent in 2018–19. Budgetary allocation for agricultural research, which stood at 0.4 per cent of the total budget in 2011–12, came down to 0.3 per cent in 2017–18.

As per convention, the Union Budget of 2019–20 was supposed to be only an interim budget. However, a full-fledged budget that included new announcements regarding the agricultural sector was presented by the government. One major announcement was a budgetary allocation of Rs 75,000 crore for the Pradhan Mantri

Kisan Samman Nidhi (PM-KISAN) scheme. PM-KISAN is a scheme to provide direct cash transfers of Rs 6,000 per year to agricultural households owning less than 2 hectares of land. The sum of Rs 6,000 is to be given in three instalments of Rs 2,000 each. This scheme is being put forward as a major intervention of the NDA-II government to ease the agrarian crisis. While this is a significant budgetary allocation, Rs 6,000 translates to a meagre Rs 3.30 per person per day for a family of five. The average cost of cultivation per hectare for wheat for one season was between Rs 60,000–70,000 in the major wheat-producing states of Punjab, Haryana, and Uttar Pradesh in 2016–17. The cost per hectare for paddy in 2015–16 was more than Rs 70,000 for major paddy-producing states, and the cultivation costs for cash crops were even higher on average.

Given the high and rising cost of cultivation and the worst price slump in 18 years,[21] this meagre transfer will hardly provide any meaningful relief to the peasantry. To make matters worse, the scheme in its present form excludes landless agricultural workers, women farmers, and tenants. The eligibility limit of 2 hectares will also exclude poor cultivators in dryland areas, who tend to have larger plots of land but are unable to use them effectively, given the poor irrigation infrastructure. Far from being a game-changer, this is a desperate attempt by the government to placate the angry peasantry. However, this measure comes too late and does too little to correct the NDA-II government's neglect of the peasantry in the previous five budgets. Moreover, despite low wage growth and rising unemployment, the MGNREGA budget has been slashed by Rs 1,000 crore in comparison to revised estimates for 2018–19.

Pradhan Mantri Fasal Bima Yojana

One of the recent significant changes in the way the State has placed itself in the policy discourse lies in its fundamental departure from its role as provider to one of regulator. And it has done this most explicitly by moving away from direct provisioning to the farmers to 'compensating' them for losses through a market-based insurance scheme. There are multiple problems with this shift in approach. Philosophically, this means that the State is absolving itself of a direct role in mitigating the problems of the people. Its role is limited to merely providing the money for the premium towards the insurance policy, even as the farmers have to bear a part of the burden. In that very process, a windfall gain is made by the insurance companies, which effectively means an ex-gratia transfer of public resources to the private corporate sector.

The government has tried to portray the revamped crop insurance scheme as a success story. Rs 13,000 crore were allocated to the PMFBY in 2018–19, an increment of over 20 per cent from the previous year. While this seems like a well-meaning gesture, the details of PMFBY are very disturbing. Before the PMFBY was launched in 2015–16, 48.6 million farmers were enrolled with the pre-existing farm insurance schemes.

As the PMFBY came along, the number of farmers buying insurance increased to 57 million in 2016–17. In the same period, the gross premium collected by insurance companies jumped from Rs 5,614 crore in 2015–16 to Rs 22,362 crore in 2016–17. The insurance claim paid to the farmers by the insurance companies in 2016 was Rs 15,902 crore, enabling them to record a profit of Rs 6,459 crore.[22] In the absence of adequate checks and balances on profit-seeking insurance companies and missing grievance redressal mechanisms, farmers ended up getting the short end of the stick, even as profits for the corporations soared.

Media reports highlighted the misery of the farmers as many of them did not receive even a single rupee for suffering crop damage, against claims made for lakhs of rupees. More than 2,000 farmers in Beed district of Maharashtra were offered compensation of less than Rs 5 in 2018.[23] As farmers became aware of the problems with the scheme, around nine million people dropped out of the scheme in 2018–19. The insurance premium collected, however, kept rising, and more than Rs 25,000 crore was collected in 2018–19. Data gathered from an Right to Information (RTI) to the Ministry of Agriculture revealed that in the two years since the PMFBY has been in place, the gross premium collected increased by a whopping Rs 36,848 crore or 348 per cent, while the number of insured increased by only 0.4 per cent.[24] A study conducted by the Indian Institute of Management Ahmedabad and supported by the Ministry of Agriculture revealed that in the first year itself, the insurance companies clocked a combined profit of more than Rs 7,300 crore.[25] The study also suggested ways to check against the 'supernormal profits' that the insurance companies can make with the existing scheme. In sum, the PMFBY is an insurance scheme that ensures corporate profits, but does not offer much to the peasantry in its current form.

Two Misadventures: Demonetisation and Cow Vigilantism

Demonetisation, which has been widely criticised for its lack of rationale and negative impact on the economy, and *cow vigilantism*, which is a political phenomenon based on communal mobilisations, are two policies/processes that are conceptually as distant from each other as one can imagine. Nevertheless, these two phenomena are united because of their successful assault against the informal economic structure of rural India, and as perhaps the greatest misadventures of the current government.

An important fallacy of the policy of demonetisation emanates from the specific economic context of India. Large parts of the Indian economy, including the entire agriculture and allied sector, are informal, and the maximal part of this informal economy earns an income lower than the lowest tax slabs in the country. At one stroke, demonetisation declared the income of millions of people, whose tax liability under the laws of the country is nil, as black income until proven otherwise.

While the policy might seem to be ill-conceived, it is, in fact, in line with the larger neoliberal policy experience, which has continuously stacked the odds against petty producers in the informal economy. Demonetisation is merely one small piece in that policy puzzle. One of the goals of demonetisation officially claimed by the government was to achieve greater 'formalisation of the economy'—an immediate and obvious corollary being the destruction of the informal economy. From banking reforms and land acquisition to the implementation of the GST, policies have militated against the informal economy and the livelihoods therein, and demonetisation fits perfectly into that neoliberal policy trajectory as a 'shock therapy'.

The impact of demonetisation on agriculture, which is primarily dependent on cash transactions, cannot be qualified as a short-term shock. This is due to the precise timing of the move in November, a month situated between the end of the Kharif season and the beginning of the Rabi season. Much of the Kharif output did not fetch remunerative prices at best, and had to be sold at throwaway prices at worst, given the severe shortage of cash. In such a situation, small and marginal farmers, constituting more than 80 per cent of the farmer households, would have resorted to purchasing inputs on credit at onerous conditions from input dealers for sowing the Rabi crops. The clear implication of this was that significant parts of the Rabi crops would have been already pledged to the lenders even before they were sown. Thus, in a single stroke, demonetisation substantially curtailed farmers' income for two seasons or a whole year.

Given the structure of Indian agriculture, overwhelmed by small and marginal farmers, such a setback to the farmers' annual income, and especially following two consecutive years of drought, has serious long-term implications for the sustenance of farmers. A significant running down of assets and savings for big and medium farmers and increasing levels of indebtedness for small and marginal holdings can be expected in this situation. For the latter particularly, there is a long-term possibility of losing assets, including land. In this sense, demonetisation has been a frontal assault on petty producers within agriculture. It is not surprising that intensified farmers' unrest were witnessed in several parts of the country following demonetisation, and this has now translated into organised farmers' agitation against the present government.

Cow vigilantism, which has afflicted the rural areas to a considerable extent, with the implicit benediction of the State, is primarily driven by the communal politics of the ruling political party. Directed at preventing cow slaughter, it has affected the sale and purchase of cattle, including buffaloes, in informal markets, and thereby hit at the core of the livestock economy. Livestock as an informal economy is a major source of primary or secondary income for small and marginal farmers, including those without land. The cattle are sold off for purposes of meat production once the milk-producing age is over, and the proceeds help the livestock farmer to purchase new milch cattle. This cyclical integral relation between the dairy farmer and the butcher is at the core of the informal livestock economy. Even as more organised meat exports and meat processing continue to grow, the informal sector is undermined by such vigilantism, thus excluding the poor from an important source of livelihood.

Added to the stagnant economic situation for agriculture, these two purportedly diverse phenomena, united by their affront on the informal economy in rural India, have exacerbated the agrarian distress immensely. Policies driven by the neoliberal ideology aimed at destroying all informal economic relations, and thereby allowing organised capital to appropriate the vacated spaces, is the fundamental contradiction that Indian agriculture faces today. The NDA-II government has callously intensified these contradictions through these catastrophic measures.

Looking Ahead

It is abundantly clear that the NDA-II government has failed to live up to its promises and tall claims vis-à-vis agriculture made as part of the *Saaf Niyat, Sahi Vikas* (Clean intent, right development) campaign. Not only do the promised *Achhe Din* (prosperous days) remain elusive to the large masses of the rural peasantry and labourers, but they have also ended up suffering from a worsening agrarian crisis. The NDA-II government continues to remain in denial about its failures vis-à-vis the rural economy. Instead of providing relief to the struggling cultivators, it is focusing on non-essentials such as the Statue of Unity.

The aggressive pursuit of neoliberal economic policies along with the politics of communal polarisation has sharpened the political contradictions in India. The peasantry is facing economic impoverishment despite high economic growth, along with a sharp rise in economic inequality. At the same time, social disparity and polarisation are on the rise, with cow vigilantism and increasing incidents of attacks on dalits in places such as Una and Saharanpur. In response to this, more than 200 peasant and other progressive organisations came together and organised a 'Kisan Mukti March' in New Delhi on 28–29 November 2018. This followed earlier, similar farmer mobilisations, including the mega Nashik–Mumbai march. Farmers from all over the country marched to the Parliament with the demand that Parliament hold a special session to discuss the agrarian crisis and identify a way out.

While the four-and-a-half years of the NDA-II government have pushed the peasantry towards greater agony and distress, the united protests all over the country provide a ray of hope. It is imperative that the mounting neoliberal assault on agriculture and associated occupations in rural India be arrested and reversed, and the dignity and well-being of the farming-labouring population be restored.

NOTES AND REFERENCES

1. The year-on-year growth rate was -0.22 for 2014–15, 0.59 for 2015–16, 6.29 for 2016–17, and 3.37 for 2017–18.

2. The growth rate of the construction sector during 2004–05 to 2013–14 was 8.15 per cent; it collapsed to 3.8 per cent during 2014–15 to 2017–18.

3. The target is perplexing because the NDA-II government's tenure ends in 2019. Also, there is no clarity from the government as to whether they mean to double the real or nominal farm incomes.

4. Utsa Patnaik, 'Agrarian Crisis and Global Deflationism', *Social Scientist* 30 (1/2), 2002, 3–30.

5. A 'scissors crisis' refers to the distress faced on account of the rising costs of production and declining output prices. Farmers' income reduced as costs are increasing without any commensurate rise in output prices.

6. Arindam Banerjee, 'Peasant Classes under Neoliberalism: A Class Analysis of Two States', *Economic and Political Weekly* 44 (15), 2009, 49–57.

7. D. N. Reddy and S. Mishra, 'Agriculture in Reforms Regime', in D. N. Reddy and S. Mishra (eds), *Agrarian Crisis in India* (New Delhi: Oxford University Press, 2009).

8. V. K. Ramachandran and V. Rawal, 'The Impact of Liberalization and Globalization on India's Agrarian Economy', *Global Labour Journal* 1 (1), 2010, 56–91.

9. NCRB data for 2015 attributes around 39 per cent of farmer suicides to indebtedness. Incidentally, the NCRB has not published the farmer suicides data after 2015.

10. R. Ramakumar and P. Chavan, 'Bank Credit to Agriculture in India in the 2000s: Dissecting the Revival', *Review of Agrarian Studies* 4 (1), 2014.

11. Possessing less than 2 hectares of land.

12. Possessing more than 10 hectares of land.

13. Utsa Patnaik, 'Neoliberalism and Rural Poverty in India', *Economic and Political Weekly* 42 (30), 2007, 3132–50.

14. A. Aggarwal, 'The MGNREGA Crisis: Insights from Jharkhand', *Economic and Political Weekly* 51 (22), 2016.

15. Food prices increased sharply across the world in 2007–08. The World Bank has estimated that this led to a global food crisis, which drove an additional 100 million people into hunger.

16. Dhananjay Mahapatra, 'Minimum support price cannot be 50% more than cost of produce, Centre to SC', *The Times of India*, 21 February 2015. Available at https://timesofindia.indiatimes.com/india/Minimum-support-price-cannot-be-50-more-than-cost-of-produce-Centre-to-SC/articleshow/46319093.cms (accessed February 2019).

17. The hike prescribes the MSP to 1.5 times the cost A2+FL and not cost C2, as recommended by the National Commission for Farmers (also known as the Swaminathan Commission). There are various concepts used in computing the cost of production. Cost A2+FL includes the cost of family and hired labour, animal labour, machinery, seeds, insecticides, manure, fertiliser, irrigation charges, depreciation, rent paid for leased-in

land, and interest on working capital. Cost C2 includes cost A2+FL, but also includes the rental value of own land. Cost A2+FL is considerably lower than cost C2, and it underestimates the cost of production. Even after the MSP hike in 2017–18, the margin over cost of production for paddy was only 4 per cent when cost C2 was considered, and not 50 per cent as is being demanded by the farmers.

18. Commission for Agricultural Costs and Prices, *Price Policy for Kharif Crops: The Marketing Season 2018-19* (New Delhi: Department of Agriculture, Cooperation and Farmers Welfare, Ministry of Agriculture and Farmers Welfare, 2018), 24. This recent CACP report noted that the 'States of Uttar Pradesh and Assam together contribute around 17 per cent to paddy production. However, prices in these two states ruled below MSP during peak market arrival period of October to December 2017.'

19. The nominal wage data is given by the Wage Rates in Rural India (WRRI), which can be converted into real terms using the consumer price index.

20. Among the occupations for which wage data is available, the representative occupation category for workers in agriculture is 'general agricultural labour', whereas the representative occupation category for non-agriculture workers is 'non-agricultural labour'. The monthly data have been corrected for inflation using CPI-Rural (2012=100).

21. Rohan Kishore, 'Worst price slump in 18 years shows scale of farm crisis', *Hindustan Times*, 15 January 2019. Available at https://www.hindustantimes.com/india-news/worst-price-slump-in-18-years-shows-scale-of-farm-crisis/story-P2niBeuqAcaxgms3HmFCTK.html (accessed February 2019).

22. Gaurav V. Bhatnagar, 'How the PM's Crop Insurance Scheme Turned into a Goldmine for 10 Private Insurers', *The Wire*, 13 November 2018. Available at https://thewire.in/agriculture/pm-crop-insurance-scheme-huge-profits-private-insurers (accessed February 2019).

23. Bani Bedi, 'Modi's Flagship Crop Insurance Scheme Wavering as Farmers Continue to Suffer', *The Wire*, 17 July 2018. Available at https://thewire.in/agriculture/modi-bjp-flagship-crop-insurance-scheme-farmers-suffer (accessed February 2019).

24. Kabir Aggarwal and Dheeraj Mishra, 'Exclusive: Under Modi's Crop Insurance Scheme, Premiums up 350% But Farmers' Coverage Stagnant', *The Wire*, 12 November 2018. Available at https://thewire.in/agriculture/narendra-modi-farmers-crop-insurance-pmfby (accessed February 2019).

25. Center for Management in Agriculture, *Performance Evaluation of Pradhan Mantri Fasal Bima Yojna (PMFBY)* (Gujarat: Indian Institute of Management Ahmedabad, 2018).

four

Employment Under the NDA-II Regime

A Reality Check

Subhanil Chowdhury

Introduction

In its election manifesto published on the eve of the 2014 Lok Sabha elections, the Bharatiya Janata Party (BJP) argued that the decade-long United Progressive Alliance (UPA) rule had been a period of jobless growth. The BJP promised that if voted to power, it would take up an agenda of economic revival and 'accord high priority to job creation and opportunities for entrepreneurship'.[1] In the run up to the Lok Sabha elections of 2014, in a political rally at Agra held on 21 November 2013, the then prime minister-aspirant Narendra Modi had promised that his government would ensure one crore jobs per year to the youth.[2] The Modi government has almost completed its tenure. Have these promises with regard to employment been fulfilled? This chapter seeks to assess the government's performance with respect to employment and job creation based on the available published data pertaining to the Indian economy.

However, measuring employment, particularly in a country like India, is not an easy task, as the question of who is to be considered as *employed* is not a simple one to answer. Most people work in the informal sector or are self-employed, and many also undertake different jobs during different times of the year.[3] Estimating employment and unemployment statistics in such a scenario requires conducting detailed and large-scale sample surveys of households. Policymakers and statisticians in India rely primarily on the employment and unemployment surveys (EUS) conducted by the National Sample Survey Office (NSSO) at five-year intervals.

To generate employment numbers on a yearly basis, the Labour Bureau (LB) under the Ministry of Labour undertook the task of conducting yearly and quarterly household surveys to estimate employment in the country since 2009–10. For the formal factory sector, the Central Statistical Organisation (CSO) conducts the Annual Survey of Industries (ASI), from which estimates of total employment in the factory sector can be obtained.[4]

The NDA-II government has practically *stopped* all these employment-related household surveys following the recommendations of the National Institution for Transforming India (NITI Aayog) Task Force, which suggested replacing them with an annual Periodic Labour Force Survey (PLFS).[5] As a result of this decision, no official measure of employment or unemployment for India has been publicly available since 2016. The last available NSSO data is for 2011–12, and from the Labour Bureau for 2015–16. The Centre for Monitoring the Indian Economy (CMIE) has started a large-scale survey covering 173,181 households.[6] In the absence of reliable government estimates, we rely on CMIE estimates for the status of employment in India, particularly since 2016. We also rely on the employment estimates generated by the Centre for Sustainable Employment (CSE), Azim Premji University, based on an analysis of the Labour Bureau data.

Employment Under the NDA-II Regime

The resignation of two members of the National Statistics Commission (NSC) in protest against the government's decision to not publish the NSSO employment data for 2017–18 has led to concern that this might be the result of the dismal employment situation in the country. Subsequently, the *Business Standard*[7] has published the basic data from the survey. This shows that the unemployment rate (6.1 per cent) in the country reached its highest level in the last 45 years in the year 2017–18. Particularly, the youth have been severely hurt because of this employment crisis. The unemployment rates among rural men, rural women, urban men, and urban women has increased drastically to 17.4 per cent, 13.6 per cent, 18.7 per cent, and 27.2 per cent, respectively. Such a huge increase in unemployment rates has occurred at a time when the Labour Force Participation Rate or the proportion of the working-age population joining the labour force has declined from 39.5 per cent in 2011–12 to 36.9 per cent in 2017–18. This shows a severe job crisis in the Indian economy. However, since the NSSO report for 2017–18 has not been officially published, we do not depend solely on it. We rely on published and verifiable data in the remaining part of this chapter to show what comes out clearly in the NSSO statistics published by *Business Standard*—far from providing one crore jobs a year, the NDA-II government has witnessed a severe reduction in employment in the country.

It is now well-established that India has experienced jobless growth since the policies of reforms were introduced in 1991. From Figure 4.1, an important fact emerges. While the GDP growth rate in the pre-reform period was significantly lower than that in the post-reform period, the trend in the employment growth rate was the exact opposite. This is particularly so during the high growth phase of the Indian economy starting from 2004, with almost negligible growth in employment.[8] According to the analysis in the *State of Working India* (*SWI 2018*) report brought out by the Azim Premji University, a 10 per cent increase in GDP now results in less than 1 per cent increase in employment, and the unemployment rate among the youth and uneducated reached 16 per cent in 2015. The question is whether the NDA-II government has, in its term, managed to break away from this pattern and increase employment in the economy.

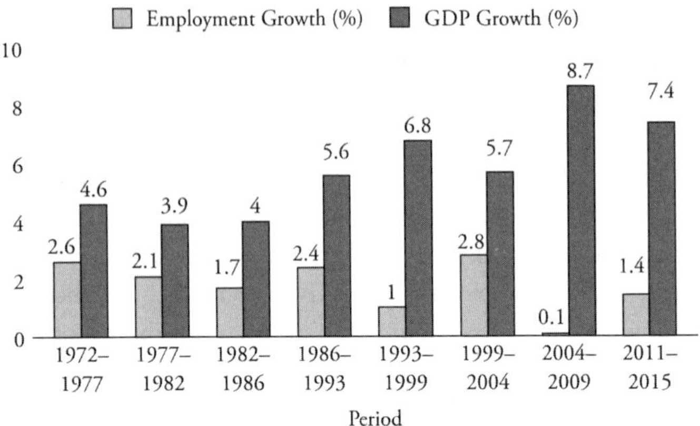

FIGURE 4.1: Employment and GDP Growth in India

Source: *State of Working India* report (*SWI*) *2018*, CSE, Azim Premji University.

In the absence of NSSO data, in this section we use two government sources which provide some data on employment during this period—the Labour Bureau annual and quarterly surveys, and the Annual Survey of Industries. Figures 4.2a and 4.2b show estimates of the labour force[9] (employed + unemployed), the total number of employed, and the unemployment rate in India from the Labour Bureau and from the NSSO-EUS for the year 2011. Three striking and important facts emerge.

First, the figures from the NSSO and LB surveys for 2011 diverge on all counts. It appears that the LB survey is over-reporting employment and the labour force as compared with the NSSO survey. Second, immediately after the NDA-II government assumed office, there was a significant decline in the labour force as well as the number of employed between 2013 and 2015—the decline amounts to 70 lakhs. Other estimates pertaining to the LB survey, while diverging in estimating the exact number of employed, agree that there has been a significant decline in the number of employed in India.[10] This shows that the employment stagnation witnessed in India before Modi came to power continued after the NDA-II government took office. Third, the unemployment rate in India has increased over the years, and this is despite the absence of any unemployment benefits.[11] This meant that the unemployment problem in India is actually more severe than may seem on the surface.

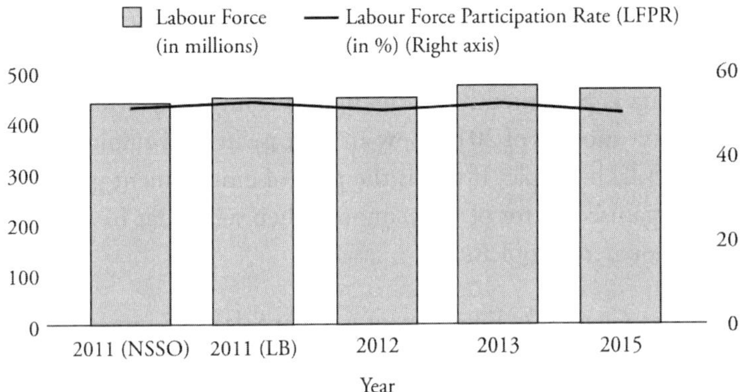

FIGURE 4.2A: Labour Force in India

Note: Values for 2011–15 are taken from the Labour Bureau Survey.

Source: *SWI 2018*, CSE, Azim Premji University.

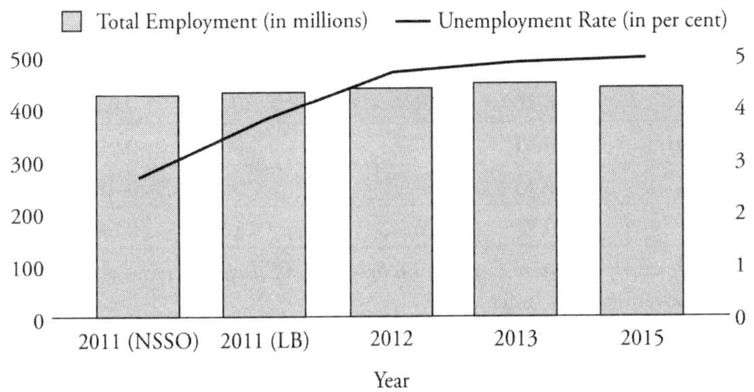

FIGURE 4.2B: Employment and Unemployment Rates in India

Note: Values for 2011–15 are taken from the Labour Bureau Survey.

Source: *SWI 2018*, CSE, Azim Premji University.

Unfortunately, we cannot go beyond 2015 as the yearly LB survey has been discontinued since 2016. Therefore, we need some other source to go beyond 2015 to understand how employment generation proceeded under the current dispensation. For this purpose we look at the Quarterly Employment Survey of the LB[12] and the ASI data on the factory sector.[13]

Table 4.1 shows that the manufacturing sector created the maximum employment in almost all the quarters, except two, for which data is presented here. The figures from the quarterly survey for the nine months of 2017 show an increase in total employment of only 3.85 lakh people. If this is the pace of employment generation in the organised sector of the economy, then we are far from solving the employment problem.

TABLE 4.1: Changes in Employment in Eight Selected Sectors (in lakhs)

Sector	Apr–Jun 2016	Jul–Sep 2016	Oct–Dec 2016	Jan–Mar 2017	Apr–Jun 2017	Jul–Oct 2017
Manufacturing	−0.12	0.24	0.83	1.02	−0.87	0.89
Construction	−0.23	−0.01	−0.01	0.02	0.10	−0.22
Trade	0.26	−0.07	0.07	0.29	0.07	0.14
Transport	0.17	0.0	0.01	0.03	−0.03	0.2
Accommodation & Restaurant	0.01	−0.08	0.0	0.03	0.05	0.02
IT/BPO	−0.16	0.26	0.12	0.13	0.02	0.01
Education	0.51	−0.02	0.18	0.02	0.99	0.21
Health	0.33	0.0	0.02	0.31	0.31	0.11
Total	0.77	0.32	1.22	1.85	0.64	1.36

Source: *Quarterly Report on Employment Scenario in Selected Sectors*, Labour Bureau, Government of India.

A more robust measure of employment in the organised sector is the ASI employment data. It is evident from Figure 4.3 that there has been an increase in the number of employed within the organised sector in India. However, there was a contraction in the total number of employed between 2012 and 2013, after which it increased to the 2012 level in 2014. But between 2014 and 2016, the increase in the total number of employed in the organised sector has been 0.71

million only. In the first two years of UPA-I (2004–06), the increase in employment in the organised sector was 1.15 million, while in the first two years of UPA-II (2009–11), it was 1.31 million. After this, the deceleration in employment set in. But the first two years of the NDA-II government (2014–16) generated only 0.7 million jobs, which is less than that of the first two years of the UPA-I and UPA-II governments.

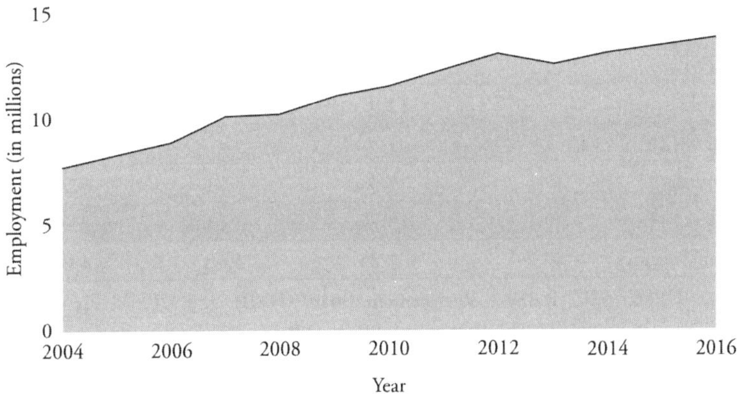

FIGURE 4.3: Employment in the Organised Manufacturing Sector

Note: Includes all employees, managerial and supervisory staff.

Source: *SWI 2018*, CSE, Azim Premji University.

In the face of a decline in the overall employment situation in the country, the government had the option of increasing employment in the public sector and other government agencies. Did the NDA-II government do that? Data on this score is not readily available. However, *The Indian Express* compiled some data, based on which Table 4.2 is constructed. It shows that during the Modi regime there has been a decline in the recruitment by Central government agencies. Particularly, recruitment through the Union Public Service Commission (UPSC), Staff Selection Commission (SSC), etc., and in Central Public Sector Enterprises (CPSEs) has fallen between 2014–15 and 2016–17. In banks, the overall recruitment has increased, but that has been solely due to an increase in the number of officers, while recruitment in clerical and other subordinate positions has declined. In short, this snapshot of recruitment by the Central government shows that it has not been able to generate public-sector employment.

TABLE 4.2 Recruitment by Various Central Government Agencies (in lakhs)

	2014–15	2015–16	2016–17
UPSC, SSC, RRB	1.13	1.11	1.01
CPSEs	15.87	15.21	15.23
Banks	12.91	13.01	13.5
(of which)			
Officers	7.3	7.71	8.29
Clerks	3.77	3.61	3.6
Subordinates	1.85	1.68	1.61

Note: UPSC, SSC, Railway Recruitment Board (RRB), and CPSEs. Figures for banks might not add up due to rounding off.

Source: Aanchal Magazine, Anil Sasi, '10 per cent quota: Pool of jobs in govt, banks, shrinking steadily', *The Indian Express*, 14 January 2019.

EMPLOYMENT TRENDS POST-2016

To analyse the employment trends from 2016 onwards, we use the information from the CMIE survey.[14]

Based on the CMIE data, it is seen that there has been a remarkable fall in the unemployment rate even as there is a marginal fall in the number of employed between 2016–17 and 2017–18 (Table 4.3). A careful look at the data, however, reveals that a fall in the unemployment rate has primarily been on account of the decline in the number of people participating in the labour market itself. As a result, the labour force participation rate (LFPR) has fallen during this period. This suggests that the employment generating potential of the economy has not increased. Had this been the case, there would have been an increase in the number of employed as well as the labour force, with many new aspirants joining the labour market after seeing others getting employment opportunities.

TABLE 4.3: Estimates of Employment and Unemployment from CMIE Data

	2016–17	*2017–18*	*2017–18 Q1*	*2018–19 Q1*
Employed	406.7	406.2	406.2	401.9
Unemployed and looking for work	33	19.9	17	23.6
Labour Force	439.7	426.1	423.3	425.5
LFPR	46.1	43.5	43.6	42.7
Unemployment Rate	7.5	4.7	4.0	5.5

Source: Mahesh Vyas, 'Employment: The Big Picture', Presentation for IC Centre for Governance, 2018. Available at https://unemploymentinindia.cmie.com/kommon/bin/sr.php?kall=wtabnav&tab=4090.

A more recent and justifiable comparison (since the LFPR remains similar between the two periods) shows that the unemployment rate has in fact risen drastically between the first quarter of 2017–18 and 2018–19 (Table 4.3). A more detailed monthly comparison of the employment situation between the two years shows that, except for July, employment has fallen in 2018 as compared to 2017 (Figure 4.4). To be precise, in the year 2018, India witnessed an employment decline of 11 million or 1.1 crore people—the polar opposite of Prime Minister Modi's promise of increasing employment by one crore each year.

The empirical evidence of this employment stagnation in the economy can be established, in a roundabout way, from another piece of government data. Every year, the Reserve Bank of India (RBI) conducts a Consumer Confidence Survey (CCS) on a quarterly basis across 13 major cities of the country, covering more than 5,000 households.[15] A negative Net Response Rate in Figure 4.5 implies that more people are reporting a deterioration in their condition as compared with those reporting an improvement.

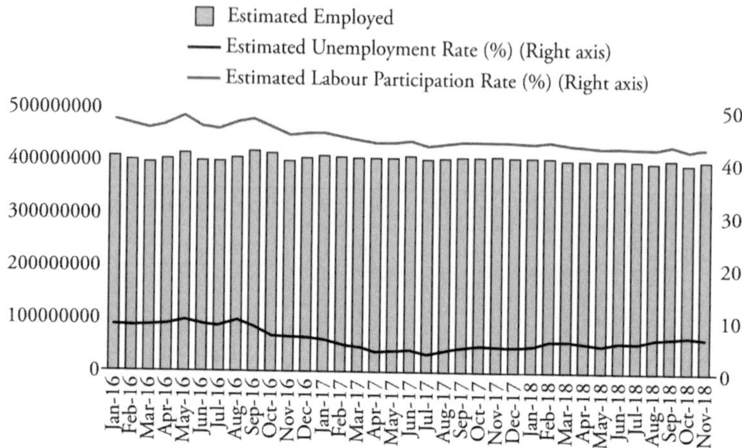

FIGURE 4.4: Monthly Estimates of the Number of Employed

Source: CMIE. Available at https://unemploymentinindia.cmie.com/kommon/bin/sr.php?kall=wtabnav&tab=4020.

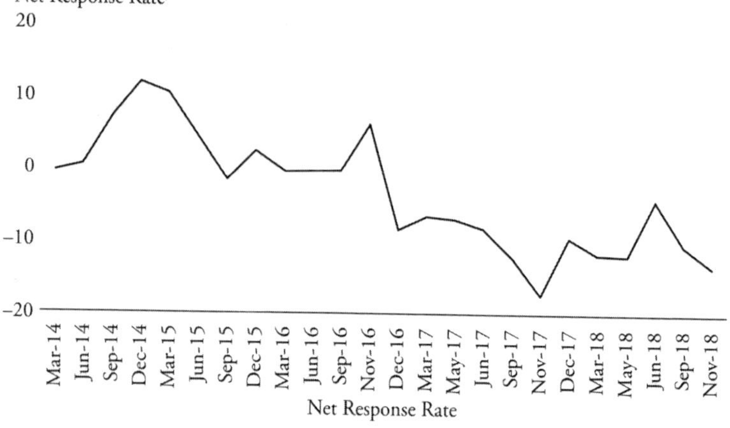

FIGURE 4.5: Net Response Rate for Current Employment Situation

Source: Consumer Confidence Survey, RBI.

It is clear that the Net Response Rate with regard to the current employment situation has consistently worsened since December 2016, immediately after the policy of demonetisation was introduced. It was a major shock administered to the Indian economy in general, and to the informal sector in particular, which is mainly dependent on cash flows.[16] Other studies based on field-level data also corroborate the basic understanding that demonetisation was detrimental for the employment situation in the country—the fall in employment has been estimated at 3.5 million, comparing four months before and after the demonetisation event.[17]

If we read these numbers from the CCS jointly with the picture of employment stagnation as painted by the CMIE data, it is clear that both in terms of reality and perception, the people of India are facing a severe job crisis under the NDA-II government. The huge rush for low-paid and low-grade government jobs even by those with higher education degrees only shows the intensity of the crisis. For example, it has been reported that to fill 9,500 posts of typists, village administrative officers, and stenographers in Tamil Nadu, nearly 20 lakh persons applied, comprising 992 PhD scholars, 23,000 MPhil holders, 2.5 lakh post-graduates, and 8 lakh graduates. It was reported that over 2.8 crore people applied for about 90,000 jobs in the Indian Railways.[18] A similar rush for government jobs has been witnessed in Uttar Pradesh, West Bengal, and other states.

Government's Response to the Job Crisis

While all the evidence available in the public domain points towards a worsening job situation in the country, the NDA-II government has adopted worrying strategies to deal with the problem, which are essentially two-fold. The first approach has been a denial of the existence of the unemployment problem in the economy. The prime minister has said that more than a lack of jobs, the issue is a lack of data on jobs.[19] While the recommendations of the Task Force on Improving Employment Data are yet to be implemented, the government started a major media campaign, claiming an increase in job creation based on various administrative and government schemes data,[20] which are not yet universally accepted as reliable sources for employment data.

For example, the government and some economists have used the Employees Provident Fund Organisation (EPFO) database to argue that there has been an increase in employment. They use the number of new registrations under EPFO to count the number of employed. This is, however, an incorrect way of estimating employment because, first, EPFO registration of workers is mandatory for establishments having at least 20 workers. Take an example of an establishment with 19 workers, none of whom were registered in the EPFO. But when an additional worker is employed, the number of workers becomes 20. This then makes registration of all workers in the EPFO compulsory. If one now looks at the EPFO data, there will be 20 new registered workers, when the increase in employment is only one. Second, the government has incentivised enrolment under the EPFO through the Pradhan Mantri Rozgar Protsahan Yojana (PMPRY). The implementation of this scheme has resulted in an increase in enrolment under the EPFO. But all such new enrolments cannot be regarded as jobs created. Further, contractual workers are also being provided EPF subscriptions, thereby increasing the number of registrations.

There is no way to judge whether the new registrations under the EPFO pertain to new employment or a simple reclassification of the already employed. The basic problem with analysing EPFO data for employment is that the methodology of the dataset is not clear. The question is, when a person changes jobs, does the EPFO merge the two policies or delete one? If it is the former, it will show up as an increase in the number of subscribers, but if it is the latter, there will be no change in the number of subscribers.[21] Also, the data released by the government does not demarcate between people who regularly make contributions to their provident fund (PF) accounts and those who do not. Thus, there is no way of knowing whether the number of workers being circulated are actively engaged in work or if these are merely dormant PF accounts.

Therefore, to claim higher job creation on the basis of EPFO data is problematic. An analysis of EPFO data for the period September

2017 to September 2018 shows that the number of new subscribers during this period was 1.57 crore. However, in the same period, one crore workers ceased to contribute while 24 lakh rejoined the scheme. The notification in this regard from the Ministry of Statistics and Programme Implementation (MoSPI) argues that: 'More analysis is required to look at the cohort of EPF subscribers before firm conclusions can be drawn on the changing pattern of employment across sectors and regions as also by gender'.[22]

The other data source being repeatedly quoted by the government is the loans provided under the Mudra scheme. In 2017–18, 4.81 crore loan accounts were in existence, with a sanctioned loan amount of Rs 2.54 lakh crore.[23] Government officials and economists claim that such a massive infusion of credit in the economy is bound to give rise to more employment. But the real question is: How many new jobs did this scheme generate? There are no estimates available on the employment generated through Mudra.[24] What is known is that 88.65 per cent of the accounts and 42 per cent of the sanctioned loans fall under the Shishu category,[25] where the loan ceiling is only Rs 50,000. With such a small loan, it is doubtful if employment can be created by an entrepreneur.

The prime minister's other claim has been that even those frying *pakoda*s and earning Rs 200 a day should be considered as employed. This is a strange claim for at least three reasons. First, as unemployment allowances do not exist in India, it is practically impossible for anybody to live without work for long. What people generally do is to join the ranks of informal workers and try to eke out a living by low-productive jobs like selling pakodas or peanuts. This is what is called underemployment, or disguised unemployment. To claim such jobs as 'employment' is not accurate. Second, if a person decides to sell pakodas for a living, this is not the result of a government initiative. Lastly, informal and unorganised labour comprises an overwhelming proportion of the Indian workforce, most of whom lack basic social security benefits. To celebrate such low-paid, low-productive jobs as gainful employment is incorrect.

CONCLUSION

Ever since economic reforms were introduced in 1991, India has been following a path of jobless growth. Most of the working people, in the absence of gainful employment opportunities, join the ranks of the informal workers to eke out a living. Narendra Modi, in the run-up to the 2014 Lok Sabha elections, promised to end this situation with a new government that would generate jobs for the people. The available data suggests that the NDA-II government has failed to keep this promise. Rather, it seems that the employment generating potential of the economy has been further eroded by policies like demonetisation.

The debate on employment in India is currently being conducted in a situation in which the government has almost stopped publishing official statistics on employment in the country, and is yet to come up with a new measure which is accepted by economists and policymakers. In this data vacuum, the government machinery is putting out various claims about job creation in the economy based on defective statistical data. However, none of this can change the basic facts about joblessness in the Indian economy. The common people continue to struggle for a living and wait for the day when the government will begin to provide them with gainful employment.

NOTES AND REFERENCES

1. See BJP's 2014 election manifesto, page 4.

2. 'One crore jobs if BJP comes to power: Narendra Modi', *DNA*, 21 November 2013. Available at https://www.dnaindia.com/india/report-one-crore-jobs-if-bjp-comes-to-power-narendra-modi-1922835 (accessed February 2019).

3. Amartya K. Sen, *Employment, Technology and Development* (New Delhi: Oxford University Press, 1975). Employment is a multidimensional concept. A person can be said to be employed if that employment generates an income for her/him, produces some useful goods or services, and if the person thinks that s/he is employed.

4. ASI is an enterprise-level survey and does not provide information regarding the household characteristics of the workers. This survey would, however, be only indicative since the organised sector employment constitutes roughly 7 per cent of the total employed in the country.

5. This makes all subsequent surveys incomparable with the earlier NSSO surveys, while the new numbers have not been published yet. Further, the NITI Aayog Task Force has advocated the use of the Goods and Services Tax Network (GSTN) to assess employment at the enterprise level and conduct a separate enterprise survey to look into establishments not covered under GST. It has also recommended that administrative data and data from government schemes be used to estimate employment numbers in India. This is a controversial suggestion from the Task Force, which we will return to later in this chapter.

6. The CMIE estimates the number of employed as well as the unemployment rate on a monthly, quarterly, and yearly basis. For details on the data and methodology, see https://unemploymentinindia. cmie.com/kommon/bin/sr.php?kall=wtabnav&tab=4000§co de=2002000000000000000000000000000000000000000 (accessed February 2019).

7. Somesh Jha, 'Unemployment rate at four-decade high of 6.1% in 2017-18: NSSO survey', *Business Standard*, 31 January 2019. Available at https://www.business-standard.com/article/economy-policy/unemployment-rate-at-five-decade-high-of-6-1-in-2017-18-nsso-survey-119013100053_1.html (accessed February 2019).

8. Subhanil Chowdhury, 'Employment and Growth under Capitalism: Some Critical Issues with Special Reference to India', IDSK Occasional Paper No. 27, Institute of Development Studies, Kolkata, 2011. Even the increase in the rate of growth of employment during 1999–2004 is suspect, particularly in terms of the quality of employment generated.

9. The labour force of an economy is defined as the number of working-age people who are working or actively searching for work. In other words, labour force denotes the total number of persons participating in the labour market for getting work. Statistically, labour force equals the sum of the number of employed and the number of unemployed.

10. V. Abraham, 'Stagnant Employment Growth: Last Three Years May Have Been the Worst', *Economic and Political Weekly* 52 (38), 2017, 13–17. Abraham, based on the LB survey data, estimates that between 2013–14

and 2015–16, the total employment in India was reduced by 0.4 per cent per annum. In absolute numbers, as per Abraham's estimates, this amounts to a reduction in employment of 37.4 lakh persons between 2013–14 and 2015–16. On the basis of sectoral employment estimates, this decline is to the tune of 53 lakh persons.

R. Kapoor, 'Waiting for Jobs', Working Paper No. 348, Indian Council for Research on International Economic Relations, November 2017. Available at http://icrier.org/pdf/Working_Paper_348.pdf (accessed February 2019). Kapoor estimates that the total number of employed in India declined from 480.4 million to 467.6 million between 2013–14 to 2015–16. This corresponds to a decline of 1.28 crore persons.

11. India has no unemployment benefit or allowance. Therefore, to remain unemployed in India is almost impossible since there is zero income for the unemployed.

12. The LB Quarterly Employment Statistics should, however, be used with caution because they do not cover the new enterprises created after the Sixth Economic Census conducted in 2013–14. What they can, however, indicate is the trend in employment generation in certain sectors on a quarterly basis.

13. It must be remembered that both these sets of data pertain only to the organised sector in the country, which is a very small proportion of the total employment in the economy. Nonetheless, we can only use this data to get some idea about employment since 2015.

14. The methodology and survey design of the CMIE data are different from the NSSO and the LB survey data. Unlike NSSO or LB data, CMIE data provides estimates of employment and unemployment at a monthly, quarterly or yearly frequency. The *SWI* report published by Azim Premji University points out that estimates of the labour force and labour force participation rates vary greatly between the last available LB survey and CMIE data (available from 2016–17). However, Vyas (2018) has pointed out that the CMIE labour force and unemployment data are comparable with the NSSO and LB survey data if we consider the 'current daily status' rather than the 'usual status' of the respondents. The NSSO collects data to generate estimates of employment and unemployment according to the 'usual status' based on a reference period of one year, the 'current weekly status' based on a reference period of one week, and the 'current daily status' based on each day of the seven days preceding the date of survey.

15. Consumer Confidence Survey, RBI, December 2018. Available at https://rbi.org.in/Scripts/PublicationsView.aspx?id=18729 (accessed February 2019). The survey asks respondents about their perceptions and expectations regarding the general economic condition, employment, price level, income, spending, etc. The report records the proportion of people saying that their current situation with respect to the respective variable has improved, and the percentage of people saying that their situation has worsened. The difference between those who report improvement and those who report deterioration is the Net Response Rate.

16. G. Chodorow-Reich, G. Gopinath, P. Mishra, and A. Narayanan, 'Cash and the Economy: Evidence from India's Demonetization', NBER Working Paper No. 25370, December 2018, National Bureau of Economic Research, Cambridge, MA. Available at https://www.nber.org/papers/w25370.pdf (accessed February 2019).

17. M. Vyas, 'Employment: The Big Picture', 2018, Presentation for IC Centre for Governance. Available at https://unemploymentinindia.cmie.com/kommon/bin/sr.php?kall=wtabnav&tab=4090 (accessed February 2019). They show that demonetisation had a significant negative impact on real economic activity and employment.

18. Madhvi Gupta and Pushkar, 'In India, Rising Joblessness is a Tinderbox Waiting to Catch Fire', *The Wire*, 24 April 2018. Available at https://thewire.in/macro/in-india-rising-joblessness-is-a-tinderbox-waiting-to-catch-fire (accessed February 2019).

19. 'More than a lack of jobs, the issue is a lack of data on jobs: PM Narendra Modi', *The Times of India*, 2 July 2018. Available at https://timesofindia.indiatimes.com/india/more-than-a-lack-of-jobs-the-issue-is-a-lack-of-data-on-jobs-pm-narendra-modi/articleshow/64827564.cms (accessed February 2019).

20. For a detailed critique of the use of administrative and government scheme data for estimating employment, see Kapoor, 'Waiting for Jobs'.

21. T. C. A. Sharad Raghavan and Priscilla Jebaraj, 'EPFO data not the right gauge of employment level', *The Hindu*, 24 August 2018. Available at https://www.thehindu.com/news/national/epfo-data-not-the-right-gauge-of-employment-level/article24764207.ece (accessed February 2019).

22. Ministry of Statistics and Programme Implementation, 'Payroll Reporting in India—an analysis of one year and way forward', Government of India, 23 November 2018. Available at http://mospi.nic.in/sites/default/

files/press_release/Payroll_reporting_analysis_24nov2018.pdf (accessed February 2019).

23. *Annual Report of Mudra, 2017–18.*

24. It is reported that the Ministry of Labour and Employment is conducting a survey of Mudra beneficiaries to assess the employment generated by the scheme.

25. *Annual Report of Mudra, 2017–18.*

Part II

Socio-economic Indicators

five

School Education
Denials and Delusions

KIRAN BHATTY

INTRODUCTION

Despite education being widely acknowledged as a crucial sector, governments have consistently failed to accord it the priority it deserves—politically as well as in policy. This is most glaringly evident in the low-budget allocations made to education, but also in the ill-thought-through policy announcements that take into account neither the capacities of the State to deliver nor the contexts in which education is to be provided. As a result, successive governments have ended up going round in circles. Was the term of the NDA-II government any different? Unfortunately, it was not. In fact, it has taken the policy space even further away from the public commitment that is needed towards education. This chapter looks at some of the developments of the past four years and how they have altered the discourse on school education.

THE STILL-AWAITED NATIONAL EDUCATION POLICY

The education sector made headlines when the NDA-II government came to power in May 2014, with the new Human Resource

Development (HRD) Minister Smriti Irani announcing the decision to formulate a new education policy. As the last National Education Policy (NEP) had been formulated more than 30 years ago (in 1986), this was seen as a welcome step. When the minister further declared that the policy would be built from the ground up, taking into account the aspirations of the people, the decision elicited even more interest. Accordingly, about 1,500 meetings around 13 themes identified by the government[1] were planned at different levels from the panchayats upwards. In addition, Irani held video conferences with select state officials, some of which were made publicly available. Two things stand out from these interactions: (i) the overwhelming focus she put on 'skill development', evident from the persistent enquiries of the state and district administrations on the level of industrialisation in their regions, accompanied by a 'request' to map skill requirements and how schools can respond to those requirements; and (ii) the use and promotion of technology. This is evident from the fact that not only was information and communications technology (ICT) a separate theme in itself, but it also figured as a policy concern in other themes.

To put all of the local-level suggestions together into a coherent policy document, a national-level committee was then set up, headed by former Cabinet Secretary T. S. R. Subramanian and comprising J. S. Rajput, Sevaram Sharma, and Shailaja Chandra, who also did their own field visits and submitted a draft in September 2016. The document was honest in recognising that the education sector was in a crisis, especially with regard to trust in the public sector's ability to deliver quality. It also pinpointed the main areas where it had failed, such as low financial allocations, insufficient decentralisation, lack of investment in teachers, and so on. However, it was remiss on two counts: (i) ignoring the role of the bureaucracy in implementation failures; and (ii) not addressing the issue of private provision.[2] Even though it was a good start, the government distanced itself from it, and later the new HRD Minister Prakash Javadekar set up an altogether new committee to reformulate the NEP—this time headed by K. Kasturirangan and comprising nine members.[3] Despite four formal extensions, this committee is yet to submit its report.

MAKING PRIVATE A MEASURE OF THE PUBLIC

In the meantime, several decisions taken at the Central as well as the state government levels provide an indication of the direction that education policy and provision is taking in the country. From the announcements made and schemes sanctioned, the major thrusts appear to be in the following areas: (i) Edu Tech or promoting the use of technology in education; (ii) promoting and strengthening private sector and non-governmental participation; (iii) promoting skill development and vocational studies; (iv) fostering cost efficiency through measures such as the merging of schools with low student population, low-cost alternatives, and contractualisation of teacher employment; (v) guidelines for ranking schools based on learning outcomes and on the financial support garnered from the private sector.

Before discussing these any further, it would be useful to place them in the perspective that has informed their creation. The main concern identified by the government appears to be that of improving cognitive learning outcomes, while keeping costs at a minimum. This is couched in the language of accountability, cost effectiveness and 'outcomes' orientation. Therefore, teachers who have been pronounced almost solely responsible for the falling learning levels are sought to be made accountable through punitive measures such as performance pays and use of technology to monitor their behaviour (for example, closed circuit television [CCTV] cameras in classrooms or biometric attendance). Low-cost options, which translate into under-qualified and low-paid teachers, are widely prescribed as effective in terms of 'costs per unit of learning,'[4] as are scale-backs on other 'inputs' (for example, toilets, which are perceived as not contributing to 'learning').[5] The concept of a fully equipped school has been portrayed as one that does not promote learning per se, implying that equipping schools with the basic infrastructure amounts to focusing on 'inputs' and not outcomes. This narrative has gained so much currency in the public domain that even the Right of Children to Free and Compulsory Education (RTE) Act is labelled as a Right to Schooling, and not Learning, because of its mandate of making schools provided for in terms of infrastructure, albeit minimally.[6]

This coming together of the accountability narrative with the outcomes and cost-effectiveness narrative on the one hand, and the private sector being perceived as the efficient alternative on the other, has created a discourse on education that has moved far from the basic principles of public education. It does so by neglecting to take into account the fact that the provision of public education extends far beyond an efficiency objective and encapsulates a range of social, administrative, and systemic functions as well. For instance, the government, system is responsible for training teachers, examination systems, curriculum development—expenditures not borne by the private sector—just as government teachers are expected to compile education statistics, respond to Right to Information (RTI) applications, manage mid-day meals, but also do election monitoring, participate in the delivery of public services, census enumeration, comply with government directives to maintain audit norms, etc., that private school teachers are not. Besides, government schools must provide education to every last child, not refusing admission to any—irrespective of 'merit' or parental support—whereas private schools can choose the children they want.[7] For these reasons, the arguments that apply to the private sector for evaluation of performance, and the punitive solutions emerging thereof, simply do not apply to the public provision of a public service. Unfortunately, from the dominant discourse and the policy response to it, it appears that, in effect, the private is being made a measure of the public.

The focus on the themes listed at the start of this section is a reflection of precisely this shift in the perception of public education. Hence, the push for technological solutions regardless of the capacity of the public sector to adopt technology; it is the measurement of learning in cognitive terms because it is relatively amenable to quantitative measures and efficiency parameters, while non-cognitive learning indicators or other goals of education such as diversity, inclusivity, etc., are neglected. The latter are not even concerns of private schools, but must be of the public. Unfortunately, public schools today do not promote these goals either, but the difference is that they can be held publicly accountable for them, whereas the private schools may not.

Edu Tech

The Central Advisory Board of Education (CABE)—the highest body to advise the government on education policy, which was reconstituted on 11 June 2015, with many more members representing the industry included—in its last meeting (January 2018) made the first major policy announcement of this government: Operation Digital Board. This appears to be an almost literal translation of the government's slogan 'Digital India' into the classroom setting. While the thrust towards digitalising basic education came in July 2015, with the prime minister calling for a linking of the Sarva Shiksha Abhiyan (SSA) with digital India and the launch of 'e-basta', the formal policy statement came with the announcement of Operation Digital Board.

The details of this operation are still to be revealed, but its express purpose appears to be to 'modernise' school education by bringing cutting-edge technology into the classroom and hence improve learning levels. While such a goal is certainly laudable, what it ignores is not only basic pedagogical concepts, but also the ground reality. The use of technology to minimise the active role of the teacher (ostensibly to reduce costs and the perceived errant behaviour of teachers) overlooks the importance of having an engaged teacher to guide the learning of students. While not ignoring the problems attributed to teachers, the point being made is that the solution does not lie in replacing them with technology, but in finding creative ways of improving their performance. The other more immediate concern, however, is of the preparedness of government-school classrooms to be part of the digital revolution. As the District Information System for Education (DISE), 2016–17, data shows, most government schools do not even have working computers (86 per cent), many do not have electricity connections (39 per cent), and none have a budget line for electricity bills. The latter are to be paid from the school maintenance grant, which is a paltry Rs 5,000/year—barely sufficient to meet the regular maintenance needs of schools. As a result, many schools rely on stealing from other connections; and where they do have a connection, the teacher or head teacher has to use personal resources to pay for it. Sustaining computer use, of the regularity required for such an operation, thus seems a distant dream.

This has not stopped the government or the private sector from promoting a 'digital-age upgrade' of schooling for 'real-time learning'. Hence 'flipped classrooms'—the name for obtaining lessons at home instead of in the classroom, social learning from social media platforms, e-books, and online proctoring—are considered the new growth areas in education. Prime Minister Modi, too, has given a boost to this sector through the launch of e-basta, a 'framework to make school books accessible in digital form as e-books to be read and used on tablets and laptops'.[8] As smart phone penetration in India was projected to be only 36 per cent in 2018, it is hard to understand how e-basta was being promoted as a game-changer in the educational life of children. It is worth mentioning, though, that the market for e-learning in India is estimated to be around USD 3 billion,[9] and has been proclaimed to be the next sunrise sector.

PROMOTING PRIVATE PARTICIPATION OR EDU BUSINESS

Perhaps the most definite enunciation of policy towards the private sector-led approach to education has come from the National Institution for Transforming India or NITI Aayog, which released its three-year action plan in August 2017.[10] The thrust of the chapter on 'Education and Skill Development'[11] is on three goals, namely: (i) orienting the system towards outcomes; (ii) providing tools to teachers and students for effective learning; and (iii) improving existing governance mechanisms and piloting new ones, each of which has been elaborated with specific suggestions. What stands out is that the education reforms being suggested are very much in line with making the system run as an efficient private-sector enterprise. In fact, it is stated in fairly unambiguous terms that:

> The provision of education can be potentially hived off into a separate publically owned vehicle, or the directorate of education can be made more autonomous and accountable. The important factors to be kept in mind for such an initiative to succeed are clear measurable goals, quality of top managers selected; independence and authority for the management to take necessary steps to reach the goals and oversight and accountability based on credible measurement of outcomes.[12]

Thus, technological fixes that will allow for monitoring quantitative outcomes as well as provide tools for learning, reducing costs of teachers by 'mobilizing local contract teachers who may not possess the qualifications of regular teachers but are nonetheless qualified to impart foundational skills ...',[13] piloting governance systems that separate the functions of 'policy making, regulation and provision', and exploring 'bolder' experiments for private participation are the specific suggestions being made. The last include 'education vouchers, local government led purchasing of school services' and public–private partnership (PPP) models, where 'the private sector adopts government schools while being publicly funded on a per child basis'.[14]

The Ministry of Human Resource Development (MHRD) as well as state education departments have also been encouraging and facilitating private participation in school education. The recently released document on Performance Ranking Guidelines issued by the MHRD explicitly includes an indicator for 'funds arranged through PPP, CSR [corporate social responsibility] etc., as a percentage of state budgets'. In other words, states that procure private funds are being ranked higher, giving an incentive to states to garner more private funds. State governments, particularly Rajasthan, have been at the forefront of promoting PPPs in various forms. In 2017, it even introduced an explicit PPP policy to allow private agencies to run government schools.

Despite a lot of discussion and support for private intervention, there is very little data in the public domain on the nature and form of the PPP models in existence. As such, it is hard to know how many schools are, in effect, functioning with private intervention, or the terms of the memoranda of understanding signed by private agencies with the government. This in particular raises serious questions about the public accountability of these initiatives. While private engagement can play a useful role in education, without clearly laid out principles of public regulation of these enterprises, there is a real danger of straying from the public commitments implied in basic education.

At the same time, private schools continue to proliferate as the quality of government schools is increasingly perceived as poor, and a shift to private seen as a status marker. As the regulatory mechanism for monitoring private schools remains underdeveloped, there is virtually no check on what passes for quality in many of these schools. In addition, the spectre of 'budget private schools' has also grown apace. Seen as an affordable option for the poor, this idea has acquired a fair degree of currency in the public domain. Unfortunately, what little is known of them is not very encouraging as far as either quality of teaching or other goals of education are concerned.[15]

SKILL DEVELOPMENT AND VOCATIONAL TRAINING

The promotion of skill development and the appeals made by the Education Minister to establish backward links with local industry show not only the influence of private industry on the education system, but also an unfortunate misreading of the goals of education and the interests of children. While the education-employment link is undeniable, the ability to determine what sort of employment a person may wish to pursue can come only after: (i) acquiring a certain level of education, and (ii) exposure to diverse streams of knowledge and opportunities. By predetermining the skills provided, not just at an early age but on the basis of local industrial demand, the child is being deprived of a more solid foundation and being straitjacketed early on—neither of which can be seen as justifiable goals. We really need to ask, then: Is the objective of public education to serve the interests of the child, or the interests of private industry? Unfortunately, in what is perhaps the cruellest irony of all, while schools are being asked to establish backward linkages with industry for skill development, industry itself has not stepped up with support, either for skill-development or through the creation or provision of jobs.[16] The sheer lack of employment opportunities should give everyone a cause for pause regarding the implications of this policy drift. In such an environment, sacrificing the intrinsic value of education for an illusory instrumental value does greater harm than good as it ends up creating a population of youth with poor overall education and low employability.[17]

This government has further chosen to promote skills that require a lower level of education and therefore a lower level of employment and less investment in human development by either the State or industry. Thus, as opposed to four years of training from class nine to class 12, creating a cadre that would seek a job at a higher end of the employment scale, now the vocational stream is offered at class nine itself.[18] It is hard to escape the sense that the State, unable to own the goals of education and its own responsibility towards the provision of a public service, is seeking ways of reducing what it apparently sees as its 'burden', thereby facilitating the exit of children from the education system sooner than desirable.

School Mergers

An issue that has grabbed headlines and worried activists working on the ground is that of school mergers. First introduced in Rajasthan, it is another example of imposing efficiency parameters on public schools without accounting for the larger goals that the system serves, such as reaching the last mile child. The almost overnight merger of schools did not consider the fact that children, especially girls, may not be able to travel the longer distances to the merged school, resulting in their dropping out. In some instances, Urdu-medium schools were merged with Hindi-medium schools, creating another situation of potential dropouts.[19] The fact that the increased pressure on the merged schools was also ignored indicates not only a response to perceived economic efficiency priorities, but also the knee-jerk nature of policymaking.

The Teaching Deficit: Vacancies and Contractualisation of Teachers

Employment of teachers as government employees follows Pay Commission guidelines and over the years, especially since the last two Pay Commissions (6th and 7th), their salary scales have increased substantially. This codification has not been taken into account by the finance ministry in its allocations to the education sector, which has only fallen over the past few years (down to 0.45 per cent of the gross domestic product [GDP]—the lowest in the last decade; see Figure 5.1). State governments are thus hard-pressed to provide teachers with the scales and grades recommended, especially for the increase in the supply of teachers, necessitated by the increase in the demand for education. As a result, vacancies and contractualisation abounds. The annual work plan and budget documents (2016–17) of the education ministry show more than 10 lakh (10,31,122) teachers' posts vacant in government schools across the country. In Jharkhand, this amounted to 38.4 per cent vacancies, in Bihar 34.4 per cent, in

Uttar Pradesh 23.4 per cent, and in Delhi 25 per cent. And this is not accounting for the teacher requirement for the millions of children currently out of school (estimates range from 6 to 40 million).

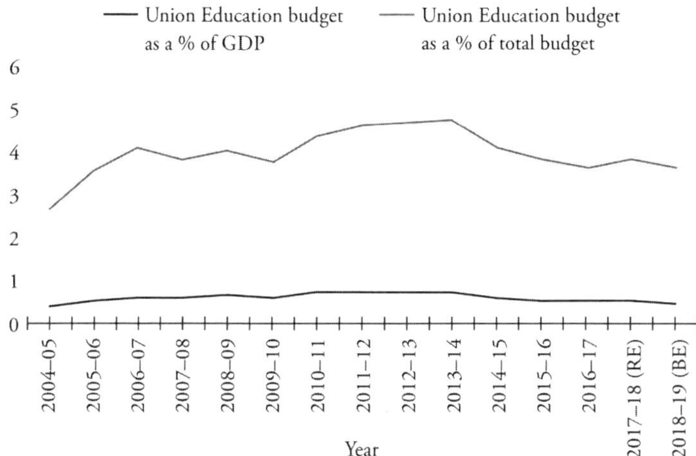

FIGURE 5.1: Annual Union Government Budget Allocations for Education, from 2004–19

Source: Compiled from the Centre for Budget and Governance Accountability (CBGA) Reports on Response to Union Budget, various years.

Teachers are also being employed as contract teachers to avoid paying them Pay Commission salaries. The form of contractualisation varies from state to state, and with the RTE banning contractualisation, it is being couched in different nomenclatures. Hence, teachers are labelled variously as '*prabodhak*', '*zilla parishad* teacher' (ZPT), 'primary assistant teacher' (PAT), and so on, and provided long-term contracts, but without the pay and benefits of regular government teachers.[20] Instead, their salaries could range from Rs 3,700 to Rs 50,000 per month, for the same post and quantum of work in the same school. While variation exists across the different categories and between states, a case filed by teachers in Gujarat showed that some of them were being paid less than even minimum wage. Despite the Gujarat High Court ordering a revision of their pay scales, the matter had to come to the Supreme Court, where it has been awaiting a hearing for the past four years.[21] Unsurprisingly, the low wage being offered attracts poorly qualified and trained teachers. According to the Unified District Information System for Education (U-DISE) 2017–18, 25 per cent of teachers today do not possess the requisite qualifications, implying that the teaching cadre has been infused with teachers ill-equipped for their job. In effect, it has led to a de-professionalisation of school teachers and played a big part in the declining learning levels noted annually.

Other Developments, Some Good, Some Not

RTE Amendments

The RTE Act is by no means a perfect legislation and does need to be amended in parts. Unfortunately, the amendments made or sought to be made by this government are a mixed bag. For instance, among the provisions under RTE that have come under attack, the one that drew the attention of this government relates to the no-detention policy as it was widely seen to be interfering in the achievement of adequate learning outcomes. An amendment abolishing the no-detention clause was passed in Parliament through the RTE (second amendment) Bill in January 2019. Having been passed, it is now up to the state governments to keep the clause or not. It is worth noting, however, that the report of a CABE sub-committee established to review the clause had clearly recommended its retention.[22] The removal of no-detention is widely recognised by pedagogists as detrimental to learning by children as it creates a spectre of 'failure' and enforces learning through fear. This is especially pernicious to children from first-generation learner families without academic support at home, who may require longer than a year to reach the required learning levels. Detaining them in the same class for failure to have crossed a 'finish line' could end up removing them from the system itself.

The other amendment that has been discussed is to extend the ambit of the RTE to pre-primary classes, which is a much-needed one. Another CABE sub-committee reviewed this suggestion, and 'in principle' recommended the extension. It is unfortunate that despite being suggested, it has not yet been carried through due to the financial implications of the extension, which have come in the way of the government's resolve.

In addition, the Central RTE Rules were also modified on 20 February 2017 to put into place: (i) benchmarks for learning outcomes based on class-wise and subject-wise learning outcomes, and (ii) guidelines for using Continuous and Comprehensive Evaluation (CCE) to achieve the said outcomes. Benchmarking learning outcomes could be useful, but much will depend on how it is implemented. Teaching to the tests, a practice whereby teachers teach solely with the purpose of enabling students to score high in tests, hence compromising actual learning, for instance, could defeat the purpose.

Textbook Changes[23]

It is an unfortunate reality of political regime change that textbooks become the site of ideological assertions, with scant regard for children's experiences or the long-term impact on their minds or even on the nation. BJP-led governments have in particular been at the receiving end of charges of making pernicious changes in textbooks—most notably that of saffronisation that was attempted by the previous NDA government. This time around, the changes are wider in nature, encompassing elements of saffronisation but extending to other areas as well, for instance, those that contribute to enhancing the nation's glory, especially its ancient 'Hindu' past, and depict Indian society as being in complete harmony with little or no conflict, inequalities or marginalisation of social and ethnic groups.

Some of the specific changes include greater space for essentially Hindu 'warriors' such as Maharana Pratap and Shivaji, or 'spiritual leaders' such as Swami Vivekananda and Sri Aurobindo, and documenting the achievements of India's ancient systems of knowledge like ayurveda, yoga, astrology, and astronomy. They also include for the first time—and in glowing terms—an introduction of flagship programmes launched by the current government, such as *Swachh Bharat* and *Beti Padhao Beti Bachao*, while toning down references to critical assessments of government and the bureaucracy. There have also been omissions, for instance, removal of references to national figures such as Jawaharlal Nehru, Sarojini Naidu, and Madan Mohan Malviya from the Rajasthan class eight social science textbooks. Also, international political thinkers, philosophers, and poets, such as T. S. Eliot, William Blake, and John Keats, to name a few, have been removed in an apparent bid to go 'local'. Urdu words have also been dropped as has the title 'Great' from Akbar, and added instead to Maharana Pratap.

The thrust seems to be on packing information into the books, making them dense to read with little analytical perspective, especially in the social sciences. In general, this government has pushed science and mathematics at the cost of social science. This foretells a missing link with the perspective and core values that social science engenders, that is, social context, critical enquiry, and democracy.

While curricula and textbooks do need upgrading from time to time, and the National Curriculum Framework (NCF 2005) brought in by the UPA government has certainly been in line for a critical review, the current changes bypass not just the government-approved NCF, but constitutional and pedagogical principles as well.[24]

Of Denials and Delusions

Learning outcomes have taken centre-stage in the debates around school education, almost to the exclusion of all else, ignoring one of the most critical gaps in the provision of schooling—the out-of-school children. Instead, figures of high gross enrolment ratios are used to assert that *all* children are in school, and that the system only needs to worry about getting them to learn adequately. Unfortunately, the government's own statistics show that the number of children out of school are anywhere between 6 million and 40 million, depending on the source one uses. Ignoring for a moment the huge discrepancy in the figures, even the lowest of them is cause for concern. In a sense, there has emerged in this discourse an invisibilisation of the out-of-school children, including the irregularly attending ones—the numbers of which are not insignificant.[25] The denial of this reality has serious consequences on education policy and its attempt to universalise basic education as well as improve learning levels.

The other aspect of policy that has the appearance of delusion is the manner in which schemes and plans have been announced without sufficient thought to the capacities in the system to deliver them, especially in terms of the financial allocations. Two such schemes are the Samagra Shiksha Abhiyan and the Pandit Madan Mohan Malviya National Mission for Teachers and Teaching (PMMMNMTT)—the former ostensibly to focus on education in a holistic fashion, and the latter to boost teacher quality and thereby learning outcomes. While both are worthy causes, what is troubling is the lack of attention to governance details and capacities necessary to implement these schemes. For instance, successive budgets have failed to allocate sufficient resources to make even a dent in the overall objectives of these schemes. Budget 2018, while emphasising teacher training, failed to increase allocations to the PMMMNMTT from the Rs 120 crore allocated the previous year (revised estimate [RE] Rs 100 crore). There was, in the same year, an increase in budgetary support of Rs 70 crore for strengthening teacher training institutes, but that appears to have come at the cost of the appointments of language teachers amounting to Rs 40 crore. In a scenario where teacher shortages are running into lakhs, this does not bode well, especially for tribal areas where language teachers would be a greater necessity.

Financial allocations for education, as seen from budgetary expenditures, have been a bone of contention between education activists and policymakers—largely those in the Ministry of Finance—for the last half-century or more. The much-quoted Kothari

Commission suggestion of 6 per cent of GDP has not just been consistently ignored, but the proportions have actually declined and currently stand at the lowest for the past few decades, at 2.6 per cent. In fact, the demands from the MHRD have also been consistently thwarted by the finance ministry, with each year's allocations falling short of what was demanded. For instance, the amount demanded by MHRD from the Budget 2017 was Rs 46,000 crore, but the allocations fell far short at Rs 29,556 crore. What is interesting to note, however, are the proclamations of grandiose schemes made each year by the finance minister, without any indication of where the funds for these schemes will come from. In the light of falling allocations, these appear to be in the realm of false promises.

When the State Gives Up on Itself

What marks the term of this government is a disturbing trend in the public sector—that of giving up on its own ability to deliver. Hence the reliance on technology as a panacea for a wide range of issues, the shift away from core educational goals towards skill development and vocational training, and faith in the private and non-government sector's role in bridging implementation gaps. It is ironic that thus far it was the citizens who were losing faith in the State's ability to provide quality education, but recent trends seem to suggest that the bureaucracy too has lost faith in its own capacities. Since even today, more than 70 per cent of the country's children are dependent on government schooling, this does not bode well. Instead of looking away from the system and adopting a minimalist approach in education governance, the government would do well to look within and fix the bottlenecks in implementation that are preventing it from delivering on its public commitments. Kneejerk reactions to existing problems will not do the trick. A sustained political commitment translated into increased resources, coupled with reforms in the governance system, is what is needed if we are to achieve even our basic goals in education.

NOTES AND REFERENCES

1. The 13 themes were: (i) Learning outcomes in elementary education; (ii) Outreach of secondary and senior secondary education; (iii) Strengthening vocational education; (iv) Reforming school exam system; (v) Revamping teacher education; (vi) Accelerating rural literacy; (vii) Promoting ICT; (viii) New pedagogies in science and math; (ix) School standards, school assessment, and school management systems; (x) Enabling inclusive education; (xi) Promotion of languages; (xii) Comprehensive education, involving ethics, physical education, arts and crafts, and life skills; (xiii) Focus on child health.

2. For a critique of the report, see Kiran Bhatty, 'The Hits and Misses of the T.S.R. Subramanian Committee Report on Education', *The Wire*, 2 July 2016. Available at https://thewire.in/education/the-hits-and-misses-of-the-t-s-r-subramanian-committee-report-on-the-new-education-policy (accessed February 2019).

3. The other eight members were: K. J. Alphonse (former member, IAS); Vasudha Kamat (Vice-Chancellor, SNDT Women's University, Mumbai); Manjul Bhargava (Professor of Mathematics, Princeton University); Ram Shankar Kureel (Vice-Chancellor, Ambedkar University of Social Sciences, Mhau, Madhya Pradesh); T. V. Kattimani (Vice-Chancellor, Indira Gandhi Tribal University, Amarkantha); Krishna Mohan Tripathy (former chairperson, Uttar Pradesh High School Exam Board); Mazhar Asif (Professor of Persian, Guwahati University); M. K. Sridhar (former member-secretary, Karnataka Innovation Council, member CABE).

4. For the use of this concept, see Geeta Gandhi Kingdon, 'The Private Schooling Phenomena in India: A Review', Discussion Paper Series No. 10612, March 2017, Institute of Education, University College, London. Unfortunately, Kingdon does not clarify what she means by the 'unit of learning'. However, one is hard pressed to imagine what a particular 'unit' of learning might entail.

5. Kiran Bhatty, 'The link between sanitation and schooling', *The Hindu*, 19 September 2014. Available at https://www.thehindu.com/opinion/op-ed/the-link-between-sanitation-and-schooling/article6423571.ece (accessed February 2019).

6. What is true is that the RTE Act did not codify learning outcomes because the constructivist approach adopted by education experts and the

establishment does not allow for such standardisation of learning outcomes across the country. The constructivist approach recognises that different parts of the country are at different levels of education progress and offer different types of learning. Hence, the outcomes are better determined or constructed from the ground upwards rather than being pre-fixed by a Central authority, especially a legal one. That said, perhaps the Act could have included a clause that requires different levels of government to set some benchmarks of learning following the constructivist approach. The complete silence on cognitive learning benchmarks was perhaps a lacuna in the Act. It has, however, been corrected through an amendment in the Central RTE Rules, as discussed in the section on RTE Amendments.

7. Clause 12(c) of the RTE is perhaps the only exception where private schools must take in 25 per cent of the incoming class from socially and economically underprivileged families.

8. Available at http://vikaspedia.in/education/interactive-resources/ ebasta#section-2 (accessed February 2019).

9. 'E-learning: India's education system needs to get online', *Hindustan Times*, 30 August 2015. Available at https://www.hindustantimes.com/ editorials/e-learning-india-s-education-system-needs-to-get-online/story-GsitwEdCHPZMmBOSjUt49K.html (accessed February 2019). See also Nilesh Christopher, 'Online education will be a $2 bn Industry in India by 2021: Google, KPMG', *The Economic Times*, 30 May 2017. Available at https://economictimes.indiatimes.com/industry/services/education/ online-education-will-be-a-2-bn-industry-in-india-by-2021-google-kpmg/ articleshow/58913744.cms (accessed February 2019).

10. NITI Aayog, Government of India, *India: Three Year Action Agenda, 2017–18 to 2019–20*. Available at http://niti.gov.in/writereaddata/files/ coop/IndiaActionPlan.pdf (accessed February 2019).

11. The fact that this chapter is titled 'Education and Skill Development' says much about the form that NITI Aayog wishes to give education policy.

12. NITI Aayog, *India: Three Year Action Agenda*, Chapter 20, 137.

13. Ibid., 137.

14. Ibid., 138.

15. Geetha Nambissan, 'Private Schools for the Poor: Business as Usual', *Economic and Political Weekly* 47 (41), 2012.

16. The website of the Ministry of Skill Development and Entrepreneurship (MSDE) (https://www.msde.gov.in/partners.html), states the following: 'Wadhwani Foundation is providing support to such initiatives on their own

or in partnership with the Ministry of HRD and/or State Governments. Now under the aegis of the new Ministry of Skill Development & Entrepreneurship, technical and project management support for skilling initiatives of the Central/State Government in the area of integration of skilling with education and entrepreneurship education would be provided in a more organized and structured manner by pooling the resources of the Central Government and the Wadhwani Foundation.' However, the Comptroller and Auditor General (CAG) of India audit for 2008–14 showed that more than 95 per cent of the funds provided to the National Skill Development Corporation (NSDC) were from government sources. It is further learnt that resources promised by private partners have not been forthcoming to date, severely impacting the objectives of the Skill India Mission.

17. Even the 'case studies' of successful employment through various initiatives under the Skill India Mission listed on the website add up to less than 50!

18. See http://mhrd.gov.in/sites/upload_files/mhrd/files/upload_document/job_roles.pdf (accessed February 2019) for the list of job roles being provided under the vocational training programme.

19. For a review of school mergers in Rajasthan, see Kiran Bhatty, 'Jumping the gun in Rajasthan', *The Hindu*, 26 November 2014. Available at https://www.thehindu.com/opinion/op-ed/jumping-the-gun-in-rajasthan/article6633517.ece (accessed February 2019).

20. What is surprising, though, is that these different categories of teachers do not get listed as 'contract' teachers and hence escape documentation in the data collection process. For instance, DISE collects data on only two categories of teachers: regular and contract. Since the governments avoid labelling them as contract teachers, by default they are counted as regular. In fact, it is hard to obtain data on the different categories of teachers and their respective pay grades from any publicly available data set. What is worse, RTIs filed by the author at MHRD and state government levels (in 2016) also came a cropper. The RTIs were shunted from one agency to the other—from the All India Council for Technical Education (AICTE) to individual schools even—to supply the information asked for and still did not reveal all the details.

21. SLP 14124/2012, and SLP 14125/2012.

22. See the Bhukkal Committee Report and other documents related to no-detention and CCE.

23. Disha Nawani, 'Modifying School Textbooks: Disregarding Children's Experiences', *Economic and Political Weekly* 53 (29), 21 July 2018. This section draws heavily from Nawani 2018.

24. In addition to these revisions which affect the government school system in particular, another change that has taken place in this period is the introduction of large international groups like Pearson in the curriculum and test design arena in India. Their entry in Tier II and III towns in partnership with local start-up groups, especially in the area of science and mathematics, is a major shift in the education landscape, the future of which is uncertain.

25. Kiran Bhatty, Radhika Saraf, and Vrinda Gupta, 'Out-of-School Children: Some Insights on What We Know and What We Do Not Know', *Economic and Political Weekly* 52 (49), 9 December 2017.

six

The Price of Freedom

The NDA-II Government's Report Card on Higher Education

Ayesha Kidwai

Mention of the topic of Indian universities today conjures up an instant imagery of protests, of State repression silencing young voices defending the right to critical thought and expression and social justice. These images, however, even as they reflect the extent of the rage, do not provide a full accounting of why there is such anger and what its causes are. Merely indexing this anger to the 'higher education system' is not particularly informative, because has Indian higher education not *always* been in the doldrums? With only one in four young people enrolled in any higher educational institution (henceforth, HEI) across the country, is this not just rage against a machine that the NDA-II government has actually been trying to repair?

In this chapter, based on the data the government has itself published, we show that the reason for the anger in universities indeed has a new cause, because where we once had growth along several parameters, four-plus years of the NDA-II government has yielded an alarming *decline* along several of them. Baldly put, higher education in India is far worse-off than it was when Narendra Modi first grasped the reins of government in May 2014. Far from even trying to repair the machine, the NDA-II government's policies have apparently been geared towards engineering its complete breakdown, and are most certainly a betrayal of the aspirations with which millions of young people voted for the Bharatiya Janata Party (BJP) in 2014.

The BJP's Electoral Promises

The BJP Election Manifesto, released in March 2014, waxes eloquent about missed opportunities and unutilised capacity, and promises policies that will make India a 'Knowledge Powerhouse' and prepare the 'World's Largest Workforce'. The BJP's core promise was to 'review and revise [the] education system' by undertaking a number of initiatives, including framing a 'National Education Policy' and raising public spending on education to '6% of GDP' so that it can deliver 'Quality education for all'.[1] Overall, the BJP manifesto did not seem to deviate too much from the UPA's preferred mode of public–private partnership (PPP) as the main engine driving the growth and diversification of government investment in higher education. It favoured a policy trajectory that facilitates State divestment in higher education, emphasises vocational and employment-oriented courses, and the use of information and communications technologies (ICT) in education in general. There are specific inflections, of course—such as the emphasis on massive open online courses (MOOCs) and skill-based short-term courses—but back in 2014, the thought that the NDA-II government would so overwhelmingly interfere with higher education on almost all fronts could not be divined from its election promises.

Policies and Schemes Implementing the BJP Manifesto

Successive governments have failed to keep the promises made in election manifestos and the NDA-II is no exception. The first casualty was the usual one of spending 6 per cent of GDP on education.

Between 2014–15 and 2018–19, the proportion of GDP spent on education actually declined—from 0.67 per cent to 0.45 per cent.[2] Others like the National Education Policy could never come to fruition, despite the setting up of two committees for the same.

Restructuring the UGC, Graded Autonomy and Eminence

The policy initiative of restructuring the University Grants Commission (UGC) and of creating a Higher Education Commission of India (HECI) was vigorously pursued by the government for about six months in 2018, but opposition from teachers and students has forced the government to put this into cold storage, at least for the time being. This opposition was on several counts,[3] which, put briefly, was along three axes:

(i) The HECI Bill creates a body, replacing the UGC, packed with non-academics—government officers and political nominees, and with no significant representation of the actual stakeholders of the higher education system—teachers and educationists. As the Bill also vests the funding of universities exclusively with the Central government on the recommendations of HECI, it is feared that HECI will serve as a gate-keeper, with obedience to the government being a precondition for funding.

(ii) The HECI Bill gives the Central government extraordinary powers to interfere in the internal governance of, and academic syllabi taught in, universities. It is feared that the innovations and specificities of HEIs across the country would be erased by forced compliance to regulations framed by a non-academic body, guided largely by the interests of the government of the day. With the Bill giving the right to HECI to both authorise and close down HEIs, to imprison and fine HEI administrators for whatever is deemed 'non-compliance', the punitive aspects of the Bill have many worried.

(iii) The HECI Bill is also opposed for the privatisation mechanism built into it, through the incorporation of the UGC's Graded

Autonomy Regulations. While most HEIs will effectively lose institutional autonomy, a few high-performing institutions will qualify to be 'let go', provided they do not rely on State funds and generate their own incomes through loans and fee hikes. In other words, the price for retaining institutional autonomy could be the complete divestment of the State's stake in the institution. This sharp right turn away from a State subsidy model has been argued to pave the way for a general user-pay principle in the funding of higher education, which will not only level the field for private players, but will also restrict access and opportunity for millions of socially disadvantaged young people of modest means.

This policy direction, in which the government establishes a choking control over less-privileged institutions through unreasonable regulations for the bulk of institutions via the HECI and hands out deregulation as a prize to a chosen few, was first spelled out in the Subramanian Committee report.[4] However, even as these recommendations were heeded—potentially good institutions *must* be given 'relaxations' and 'total autonomy', but 'poor managements' should be abolished or discouraged through 'appropriate checks and controls'—its scathing observations on how the current system of the political nomination of vice-chancellors (VCs) is 'prone to manipulation, which militates against the appointment of competent persons as VC with vision and leadership'[5] were ignored. The government will continue to appoint VCs for both 'poor' and 'potentially good'[6] institutions, with the result that even institutions given graded autonomy will never be free of government agendas. Something of this can already be seen at Jawaharlal Nehru University, which was granted graded autonomy in 2018, without its Executive Council even asking for it. The first measures it has taken—online certificate courses in Hindu rituals, *vastu shastra*, and religious tourism—are designed to fulfil the skill-oriented courses promised in the BJP manifesto.

The graded autonomy regulations and the HECI Bill are all based on the premise that excellence is contingent on ushering in private investment in the sector. From this position, it is but a small leap to equate a plentiful supply of private capital with a promise of at least a potential for excellence. That leap was made via a public announcement of the yet-to-be founded Jio Institute as a government-designated 'Institution of Eminence', which caused the government a great degree of embarrassment. In the laughter that followed, however, what was drowned out was the fact that the awards also meant the deregulation of three high-performing public institutions—the Indian Institute of Science (IISc), Indian Institute of Technology (IIT) Bombay, and IIT Madras—albeit after a cash injection of Rs 200 crore per annum from taxpayers' contributions. These institutions are now permitted to do essentially five new things—admit foreign students up to 30 per cent of student strength with fees fixed without restriction, recruit foreign faculty up to 25 per cent of faculty strength with differential incentives, offer online courses up to 20 per cent of their programmes, fix differential fees and remunerations, and be flexible about the years needed to complete a degree.

In other words, for Indian students, the number of seats reduces to 70 per cent of what it is currently, and for Indian researchers, jobs fall by 25 per cent. With the requirement that these institutions must raise funds for all new programmes through resources earned from fees and other charges, new programmes launched by these institutions will be accessible to only a few. Coded into the tag of eminence is also a deafening silence about the reservation policies of India, which suggests that freedom is another word for losing the agenda of social justice altogether. It is entirely unclear why a causal link has been made between online courses and flexibility in years with a degree and excellence, but assuming there is some rational basis for this connection, why should this policy be available only to those who pay a higher fee in these HEIs?

Skilling India and Teacher Training

The national agenda for skill development got off to a good start. The India Apprentice Act was amended in December 2014 itself (ignoring protests by workers' unions), a Ministry of Skill Development and Entrepreneurship (MSDE) instituted in November 2014, and a National Apprenticeship Promotion Scheme (NAPS) launched in August 2016 and given a budget of Rs 500 crore. However, by 2018–19, according to the *Thirty-Sixth Report of the Standing Committee on Labour*,[7] NAPS has had a 'dismal performance', utilising only 44 per cent of the money allotted to it in 2017–18. The umbrella scheme for Apprenticeship and Training also recorded an unspent balance of close to 50 per cent.

In fact, the Standing Committee on Labour pulled up MSDE for failing to 'make concerted efforts for full utilisation of allocated funds in implementing their schemes at all costs'.[8] All skill development schemes faced huge cuts in the Union Budget of 2018–19, but this was at least in part because the MSDE could never spend the money allocated to it in the first place. For two consecutive years, in 2016–17 and 2017–18, the actual expenditure of the ministry was significantly lower than the revised estimate, and about 22–29 per cent of funds were left unutilised. The NDA-II government continued down this route—there have been good intentions, but no plans going forward on how skills are to be developed. Hence, while money could be spent in an initial thrust and various schemes launched, they could not be sustained.

The MOOCs scheme has been more successful, at least as far as utilisation of the budget is concerned. Over the past three years or so, over Rs 200 crore have been spent on MOOCs. The output, however, is dismal, to say the least, as the Swayam portal developed to deliver MOOCs lists only a grand total of 285 courses—264 in engineering, three in mathematics, two in science, and one in the humanities. Many of these courses are merely announced, with nothing beyond an introductory video. Furthermore, most of them seem to involve no evaluation at all, so that taking a course merely requires watching the videos. This should make even the suggestion that these courses be prescribed by universities unacceptable. But this is exactly what universities have been asked to do by the UGC through its *Credit Framework for Online Learning Courses (through*

SWAYAM) Regulation 2016,[9] and several universities have already signed up to replace their taught courses with actual evaluations. In short, while the NDA-II government has succeeded in putting these courses online, and has indeed kept them open, the 'massive' part has not been met.

The government's flagship scheme in this regard, the Pandit Madan Mohan Malviya National Mission on Teachers and Teaching (PMMMNMTT), has proved to be a failure. From the information available to the *295th Report on the Parliamentary Standing Committee on Human Resource Development* (henceforth, Standing Committee HRD),[10] only 48 proposals were approved until March 2018 for institutional arrangements under various components of the PMMMNMTT scheme, and a paltry sum of Rs 153.38 crore released between 2014–18. This led the Standing Committee MHRD to express serious concern that the department's attitude towards implementation of the scheme was both 'lackadaisical' and 'lethargic'. Other budgetary allocations for the professional development of teachers have also been abysmal, indicating that neglect of, rather than a commitment to, teachers' professional development is the big policy story.

POLICIES NOT PROMISED BUT RELENTLESSLY PURSUED

Mission: Instrumentalise and Undermine the UGC

The NDA-II inherited a UGC that had long departed from being a body that was established, according to the preamble of the UGC Act, 1956, 'to make provision for the co-ordination and determination of standards in Universities'.[11] Particularly since 2016, the NDA-II government, taking advantage of the UPA-II's earlier attempts to abuse the UGC's power to make binding regulations, has sought to transform the UGC into a regulator which prescribes uniform standards by diktat and demands absolute compliance. While the UGC Act actually conceives the determination of standards as being a process, created by dialogue and guidance towards a goal that is amenable to plural interpretations and sensitive to the social and geographical milieu in which the HEI is located, a regulator sets targets that define the benchmarks of eligibility for funding.

Even prior to 2014, the UGC Act's language of 'recommendation' and 'advice', and 'reasonable time', and its understanding of 'coordination' as involving due respect for the autonomy of HEIs and the various objectives for which they were constituted, had begun to be abandoned. Under NDA-II, this trend has become the norm for the manner in which the UGC deals with HEIs today. All HEIs are placed in a subordinate relationship to it, and UGC regulations have been weaponised as a means to engineer a dull uniformity across the country that has proved exceedingly harmful. Nowhere is this more evident than in the assaults on undergraduate education through the forced imposition of the semester system and the UGC Choice Based Credit System (CBCS) regulations, and on research degrees through the UGC regulations regarding the award of MPhil and PhD degrees.

It is not as though the UGC as an institution has gained in terms of power and pelf. In fact, its budget has suffered great drops, as Table 6.1 shows. The UGC budget has stagnated since 2016–17, which has meant that the real sums available to the UGC for its schemes for teaching, research, doctoral and post-doctoral fellowships have shrunk. Funding to these schemes has long been delayed and erratic, and in many cases several schemes have not even been offered over the past two years.

TABLE 6.1: Allocations for UGC (in crores)

FY 2014–15		FY 2015–16		FY 2016–17		FY 2017–18		FY 2018–19
Budget Estimate	Revised Estimate	Budget Estimate	Revised Estimate	Budget Estimate	Revised Estimate	Budget Estimate	Revised Estimate	Budget Estimate
8977.71	9099.29	9615.45	9315.45	4286.94	4471.92	4691.94	4922.74	4722.75

Source: *Detailed Demands for Grants* (for financial years) *2014–15, 2015–16, 2016–17, 2017–18, 2018–19*, Department of Higher Education, MHRD.

Mission: Reduce Central Liability on Higher Education in States and Union Territories

The sharp fall in the UGC's budget in 2016–17 was by over Rs 5,000 crore, to less than half of what it was in 2014–15. This was because of a policy decision to directly disburse grants to HEIs in the states and the union territories (UTs) through the Rashtriya Uchchatar Shiksha Abhiyan (RUSA), and not through the UGC. These grants were for the development of infrastructure at the university level as well as maintenance grants to recognised colleges affiliated to them. Plan grants were matched by state government funding. In addition, many targeted schemes for developing capacity in teaching and research were also implemented. The funding UGC gave was contingent on both need being demonstrated, as well as adherence to minimum standards of quality.

Under RUSA, all of this has changed as now all funding is 'norm-based' and 'outcome dependent' according to MHRD.[12] Both universities and their affiliated colleges and the states and UTs now have to satisfy a whole host of prerequisite criteria to even be able to apply for funds—from accreditation by the National Assessment and Accreditation Council (NAAC), to implementation of digital management systems, to compliance with UGC CBCS regulations and the semester system, continuous internal evaluation, and admission tests. Only applications from universities that have reformed their affiliation system by instituting affiliation reforms, and from states that have no more than 15 per cent of faculty positions vacant, and have instituted a State Higher Education Council and developed a State Perspective Plan are entertained. Once grants are given, HEIs must meet performance targets acceptable to the government—if they do not, funding will come to a halt. It is worse if they succeed—they will be rewarded with the divestment misleadingly named autonomy.

Fulfilling most of these prerequisites is simply not within the HEI's control. For one, the pace of NAAC accreditation is very slow—as of 2 November 2018, only 11,816 colleges had been accredited by NAAC in its three-stage process. Undoing a long history when affiliation was the encouraged mode of university development, even if it was to be attempted, takes time, and unfilled vacancies in the state are often due to a number of factors well beyond the state's control. The implementation of CBCS has time and again proved to be a virtually impossible task, because colleges and universities simply do not have enough classrooms and laboratories to accommodate timetables that allow a selection of courses in a cafeteria mode. A semester system is not suitable for many contexts, for example, in areas that have a long winter and inaccessible terrain. And certainly no HEI can get a state government to speed up its bureaucratic processes to get the policy architecture in place so that it can apply for a RUSA grant.

The net result of this has been that colleges and universities across the country are starved of funds, and are in a state of complete disrepair and stagnation, both in terms of infrastructure and academic development. Worst affected are the colleges, which effectively are the units that cater to nearly 80 per cent of all students enrolled across India, who have historically received support for much of their development from the UGC grants. As a result, across the country, fees have been hiked by college administrations to cover much of the deficits towards running expenses, thereby passing on the cost to the student and her family. And several important schemes have suffered as well—particularly in the sciences, which require greater investment down to the college level. Programmes like Inter-University Centres, Departmental Special Assistance, Committee for Strengthening of Infrastructure in Science and Technology, the Major/Minor Research Projects have all taken a hit, and young scientists who returned to Indian universities under the Faculty Recharge Programmes were not paid their salaries for many months in 2017–18.[13]

For 2016–17 and 2017–18, Rs 1,300 crore per year were allocated to RUSA in the Union Budget, but even this sum is not being utilised. In its replies to the Standing Committee HRD, the ministry has reported that as of 30 September 2017, Rs 2,319.53 crore had been approved, of which the Central share was Rs 1,413.015 crore.

However, only Rs 812.95 crore was actually released. The ministry also reports that 'an additional amount of Rs 1300 crore was sought as supplementary grants in Financial Year 2016–17 for RUSA', but this request was 'not granted'. All these figures are far less than what UGC would have disbursed to state universities and colleges in one year.

Mission: Divest from Central Institutions

The lot of Central institutions has not improved either. The established Central universities (CUs) have seen their budgetary allocations slashed and now wrestle with the threat of divestment and privatisation via the unasked for 'reward' of autonomy, while the fledgling ones, established between 2009 and 2016, are not funded anywhere close to what they require for their development. Like with state universities, MHRD has demanded that in order to receive grants from it, all CUs must enter into a memorandum of understanding (MoU) with it that clearly specifies targets to be achieved in conformity with the priorities of the government of the day, which often have very little to do with the concerns of an HEI. Hence, in the current round of MoUs being signed, there is more concern for targets pertaining to digital security and surveillance, MOOCs, skill development, and skill-oriented online courses, as compared to the development and expansion of academic programmes, research, and policies for social inclusion. In other words, HEIs are being made the instruments of implementation of the NDA-II government's electoral promises.

The bulk of Central government funding is overwhelmingly directed away from CUs, leading the Standing Committee HRD to observe that the increase in budget for Central universities is meagre and should be given greater priority. While the budget for technical and management institutions has seen an increase of 57.76 per cent and 41.1 per cent, respectively, that for CUs has seen an increase of just 2.31 per cent.

Table 6.2 shows that budgetary allocations for CUs have stagnated, and as a share of the budget for autonomous bodies, their budgets have been low (around 33 per cent) and declining. Although the IITs and Indian Institutes of Management (IIMs) have got a better deal, it is not the students who have benefited. The six new IITs established in 2015–16 are woefully short of faculty and have very little infrastructure, and across the IITs, reports of fee hikes have become all too frequent.

TABLE 6.2: Expenditure on Autonomous Bodies

	2016–17 (Actuals)	2017–18 (Revised Estimate)	2018–19 (Budget Estimate)
Total Central universities	6,356.26	7,291.42	6,475.23
Total Indian Institutes of Technology	5,379.70	8,244.80	6,326.00
Total Indian Institutes of Management	722.56	1,068.00	1,036.00
Total National Institutes of Technology	2,860.41	3,668.17	3,203.40
Total Indian Institutes of Science, Education and Research (IISERs)	1,198.52	650.00	715.00
Total Indian Institutes of Information Technology (IIITs)	175.51	369.45	363.92
Total autonomous bodies	17,838.82	23,364.85	20,131.45
% share of CUs	35.63	31.21	32.16
% share of institutes of national importance (INIs)	57.94	59.92	57.84

Source: Detailed Demands for Grants, 2018–19, Department of Higher Education, MHRD.

Both types of Central institutions have been ordained a choice between a future of underdevelopment or indebtedness—they must meet most of their developmental and day-to-day functioning budget (effectively all their expenses, barring salaries) through 'internal resource generation'. For development, earlier funded by the government, they can now only take a loan from the Higher Education Financing Agency (HEFA), MHRD's joint venture with Canara Bank. But as the principal part of a loan from HEFA[14] can be repaid only through the 'internal resource generation' of the institutions earned through fee receipts, research earnings, etc., to be eligible to apply for a loan, a sharp escalation in receipts over a short period of time will be needed. Further, HEIs are required to place a specific sum from these earnings in escrow[15] for a period of 10 years, and to use the Plan assistance they get to service the interest portion of the loan. Taking a HEFA loan would mean an effective decrease in the usable grant from the government. The obvious consequence is that internal receipts will have to be pegged at a level that covers both the escrow amount and day-to-day functioning of the HEI over the next 10 years.

All these policies and financial decisions, taken together, make the overall plan of the NDA-II government one that spreads the strategy of the 'user pay' principle across higher education. The people end up essentially paying *thrice* for a right that they gave themselves via the Republic—through the taxes they pay, the education cess on personal income tax, and the fees and other charges HEIs will take from them.

POLICY IMPACT: BREAKING A SYSTEM THAT IS NOT FIXED

The impact of the NDA-II government policies, which are really still in the process of becoming, cannot be expected to be recorded so soon in the statistics provided in the *All India Survey On Higher Education (AISHE)*.[16]

However, a close scrutiny of the data for the past few years reveals a picture that is quite disturbing, indicating that the hammer being brought down upon the entire publicly funded higher education system has already inflicted significant damage. As discussed later, even though this hammer has always come down in favour of private institutions, the NDA-II government has chosen to wield it with greater strength than ever before, yielding significant changes in the quantitative data in the *AISHE* reports.

Growth of Higher Education Institutions

While the Gross Enrolment Ratio (GER)[17] for higher education has risen from 21.5 per cent in 2012–13 to 25.8 per cent in 2017–18, there has been a relative slowing down of the growth rate since 2014–15 (Figure 6.1).

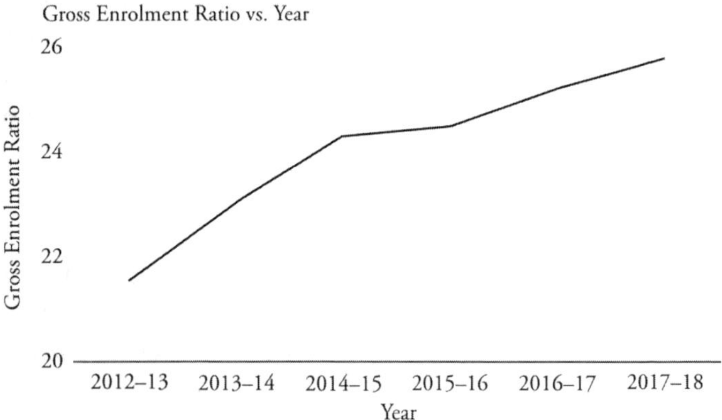

FIGURE 6.1: Gross Enrolment Ratio (GER, in %) in HEIs from 2012–18

Source: *AISHE Report 2017–18*, Tables 47 and 52.

In fact, the number of new students entering the system each year has consistently declined since 2014. In 2017–18, new enrolment in HEIs was just about 9.2 lakhs, as compared to 21.6 lakhs in 2013–14. As it is highly unlikely that the desire for an undergraduate education suddenly deserted the population a year after the new government came to power, the explanation most likely lies in the fact that HEIs have already begun to suffer.

In most instances, entry into the higher education system is through colleges, and one glance at the availability of colleges in the same period reveals the reason for this shortfall—there are simply not enough seats available. In the NDA-II government's tenure, not only has college density (number of colleges per lakh population) stagnated, but the average enrolment per college has also actually come down, as shown in Table 6.3.

TABLE 6.3: Limited Intake Capacities of Colleges

	2012–13	2013–14	2014–15	2015–16	2016–17	2017–18
Average enrolment per college	715	742	731	721	659	698
Colleges per lakh population	25	26	27	28	28	28
Maximum capacity of colleges per lakh population	17,875	19,292	19,737	20,188	18,452	19,544

Source: *AISHE Report 2017–18*, Tables 42, and 47.

Amongst Centrally-funded institutions, CUs have not grown at all, with only institutes of national importance (INIs) being added. This has transferred the burden of the expansion of higher education to state universities and private universities, the latter having recorded the fastest growth on average (Figure 6.2).

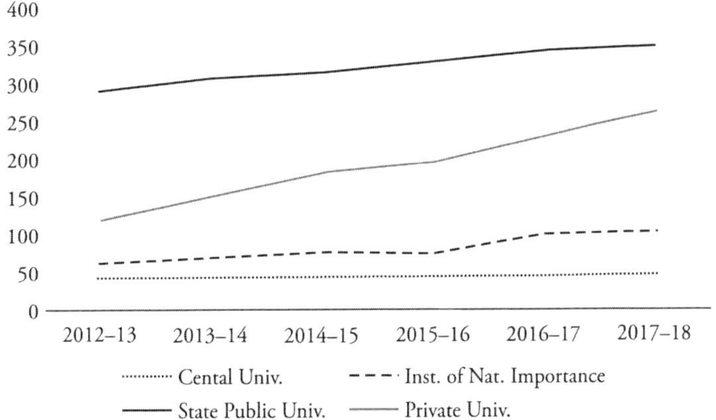

FIGURE 6.2: Growth in Number of HEIs by Type from 2012–18

Source: *AISHE Report 2017–18*, Table 41.

Undergraduate and Postgraduate Education

This sluggish growth in publicly funded educational institutions is reflected in undergraduate and postgraduate enrolment figures. The enrolment in private universities is growing at a faster rate than any other, so much so that their share in total enrolment is now even higher than that of Central universities, and second only to state universities as far as undergraduate education is concerned. Further, despite garnering handsome allocations in the MHRD budget for several years, the INIs have the least enrolment and show no increase in their share. While CUs always had a small share in postgraduate education, the share of state public universities, which has been fairly high, has also been declining (see Figures 6.3a and 6.3b).

The ongoing transfer of undergraduate education from CUs to private universities is, it is important to note, a well thought-out plan. As successive *AISHE* reports have made clear, more than a third of students at the undergraduate level opt for arts/humanities programmes. Publicly-funded HEIs, and particularly CUs, have developed curricula that are responsive to both intellectual needs and pedagogical obligations, and hence rank high amongst students'

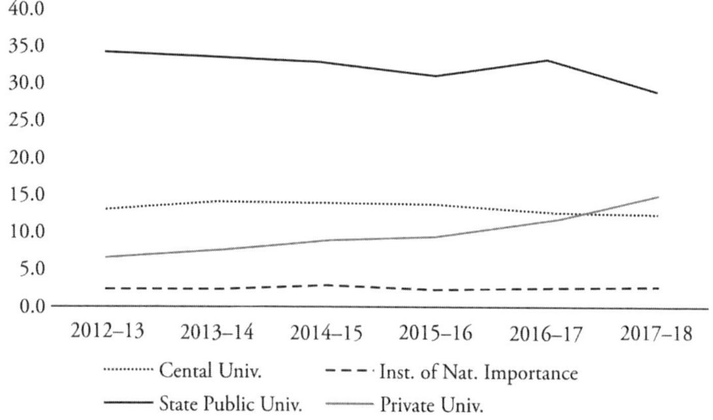

FIGURE 6.3A: Undergraduate Enrolment in HEIs by Type from 2012–18

Source: *AISHE Report 2017–18*, Table 50.

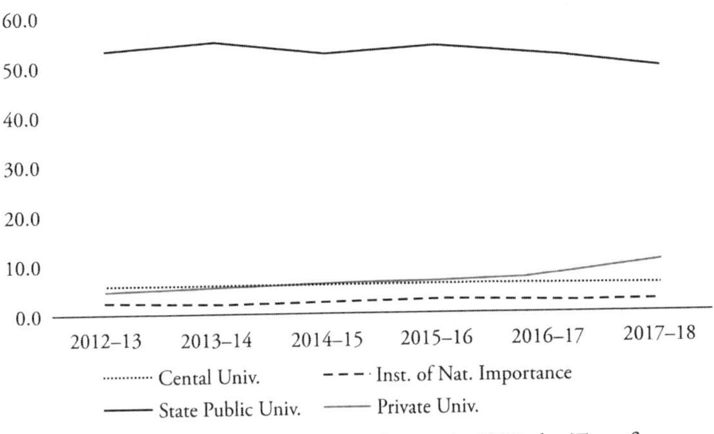

FIGURE 6.3B: Postgraduate Enrolment in HEIs by Type from 2012–18

Source: *AISHE Report 2017–18*, Table 50.

preferences. Restricting the intake of these universities through financial starvation, MoUs, HEFA loans, and mindless UGC regulations is to level the field for private players. Perhaps even the attacks on freedom of thought and expression that many of the public universities have seen is part of a package in which liberal, humanist values come to be perceived to have only one true refuge in the nation—the profit-making private university.

Missing Research Students and Teachers

The MPhil degree is dying, without any policy announcement that it is being eliminated. Across all institutions, MPhil enrolment figures have fallen even well below 2012 levels (Figure 6.4). Private institutions have no interest in investing in MPhil degrees, so the 18,000-odd MPhil students left in the country study mainly in the public institutions. For both Central and state universities, however, in which enrolment had started growing exponentially since 2014, the UGC MPhil Regulations 2016 caused a reduction in seats by over 50 per cent.

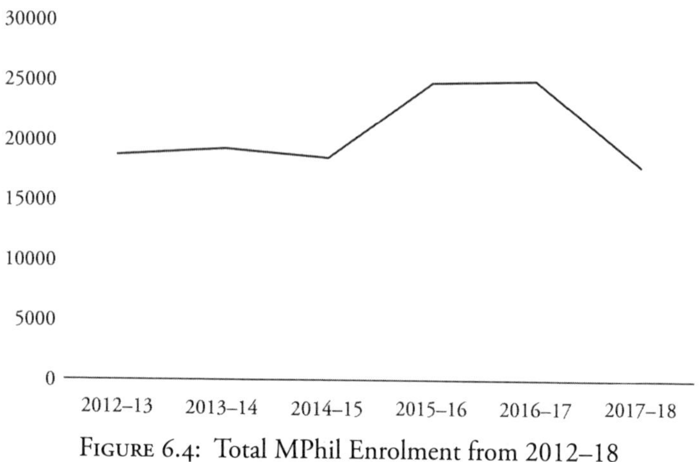

FIGURE 6.4: Total MPhil Enrolment from 2012–18

Source: *AISHE Report 2017–18*, Table 50.

The UGC/MHRD's decision to wind up the MPhil degree was not taken with the best interests of the specificities of Indian higher education in mind. A degree whose popularity has waned internationally, in India, the MPhil is important because Master's level curricula do not involve any component of independent research.[18] The MPhil provides students, especially those from disadvantaged sections and women, an opportunity through which they can first be trained in independent and original thought on a smaller scale before making the transition to a PhD. It therefore not only serves to enhance the originality and contribution of doctoral work, but it is also for many the only research degree they can afford to spend time on. The MPhil also provides essential training for potential faculty in HEIs as the degree has been a desirable qualification for recruitment at the assistant professor level. In a country with such hunger for qualified faculty, winding up an MPhil degree is a guaranteed way to reduce the pool from which such faculty are sourced (Figure 6.5a).

The loss of the MPhil degree is not the PhD degree's gain, for publicly funded social science and humanities education at least. PhD students have usually comprised just 0.5 per cent of total enrolment for several years, and this figure has not improved in the the past five years. As is the new normal, it is private universities that show the most consistent rate of growth, whereas the share of PhD students for both state and Central universities has declined by several percentage points since 2012–13 (Figure 6.5b). Significantly, all Centrally-funded institutions—both INIs and CUs—suffered sharp reductions in PhD enrolment between 2015–17, which means that much of their recovery in 2017–18 is to make up the deficits of these two years.

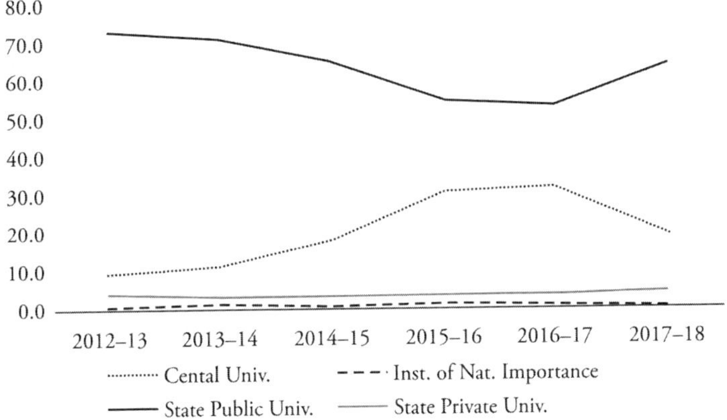

FIGURE 6.5A: MPhil Enrolment in HEIs by Type from 2012–18

Source: *AISHE Report 2017–18*, Table 50.

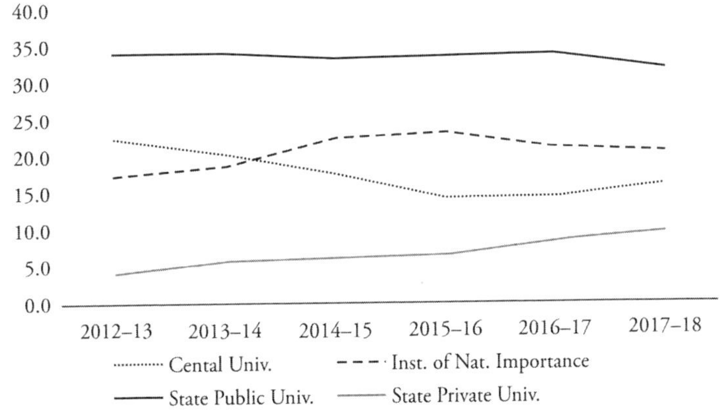

FIGURE 6.5B: PhD Enrolment in HEIs by Type from 2012–18

Source: *AISHE Report 2017–18*, Table 50.

The research degrees crisis is complemented by the fact that a very large number of faculty positions have simply vanished from the system, all the way from professor down to temporary teachers. In all, 2,07,668 teaching positions are either left vacant or have been scrapped, the greatest number being at the initial recruitment level of assistant professor. It is not as if there were enough faculty positions given to HEIs in the pre-NDA-II years, but there still was a modest growth in permanent faculty positions, and a greater growth for temporary/contractual positions. Since 2015–16, there has been a decline in the rate of growth, which, by 2017–18, has brought down the total number of teachers to less than what it was in 2012–13 (Figure 6.6).

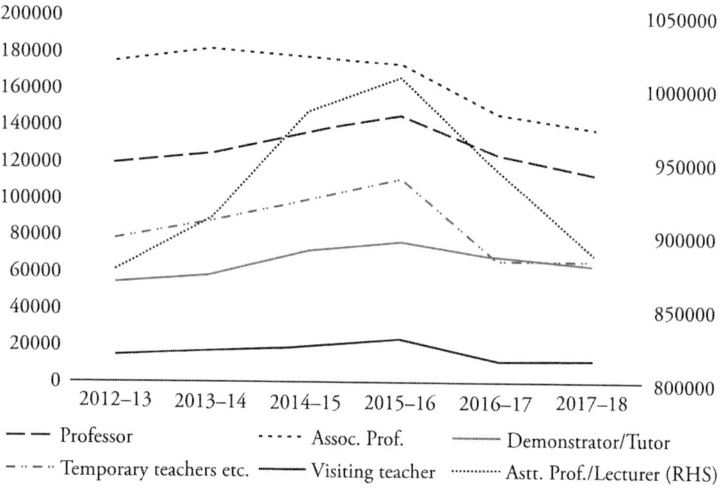

FIGURE 6.6: Number of Faculty Positions at Different Levels from 2012–18

Source: *AISHE Report 2017–18.*

This fall is at least partly due to the fact that recruitments have not been made against a number of sanctioned positions for HEIs. In July 2018, the HRD Ministry informed the Lok Sabha that 11,778 (nearly 36 per cent) sanctioned positions were vacant in just Centrally-funded institutions (no consolidated record of vacant positions in the state HEIs is available). After three years of continuing decline and underfunding of HEIs, the government's protestations that it is doing all it can to hasten the speed of recruitment ring hollow. As a result, pupil–teacher ratios have worsened. Against the MHRD's professed ideal of one teacher to 15 students, the ratio in universities and colleges has worsened significantly, from 21 in 2012–13 to 30 students in 2017–18.

Many of these vacant positions are for reserved groups. Since July 2018, all recruitment in universities had been put on hold by the UGC because of a stay in the Supreme Court. In January 2019, the Supreme Court has vacated the stay and upheld the Allahabad High Court judgment mandating a department-wise roster for the reservation of faculty positions.

One would think that a government that came to power with promises of enhancing teaching and research would be able to see that its policy of discouraging MPhil/PhD research in publicly-funded universities has contributed to the shortage of qualified candidates for teaching positions. One would not expect it to make the recruitment of teaching faculty at the undergraduate level even more difficult. But with the UGC Regulations 2018, it has done exactly that— by 2021–22, having a PhD will be mandatory for recruitment for even undergraduate teaching at the college level. Given the declining availability of research seats in public universities, the difficulties of doing a PhD full-time (the UGC MPhil and PhD Regulations ban open universities from awarding PhD degrees), there is no doubt that the paucity of teachers will only continue to grow.

Social Justice

When a compact that flows from the Constitution is replaced by a contract, a service provider, and a client who must pay, it is only to be expected that the State's decision to default on its agreement will have a catastrophic impact on other guarantees given in the Constitution, such as reservation for socially disadvantaged categories, women, and the disabled, the advancement of minorities and protection of their rights. Given that the system is not broken yet, the one 'achievement' of the government appears to be that it has not been able to reverse the slowly increasing share of reserved categories in total enrolment—from 2012–13 to 2017–18, the share of Scheduled Castes (SCs) had gone up from 12.8–14.5 per cent, Scheduled Tribes (STs) from 4.4–5.2 per cent, and of Other Backward Classes (OBCs) from 31.2–35.2 per cent. This is owing to the fact that reservation still remains an obligation on the State. But this obligation exists only as long as the State has a responsibility to citizens by providing them higher education, there being no reservation for the private sector. As the State moves away from the HEIs that it owns, only 'users who can pay' will occupy the levelled ground, and the downtrodden will not be amongst them.

The same is true for minorities, whose educational status remains as abysmal today as in 2012–13, and also of women, who will perhaps be the greatest losers of all. Many will lose twice—once because of their gender, and once because of their religion or caste. While thus far there has only been progress, with gender parity having reached 97 women per 100 men, it is a social reality that an education that costs more will have significantly less enrolment for women. This is visible in the gender composition of private universities in the *AISHE* data—in 2017–18, total enrolment was 66 per cent men to 34 per cent women for private HEIs, as compared to CUs, where the share of women in total enrolment was 48 per cent.

Those who have the most to lose must shout the loudest, especially since the objective of the policies is to silence them. Public universities across India have been shouting out loud since 2016—the year that saw many of the NDA-II government's major policy measures to liquidate publicly-funded higher education being fully rolled out—and faced brutal repression. In the beginning, the uprisings were themed around the right to dissent and freedom of thought and expression, but they have really been about much more—the survival of the public university as an inevitable product of a democratic society.

WHAT'S THE DIFFERENCE?

The data discussed in the preceding section speaks to how the NDA-II government's policies have contributed to a rapid growth in private institutions (their share of ownership is now up to over 40 per cent in terms of management alone). The precision with which this has been done is no mean achievement. To systematically depress growth in a higher education sector as huge as India's requires more than mere neglect.

Rather, across all levels of higher education, a uniform strategy has been deployed: (i) the way budgets are presented and expenditure is done have changed so that funding cuts are not obvious; (ii) the evaluation metrics of 'quality', 'performance', and 'outcome' are used as the primary instruments to restrict demands for grants by HEIs; and (iii) tamper with institutions and practices so as to depress the public higher education sector, to the advantage of the private sector.

Yet, the quantitative data does not tell the whole story, as it cannot capture the extreme social stress that publicly-funded HEIs have experienced in the processes employed to level the field. Amidst almost daily news of police forces marching all over campuses, and caste, communal, and gendered abuse in universities, hundreds of thousands of students and teachers have protested at sudden changes in university policies of admission, funding, the right to ask questions about them, indeed, the right to ask any question at all. Many students have been compelled to suicide; others have spent long periods in incarceration.

Neoliberal policies have been relentlessly pursued since the 1990s, which is why only one in four students have access to any form of higher education. But the growth rate along several parameters has never plummeted like it has done in the past five years, and certainly the degree of government control has never been so high. So what has the NDA-II government done that is different?

The NDA-II government has altered the character of publicly-funded education and its employees' and students' relationship with the State. The State is now a venture capitalist, and State-funded HEIs—the small companies to which it brings capital investment with a view to reaching a higher growth rate and a quicker sale—must show a return on this investment, which must take the form of repayments of loans, assurance of steady progress towards divestment, growth by the parameters it defines, and of course, the complete transformation of the HEI into a service provider, where every service rendered must be monetised.

Furthermore, the conditions the venture capitalist sets demand the adoption of its managerial and technical prescriptions about how the company must be run. A plurality of practices sourced from a variety of perspectives is anathema to it. Adherence to the rapid changes in modes of functioning that the venture capitalist demands is obligatory—employees must not harbour the illusion that they serve knowledge or their students, and students must know that service comes only to those who pay. Appeal to the idea that the universities are spaces of critical thinking and rationality as well as sites of diversity and social responsibility are seen as articulations of rank disobedience, embodying 'non-compliance' and resulting in 'non-performance'. And because higher education is now the work of the venture capitalist, all protest and dissent is viewed as sedition and anti-national.

Notes and References

1. *BJP Election Manifesto 2014*, 23–24. Available at http://www.bjp.org/images/pdf_2014/full_manifesto_english_07.04.2014.pdf (accessed February 2019).

2. Vikram Singh, '4 Years of Systematic Destruction of Education Under Modi Regime', *NewsClick*, 15 June 2018. Available at https://www.newsclick.in/4-years-systematic-destruction-education-under-modi-regime (accessed February 2019).

3. Ayesha Kidwai, 'The HECI Bill: Liquidating the States' Stake in Higher Education', The Hindu Centre for Politics and Public Policy, 17 July

2018. Available at https://www.thehinducentre.com/the-arena/current-issues/article24442608.ece (accessed February 2019).

4. Sabyasachi Bhattacharya, 'Elusive education policy', *Frontline*, 2019. Available at https://frontline.thehindu.com/columns/sabyasachi-bhattacharya/article24207852.ece (accessed February 2019).

5. *National Policy on Education 2016: Report of the Committee for Evolution of the New Education Policy*, Ministry of Human Resource Development, Government of India, 30 April 2016. Available at http://nuepa.org/new/download/nep2016/reportnep.pdf (accessed February 2019).

6. Ibid.

7. *Demands for Grants (2018-19): Thirty Sixth Report of the Standing Committee on Labour* (New Delhi: Ministry of Skill Development and Entrepreneurship, Lok Sabha Secretariat). Available at http://164.100.47.193/lsscommittee/Labour/16_Labour_36.pdf (accessed February 2019).

8. Ibid., 9.

9. These and other UGC regulations cited in the article are available on the UGC website https://www.ugc.ac.in/page/ugc-regulations.aspx (accessed February 2019).

10. *Report No. 297: Action Taken by the Government on the Observations/Recommendation contained in the Two Hundred Eighty Eighth Report on the Demands for Grants 2017-18 of the Department of Higher Education (Ministry of Human Resource Development)*, Rajya Sabha Secretariat, New Delhi, January 2018. Available at http://164.100.47.5/newcommittee/reports/EnglishCommittees/Committee%20on%20HRD/297.pdf (accessed February 2019).

11. The University Grants Commission Act, 1956, 6. Available at https://www.ugc.ac.in/oldpdf/ugc_act.pdf (accessed February 2019).

12. *Handbook of RUSA 2.0.* Available at http://rusa.nic.in/wp-content/uploads/2018/04/draft-guidelines.pdf (accessed February 2019).

13. G. S. Mudur, 'Research recharge hits doldrums', *The Telegraph*, 9 October 2017.

14. See http://hefa.co.in/apply-for-loan/ (accessed February 2019).

15. Escrow is a legal concept in which a financial instrument or an asset is held by a third party on behalf of two other parties that are in the process of completing a transaction. Money, securities, funds, and other assets can all be held in escrow by a third party, to take effect only when a specified condition has been fulfilled.

16. Available online at http://aishe.nic.in/aishe/reports (accessed February 2019).

17. The Gross Enrolment Ratio is the percentage of students enrolled in higher education out of the total population between 18 and 23 years.

18. Mary E. John, 'No place for scholarship', *The Hindu*, 12 April 2017. Available at https://www.thehindu.com/opinion/lead/no-place-for-scholarship/article17932036.ece (accessed February 2019).

seven

Painting a Picture of Ill-health

Indranil Mukhopadhyay and Dipa Sinha

Health and healthcare for all has been a neglected subject in India's politics and public policy for a long time. The health outcomes in India are poor and lower than what would be expected, given the growth rates in the economy. One largely recognised problem in the country is the burden of out-of-pocket spending (OOPS) on healthcare that households must bear in the absence of accessible and free quality healthcare services in the public health sector, as well as the lack of insurance coverage. The BJP, in its manifesto for the 2014 elections, promised to 'Increase the Access, Improve the Quality and Lower the Cost' of health services with the goal of providing 'Health Assurance to all Indians and to reduce the out of pocket spending on health care'.[1] However, during the first three years the government undertook no major initiative, even though there was mention of an expanded and new health assurance scheme in the finance minister's speech in 2016.

Budget 2018, the last full budget of this government, announced the Ayushman Bharat programme, which was celebrated as the 'world's largest government-funded healthcare programme'. This scheme, which has been renamed multiple times since its conception, was hailed by many as one that would revolutionise the health sector in the country. It promises to provide a cover of up to Rs 5 lakh per family per year for secondary and tertiary care hospitalisation to over 10 crore households (approximately 50 crore people). Currently known as the Pradhan Mantri Jan Arogya Yojana (PMJAY), the scheme is already being portrayed as a success by the Central government, with numbers of health insurance cards issued and patients who have received cashless services being publicised almost daily on social media and in the press. The prime minister has been given the credit for this scheme, which has been christened 'Modicare' by the media.

However, there are a number of serious concerns raised on whether such an insurance-based strategy is most desirable in the Indian context. The budgets that have been allocated for this scheme, as many have shown, are highly inadequate. The ability of such a scheme to truly reduce the burden of healthcare expenditure that households face has also been questioned. It has been argued that such a scheme would only serve to increase the profits and growth of the private healthcare sector in the name of providing free healthcare to the poor. Further, the credibility of the present government's commitment to public health is also undermined by the fact that the overall Central government health budgets have been declining in real terms during its term. This chapter looks at some of these issues in detail.

HEALTHCARE IN INDIA: A STORY OF CONTINUED NEGLECT

In terms of public expenditure on health as a percentage of gross domestic product (GDP), India ranks amongst the lowest in the world. According to the *National Health Profile 2018*,[2] the data for 2015 shows that the average public expenditure on health among lower middle-income countries was 2.5 per cent of GDP, while in India it was 1.0 per cent. Health in India is a state subject and for a long time the Central government was largely concerned with medical education and research, family planning, and certain vertical disease control programmes. There was an absence of a comprehensive effort towards setting up a public health system that addressed the preventive, curative, and promotive aspects of healthcare for the entire population.

Public investment on health was further squeezed since the introduction of economic reforms in 1991 from the sub-critically low levels that prevailed earlier. This led to a virtual collapse of the public health infrastructure in rural areas and halted the expansion of health services experienced in the 1970s and 1980s. The trend was somewhat reversed with the launch of the National Rural Health Mission (NRHM) in 2005, and there was some movement towards rebuilding the government healthcare system in rural areas. However, with the change in government in 2014, this process has suffered a setback. As we will see in the following sections, despite the claims in their manifesto, the NDA-II government has not only ignored health, but it has also halted whatever little progress was made by taking investments away from existing programmes, including those that were doing well.

Although the National Health Policy 2017 promises to increase public expenditure on health to 2.5 per cent by 2025, the budget allocations of the Central government reduced during the first few years of the NDA-II government (Figure 7.1). As a result of the budget cuts in the initial years and minimal increase later, as a proportion of GDP, the Union government's expenditure on health has remained extremely low. It peaked at 0.3 per cent towards the end of UPA-I, but then saw stagnation throughout UPA-II and then declined towards the end. The decline continued in the first few years of the NDA-II government. The Union government's spending on health as a percentage of GDP reached an all-time low in the last four decades in 2015–16, even lower than the much-tainted early 1990s.[3] Although there has been some revival in the past two years, it is nowhere near adequate and still does not match the peak attained earlier (Figure 7.1).

The low budgetary allocation for health is reflected in India's poor aggregate health outcomes when compared to other BRICS countries like Brazil, Russia, China, and South Africa, and some Asian neighbours. Over the last few decades, South Asian neighbours like

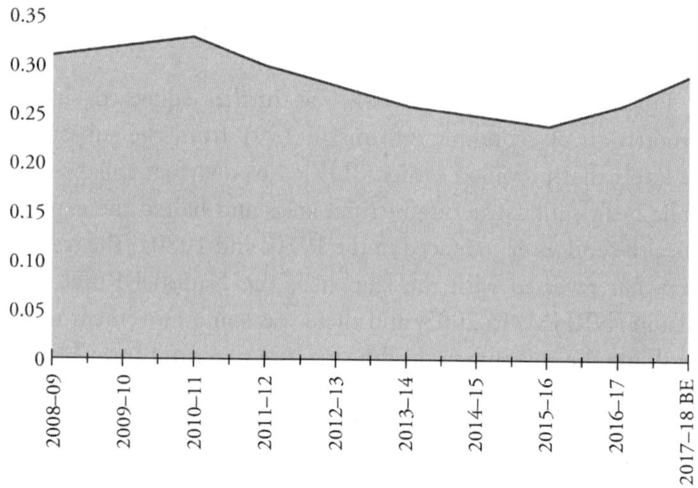

FIGURE 7.1: Union Government Expenditure on Health as a Percentage of GDP

Source: *Expenditure Budget*, Vol. 2; Union Budget, various years (2008–18); available at www.indiabudget.nic (accessed December 2018). GDP figures are from *Economic Survey 2017–18*; available at https://mofapp.nic.in/economicsurvey/economicsurvey/index.html (accessed December 2018).

Bangladesh and Bhutan have also surpassed India in terms of health outcomes. For instance, life expectancy at birth was 68.8 in India in 2016, while that of China was 76.4. Other South Asian countries, barring Pakistan and war-ravaged Afghanistan, are also ahead of us. Child health outcomes in India rank the worst among the BRICS countries, and also in comparison to neighbouring countries such as Bangladesh, Nepal, Bhutan, and Sri Lanka. It is noteworthy that the per capita incomes of Bangladesh and Nepal are much lower than that of India. One of the key factors leading to poor health outcomes in India is poor public spending on health, and consequently a higher share of out-of-pocket expenditure. Governments in BRICS countries like Brazil, South Africa, and China, which have made significant efforts in recent times towards provisioning of universal access to health, spend higher proportions of GDP on health. Governments in nearby countries like Sri Lanka, Thailand, Malaysia, and Nepal mobilise more resources towards health than India (see Table 7.1).

TABLE 7.1: Comparison of India with BRICS Countries, South Asian Countries, and Some Asian Nations in Key Health Indicators

Countries		Life expectancy at birth (years): 2016	Under-five mortality rate (per 1000 live births): 2016	Out-of-pocket spending as % of current health expenditure	Domestic general government health expenditure as % of GDP
BRICS Countries	Brazil	75.1	15.1	44	3.91
	Russian Federation	71.9	7.7	40	3.00
	India	68.8	43.0	65	0.93
	China	76.4	9.9	36	2.89
	South Africa	63.6	43.3	8	4.36
SAARC Countries	Afghanistan	62.7	70.4	77	0.52
	Bangladesh	72.7	34.2	72	0.42
	Bhutan	70.6	32.4	20	2.55
	Nepal	70.2	34.5	55	1.17
	Pakistan	66.5	78.8	65	0.77
	Sri Lanka	75.3	9.4	50	1.68
Other Asian Neighbours	Thailand	75.5	12.2	12	2.90
	Vietnam	76.3	21.6	45	2.68
	Indonesia	69.3	26.4	37	1.40
	Malaysia	75.3	8.3	38	1.92

Source: *World Health Statistics 2018: Annex B*; available at http://who.int/entity/gho/publications/world_health_statistics/2018/en/index.html (accessed December 2018).

UNDERMINING GAINS THROUGH BUDGET CUTS

National Health Mission

The National Rural Health Mission (NRHM) was launched in 2005 to provide accessible and affordable healthcare to rural populations by strengthening the primary healthcare system, including primary health centres and sub-centres as well as strengthening community-level services by the appointment of accredited social health activists (ASHAs) at the village level. The NRHM included components aimed at improving health infrastructure and human resources and decentralised planning for health with community participation. Despite its many limitations, NRHM has been recognised for its contribution towards improving health outcomes in the country, especially those related to maternal and child health. After the introduction of NRHM, the annual rate of decline in infant mortality rate (IMR) saw a steeper fall in the years of UPA rule as compared to the NDA government of 1998–2004 (Figure 7.2).

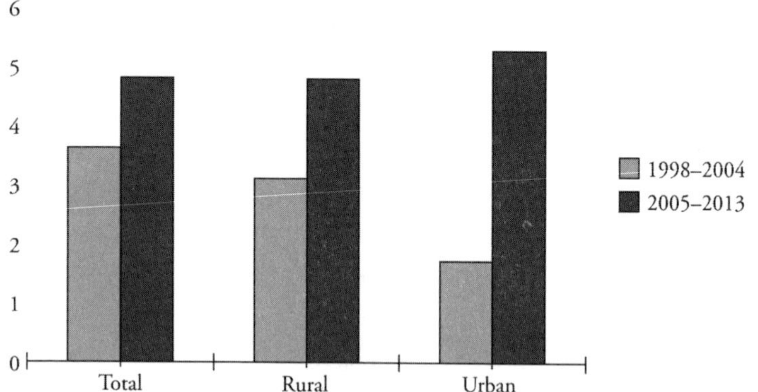

FIGURE 7.2: Annual Rate of Decline in Infant Mortality Rate (IMR)

Source: *SRS Statistical Report 2016*; available at http://www.censusindia.gov.in/vital_statistics/SRS_Reports__2016.html (accessed December 2018).

Similarly, since the introduction of NRHM (2005), certain other key health indicators showed considerable improvement after a prolonged period of stagnation. For instance, the increase in institutional deliveries (Figure 7.3a) and full immunisation (Figure 7.3b) was much faster in the period after 2005, indicating the success of the NRHM. With the launch of a mission for urban areas as well, the NRHM later became part of the National Health Mission (NHM) in 2013.

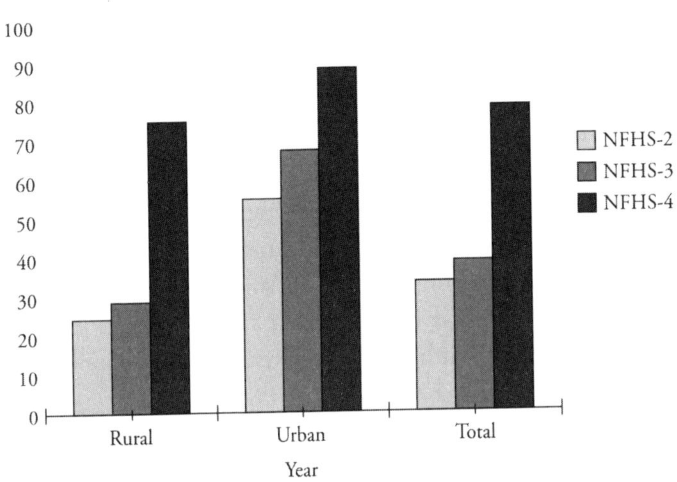

FIGURE 7.3A: Improvements in Key Health Indicators post-NRHM:
Percentage of Child Deliveries in Health Facilities

Source: *NFHS-2*, *NFHS-3* and *NFHS-4*, National Family Health Survey, India;
available at http://rchiips.org/nfhs/nfhs3.shtml (accessed February 2019).

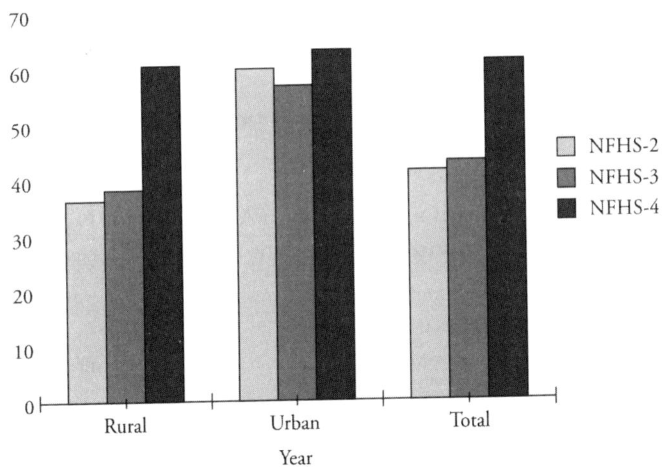

FIGURE 7.3B: Improvements in Key Health Indicators post-NRHM:
Percentage of Children who Received Full Vaccination by
12–23 Months of Age

Source: *NFHS-2*, *NFHS-3* and *NFHS-4*, National Family Health Survey, India;
available at http://rchiips.org/nfhs/nfhs3.shtml (accessed February 2019).

However, with the change in regime, instead of building upon the limited progress achieved earlier and strengthening the government health system, the new government began its journey by cutting NHM allocations. Repeated budget cuts since 2015 resulted in the virtual paralysis of NHM. Allocations for these schemes have been either reduced or have remained stagnant, implying decline in real terms. While there was a significant increase in NHM budgets during the UPA governments, despite some slowdown during the UPA-II period, there has been a drastic fall in budgets during the NDA-II government, with a negative average annual rate of growth of –0.5 per cent (Figure 7.4).

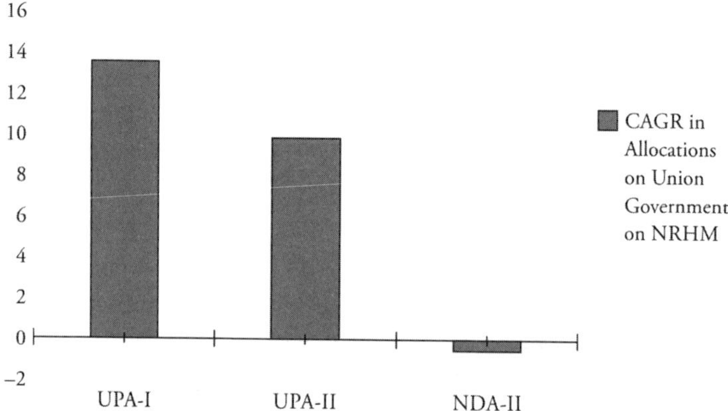

Figure 7.4: Comparison of Growth in Allocations for NHM by Union Governments, at Constant (2004–05) Prices

Note: This figure gives the compound annual growth rate (CAGR) for each of the periods.

Source: MIS, National Health Mission; available at http://nhm.gov.in/component/content/article.html?id=405 (accessed December 2018).

Soon after the NDA-II government came to power, there was a reduction in the Central government's allocations for NHM, even in nominal terms. Allocation fell from Rs 19,133 crore in 2014–15 to Rs 14,827 crore in 2015–16. Since then there has been some increase in allocations for NHM, but only in nominal terms. Allocation for the year 2017–18 is actually equivalent to what was spent during 2011–12 in real terms. Taking into account the increasing population and increased demand for healthcare, this is a significant decline.

At the same time, state governments have continued to increase their contributions to the NHM. Expenditure incurred by states has increased over the years and surpassed allocations from the Union government (Figure 7.5). This was mainly because states started putting their own resources into NHM, while utilisation of Union budgets also increased considerably. This is important to note because the argument is often made that fund allocations are not increased because of the lack of fund absorption at the state level.

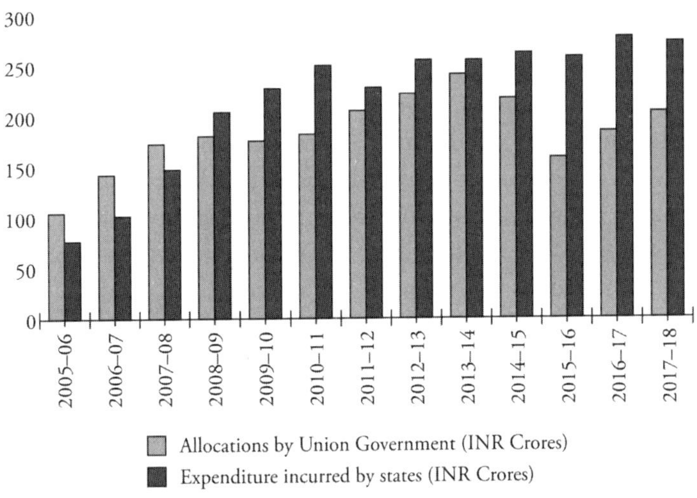

FIGURE 7.5: Allocations for NHM by Union Governments, and Expenditure Including State Contribution (in crores), at Constant (2004–05) Prices

Source: MIS, National Health Mission; available at http://nhm.gov.in/component/content/article.html?id=405 (accessed December 2018).

Integrated Child Development Services

A similar lack of budgetary support is seen in the case of the Integrated Child Development Services (ICDS) programme as well.

ICDS addresses the health and nutrition needs of children under the age of six, pregnant and lactating women, and adolescent girls. It is the main platform through which all the nutrition services for these target groups are provided by the government. Although ICDS was neglected for a long time, following Supreme Court orders in 2001, there was considerable expansion of the programme. A number of researchers and experts have recommended that the ICDS be strengthened with better resources aimed at improved infrastructure, well-paid and trained human resources, and higher allocations in order to provide better quality supplementary nutrition.

Much of the budgetary increases during the UPA period went towards expanding this programme—the number of *anganwadi* centres increased from around six lakhs to almost 14 lakhs in this period. What was expected from the NDA-II government was a continued enhancement in resources so that the quality of the programme could be improved. However, the second budget of the NDA-II government saw a drastic cut in allocations for ICDS (to half). It was only after outcry from civil society and their own Minister for Women and Child Development that the allocations were reinstated in the revised Union Budget for 2015–16 (from Rs 8,246 crore to Rs 15,393 crore). Central government budgetary allocations for ICDS have declined at a constant pace since 2014–15, only to recover marginally since 2017–18 (Figure 7.6). Similar to the NHM, the growth in the ICDS budget also shows a significant increase in the UPA period (higher during UPA-I), but a negative growth rate during the NDA-II, indicating a fall in budgets in real terms during the present government (Figure 7.7).

These changes in budgets also need to be seen in the context of changes in the fiscal architecture brought about by the Fourteenth Finance Commission, where on the one hand, devolution of general-purpose grants to state governments has gone up, and the funds for sector-specific Centrally Sponsored Schemes (CSS) are being squeezed on the other. One likely impact of this is a resultant lower social-sector spending, particularly in states with an unfavourable fiscal situation or lower priority towards the social sector. Enhanced

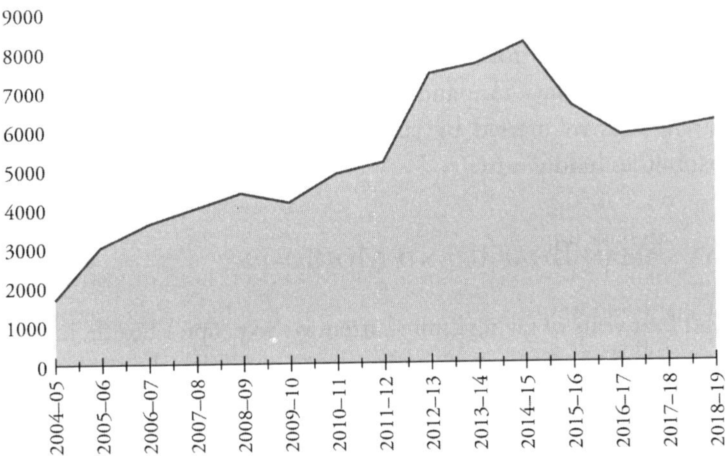

FIGURE 7.6: Union Government Budgetary Allocations for ICDS at Constant (2004–05) Prices

Source: *Expenditure Budget*, Vol. 2; Union Budget, various years (2004–19); available at www.indiabudget.nic (accessed December 2018).

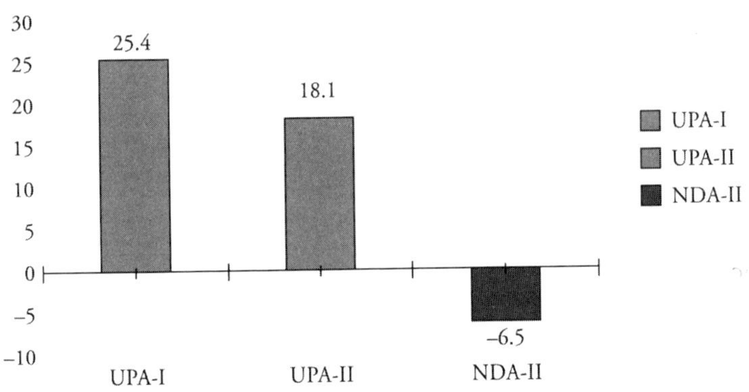

FIGURE 7.7: CAGR of Allocations for ICDS by Union Governments versus Tenure, at Constant (2004–05) Prices

Source: *Expenditure Budget*, Vol. 2; Union Budget, various years, available at www.indiabudget.nic (accessed December 2018).

public spending, as recommended in various policy documents including the High Level Expert Group (HLEG)[4] report, plan documents, and the latest National Health Policy 2017,[5] requires a coordinated effort from both the Centre and the states, particularly in areas of primary care and preventive health services. Under the current regime, marred by cutbacks in spending on health, such possibilities hardly exist.

Ayushman Bharat and Modicare

After four years of giving limited attention to people's health, in their last full budget, the finance minister announced that the government would be introducing a new and expanded health insurance scheme. This became the highlight of Budget 2018, with the media dubbing this initiative 'Modicare', evoking the American Affordable Healthcare Act ('Obamacare'). This scheme is basically an expansion of the Rashtriya Swasthya Bima Yojana (RSBY) and numerous other government-funded health insurance (GFHI) schemes run by state governments.

The main provisions promised in the PMJAY include hospital coverage of up to Rs 5 lakh for about 10 crore families. Therefore, about 40 per cent of the population will be identified as beneficiaries of this scheme. The eligible families are being identified using the Socio-Economic Caste Census (SECC) database that was collected in 2011. The Centre and states share the costs of the scheme in a 60–40 ratio. It took the government a long time to convince all the states to come on board this scheme. Even now, some states such as Delhi, Odisha, and West Bengal have refused to be part of this scheme and most recently, following the Assembly elections in the state and change in government, the Congress government in Chhattisgarh announced that it would withdraw from the PMJAY and would rather provide universal healthcare to the people of the state by strengthening the public healthcare system. Therefore, even in this short span, implementation of the scheme has not been smooth.

In order to benefit from the insurance cover, patients will have to access any private or public-sector hospital empanelled to provide services. Various packages have been negotiated with health providers for the costs at which the services are to be provided, and for the patient, it is supposed to be cashless. Further, for tier-II and tier-III cities, various incentives and subsidies are being doled out for private investors to set up hospitals.

If a person is admitted to a hospital, all the services—tests before admission, everything required during admission, including all tests, drugs, consumables, post-surgery care, and even transportation and food for the patient—are supposed to be free. The hospitals will sign a written contract stating that they will not charge any patient a single rupee under this scheme. On the face of it, PMJAY seems a beneficial policy, particularly from the patient's point of view. The earlier government scheme, the RSBY, had a lower cover amount of Rs 30,000. The experience of this scheme has a number of lessons for the PMJAY as well.

An Expensive Strategy Poorly Funded

While there are several issues with this insurance-based strategy, as discussed below, it is seen that the current budgetary allocations for the PMJAY are themselves inadequate to deliver on what it promises. The Union Budget of 2018–19 made a provision of Rs 2,000 crore for this scheme. Even accounting for the states' share of 40 per cent, the budget for PMJAY annually comes to around Rs 3,300 crore, that is, Rs 330 per family as 10 crore families are to be covered. The government's own estimates, along with the NITI Aayog, have set a premium of Rs 1,100 per family for an annual coverage of Rs 5 lakh. It has been reported that the Ayushman Bharat National Health Authority has asked for Rs 10,000 crore for the implementation of the scheme, which is five times higher than what has been allocated. Many others, including those from the insurance industry, have stated that the government's premium estimates are very low and not sustainable for the kind of cover expected.[6] It is therefore unrealistic to expect that this scheme will be able to achieve what it claims it will on the face of it.

Based on current market rates, the premium for a cover of Rs 5 lakh is around Rs 30,000. While the premiums for PMJAY would be lower, given the economies of scale, the PMJAY also targets a poorer section of the population. This section faces a higher disease burden, including pre-existing conditions which ordinary insurance schemes do not cover. In balance, it is not clear how much lower the actuarial premium for this public scheme will be, but it can be safely assumed that it would be higher than Rs 1,100.

A further issue with an insurance-based strategy is that it is known to come with escalating costs. The RSBY, for instance, with a coverage of Rs 30,000, had a premium ranging from Rs 350 to more than Rs 900, with the premium increasing each year. The likely consequences of the implementation of the PMJAY scheme and its widespread use are a considerable increase in healthcare costs, as reimbursements would increase and so would premiums. This is already being experienced in states like Kerala where the claims under RSBY are high, and premium prices have shot up significantly over the years. This strategy of insurance-based healthcare is therefore not cheap.

Further, the insurance-based schemes are narrowly focused on providing secondary and tertiary care, often to the neglect of primary care. With increasing budgets for the insurance scheme, funds are diverted away from the provision of primary care, as seen in the case of Andhra Pradesh with the Arogyasri scheme. Insurance is therefore definitely not cheaper than direct public provision of healthcare services for all. Recent reports in the media suggest that there is already a tussle in the Health Ministry for funds for NHM, and the worry that the PMJAY is squeezing the budgets for everything else.[7] Hence, as an overall strategy to improve 'efficiency' or reduce costs, there is little in favour of the PMJAY.

Uneven Access

One of the arguments given in favour of PMJAY, and generally for any insurance-based strategy, is that it allows users access to a larger number of health facilities by opening up the option of private hospitals. This becomes crucial in contexts where public facilities are poor or access is difficult, which is the case especially in rural areas and backward states. In such a situation, the ability to get cashless treatment in private hospitals, it is argued, would increase the choices available to patients and could also improve public facilities because of the competition created. This argument might have been valid if private hospitals were available in remote areas. However, the well-documented reality in India is that private hospitals have either grown where public hospitals already exist, or in metropolises, state capitals, and other big cities where there is greater purchasing power. Almost half of the private hospitals and two-thirds of the corporate hospitals are located in the few five million-plus cities, where the bigger government hospitals and medical colleges are also available. There are hardly any private hospitals in rural areas and remote parts of the country. In a recent study based on Chhattisgarh's experience with RSBY, Nandi, et al.[8] found that although government-funded health insurance coverage is higher in more vulnerable districts, the availability of hospital services is inversely proportional to such vulnerability. As a result, equitable enrolment in health insurance schemes does not automatically translate into equitable access to healthcare. Access to healthcare depends on availability as well.

In this context, the earlier point made about the squeeze on overall health budgets as a result of the burden of insurance premiums to be paid is worth reiterating. While on the one hand the private sector does not exist in remote parts of the country, there is the danger of worsening access and quality due to declining budgets for the public healthcare system.

No Reduction in Out-of-Pocket Health Expenditure for Families

The most important claim of this scheme is that it will reduce the out-of-pocket spending on healthcare for families. However, evidence suggests otherwise. First, it is seen that more than two-thirds of out-of-pocket expenditure on health is incurred on account of outpatient care, which is not covered under the PMJAY. The PMJAY covers only hospitalisation expenses, like the existing state government funded health insurance (GFHIs). The evidence from these schemes and RSBY shows that healthcare is seldom 'free', particularly when it is sought at private hospitals. A study based on National Sample Survey Office (NSSO) data looked at hospitalisation cases and found that out of every 100 under various GFHIs, only three get cashless treatment.[9] This, the authors suggest, could be due to the lack of an appropriate regulatory regime and poor monitoring and governance, leading to different forms of co-payment and manipulation.

Further, even when they are insured, people spend more money when admitted to a private hospital than what they would have spent seeking care in public hospitals. For example, when a person without insurance is admitted to a government hospital, they spend on an average Rs 4,560 on a hospitalisation episode. In contrast, if a person with a GFHI card is admitted to a private hospital, they spend Rs 18,081 on an average.[10] The GFHIs push patients towards private hospitals with the assurance of free care, where they actually end up incurring huge expenses.

Though the insurance schemes are meant to provide free hospitalisation to the poorest two quintiles, growth in hospitalisation expenses for these sections between 2004–05 and 2011–12, after the introduction of RSBY, have been the highest.[11] A sharp increase in hospitalisation expenses among poorer quintile groups points to the limited efficacy of the GFHIs, which are supposed to cater to the hospitalisation expenses of the poor.

Further, PMJAY is not universal but targets 40 per cent of the population. Numerous studies, especially in the context of the public distribution system (PDS), have shown the inclusion and exclusion errors in such targeting. The burden of healthcare expenditure affects a much wider section of the population. In fact, for most households except the very rich, a serious health condition for any member in the family can lead to a catastrophic financial burden. Existing evidence suggests that GFHI schemes have not resulted in any reduction in out-of-pocket expenditure.

Poor Regulation of the Private Sector—Markets for Health Always Fail

One of the main reasons why private hospitals are able to continue charging patients with insurance is the absence of any government regulation of the private sector in health. The Clinical Establishments Act, which is supposed to lay out the standards to regulate the private sector, has not even been ratified by most states. Furthermore, the Act in its current form is very weak. One of the crucial components of the legislation should be to regulate the prices of medical services, which is not included in the current Act. Without regulation, private hospitals have the incentive to overcharge patients by providing unnecessary procedures, sometimes those that might even be harmful to the patient's health. Reports on the rise in the number of hysterectomies conducted in Andhra Pradesh or cataract surgeries in Chhattisgarh have been linked to the introduction of state-provided health insurance and the opportunity it provided to private hospitals to profit from these procedures, which were often not required.

When the NITI Aayog came up with procedure rates under PMJAY, there was a considerable hue and cry among the industry and medical associations that prices were very low and would thus result in compromises in the quality of care. Though this reaction is understandable as a strategy to negotiate for higher prices, one also needs to appreciate the dangers of such a partial regulation of prices. It must also be recognised that countries like China, where GFHI is being rolled out, have very strong regulatory mechanisms in place, along with a well-functioning public health system. India has neither.

The lack of regulation of prices in the open market creates the possibility of the private sector charging higher prices from patients who are not covered by the GFHIs in order to cross-subsidise the lower rates provided by GFHIs. It is therefore likely that healthcare will become even more expensive for those who are not insured. Given the issues with identifying the poor as well as the fact that a large number of people who are above the poverty line are also in informal occupations and have vulnerable livelihoods, an increase in healthcare costs could be catastrophic to the officially non-poor.

As the private sector becomes more organised and forms oligopolies or monopolies, which is inevitable without any regulation and no expansion in government services, they would lobby for higher prices under GFHIs and also charge higher prices in the open market, and the government and patients would have little choice but to accept their demands. Like we see in the United States, corporate chains would thus start dominating the healthcare market and have greater control over prices—healthcare costs would thus be bound to increase.

This trend can already be seen in the changes that have taken place in the private sector in health in recent years. There is a shift from the earlier model of largely doctor-owned hospitals and nursing homes to a larger penetration of corporate and a completely commercialised private sector in healthcare. Big corporate hospital chains are acquiring smaller nursing homes, with a larger presence of multinational corporations (MNCs) in the market. A large part of the funding comes from share markets, angel investments, and other forms of hot money, where faster and higher returns are the major consideration and medical ethics are being increasingly compromised.[12] There is a real danger of unethical practices, overcharging, and unnecessary medical procedures, with patients suffering as a result. The recent cases of medical neglect and overcharging in Fortis and Max hospitals in Delhi are a reflection of this trend.[13] This situation calls for stricter forms of regulation of clinical and medical standards. Poor patients visiting these big hospitals will be even more voiceless in the absence of a strong regulatory framework and redressal mechanism.

An insurance-based strategy, such as the PMJAY, requires not only a well-functioning healthcare system, but also a regulatory mechanism for the healthcare providers, health insurance agents, and mechanisms within the justice system for response in case of violations. In a recent article in *The Indian Express*, Jishnu Das, et al.[14] have argued that a complex regulatory mechanism is essential for the PMJAY to work. However, the current regulatory framework for insurance in India is extremely weak. A recent study by Ila Patnaik, et al.[15] shows that all 17 insurance ombudsman offices in India are vacant and there is a backlog of over 9,000 complaints. There is no independent grievance redressal mechanism that is easily accessible to patients, nor does the law provide for strong provisions of penalties and compensation.

The Elusive Promise of Free Medicines

During his first Independence Day address to the nation after becoming Prime Minister, Narendra Modi had promised that his government would ensure free medicines for all. This is a significant promise in a country where it is estimated that 3.68 crore people fall below the poverty line because of their expenditure on medicines.[16] Expenditure on medicines constitutes more than 70 per cent of the total out-of-pocket expenditure on healthcare. In Tamil Nadu and Rajasthan, experience has shown that providing free good quality medicines from public facilities improves access significantly and also helps to contain market prices.[17] However, there has been no expansion in the free medicine initiatives. In fact, under pressure from the pharmaceutical industry and retail pharmacies, the BJP government in Rajasthan tried to cut budgets and even halt the 'Chief Minister's Free Medicine Scheme' in the state. After much resistance from civil society and health movements, the government was forced to continue with the scheme.[18]

The NDA-II government's performance in controlling the consumer prices of medicines has also been abysmal. The current Drug Price Control Order (DPCO) has been operational since May 2013. In the 64 months since its implementation, the point-to-point inflation rate of medicines has often been higher than the general

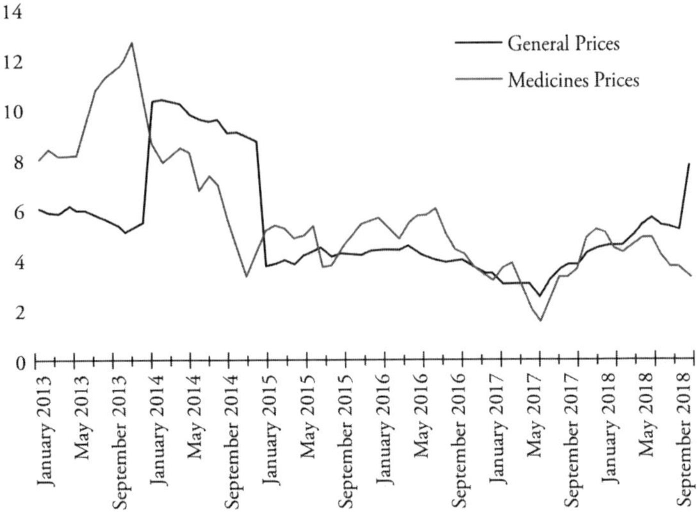

FIGURE 7.8: A Comparison of General Prices with Medicine Prices from 2013–18

Source: Consumer Price Index (industrial workers); CPI Warehouse, Ministry of Statistics and Programme Implementation, Government of India.

inflation. Over the past two years, since November 2016, we have experienced a higher inflation in medicine prices as compared to general inflation (Figure 7.8).

One key reason for less effective price control is that only 10 per cent of the market is under price control because fixed drug combinations (FDCs)—which constitute a big share of the medicine market—are left out of the purview of price control. Even though many FDCs have been banned, they continue to be sold in the open market mainly because of the unwillingness of the current political regime to crack down on the pharma industry.

There are several problems with the current DPCO. It is based on market prices and not on the cost of input prices, with the ceiling price of essential medicines now being determined on the basis of the average price of all brands of medicines having a market share of at least 1 per cent. A market price-based formula remains biased towards the price of market leader(s), which is often on the higher side and does not take into account the price of inputs. So the market price-based formula has been beneficial to big pharma, who have been active supporters of DPCO 2013. The new DPCO works against firms which are more efficient in terms of lower costs of production because ceiling prices tend to gravitate towards weighted average prices.

Health movements have been constantly advocating for a cost-based price control formula, without much success. A comparison of the system of market-based pricing with cost-based pricing shows that the latter could effectively bring down prices by two to four times for a select set of medicines.

CONCLUSION

Despite the considerable build-up around the launch of the PMJAY, the story of the health sector in the past five years has been one of a funds crunch undermining previous gains, allowing increasing space for private-sector involvement and changing the basic commitment of the State—from guaranteeing the provision of free medical care at all levels to providing insurance cover for hospitalisation for 40 per cent of the population.

In the previous 10 years, corresponding to the UPA-I and II governments, some rudimentary efforts were made to bring public healthcare services to the centre-stage through the National Health Mission. With the launch of the PMJAY, this government has paved the way for a private sector-led health provision model, which favours profits over health outcomes. In the name of reducing the burden of out-of-pocket health expenses for the masses, there is a danger of increasing healthcare costs for all. With the experience of the NHM and RSBY in front of them, the NDA-II government, if it were truly committed to assuring the health of the people, would have chosen to go the NHM route rather than expanding insurance. Instead, their efforts to expand primary healthcare through 'Health and Wellness

Centres' have been feeble, while the entire attention and propaganda have been geared towards the expansion of the PMJAY, which has been prematurely called the world's largest health programme.

There have been numerous efforts in the past to forge public–private participation (PPP) in the health sector to help expand the private sector, often at the cost of public services. However, the objective of orienting the private healthcare sector to public goals has remained largely unsuccessful. As the private sector becomes more organised and big hospital chains start dominating the market, which is inevitable without regulation and no expansion in government services, it will become increasingly difficult for governments to intervene. On the other hand, there would be further lobbying for higher prices under GFHIs, insurance premiums would go up, and governments and patients would have little choice but to accept their demand. PMJAY has the potential to truly become the world's biggest scheme, not in terms of the provision of free healthcare, but rather, in terms of how much money it consumes while a majority of the population continues to find access to quality healthcare unaffordable.

What is needed is an alternative framework of healthcare delivery where the right to healthcare is seen as a justiciable right. This needs the enactment of appropriate legislations both at the Centre and the states to ensure universal access to good quality and comprehensive healthcare, including the entire range of primary, secondary, and tertiary services for the whole population. This would entail an expansion in public expenditure on health, financed primarily through general taxation, to 3–5 per cent of the GDP.

The fiscally prudent way to reduce the high burden of out-of-pocket expenditure and improve equity in access to quality care would be to expand and strengthen the public healthcare system to ensure quality and availability of healthcare entirely free of user fees. Universal access to the entire range of essential drugs and diagnostics at public facilities with a matching human resource policy and much better governance and management would be crucial. The focus should be on strengthening public systems, with private healthcare resources (with preference for the non-profit sector) being selectively used, rather than using public resources to strengthen private healthcare providers, as proposed under PMJAY.[19] Unfortunately, the current government has been taking the health sector in the direction of greater commercialisation and uncontrolled profits.

While its claim to be the world's biggest health scheme may be questionable, it can be safely said that this is the biggest public–private partnership effort in healthcare in India.

Notes and References

1. *BJP Election Manifesto 2014*, 25. Available at http://www.bjp.org/images/pdf_2014/full_manifesto_english_07.04.2014.pdf (accessed February 2019).

2. Central Bureau of Health Intelligence, *National Health Profile 2018*, 13th Issue, Ministry of Health and Family Welfare, Government of India, 2018. Available at https://www.cbhidghs.nic.in/index1.php?lang=1&level=2&sublinkid=88&lid=1138 (accessed February 2019).

3. Indranil Mukhopadhyay, 'Healthcare at ICU doors as government spend drops, again', *BusinessLine*, 5 February 2017. Available at http://www.thehindubusinessline.com/specials/pulse/healthcareaticudoors-asgovernmentspenddropsagain/article9522766.ece?css=print (accessed February 2019).

4. *High Level Expert Group Report on Universal Health Coverage in India*, Instituted by Planning Commission of India, November 2011, Government of India, New Delhi. Available at http://planningcommission.nic.in/reports/genrep/rep_uhc0812.pdf (accessed February 2019).

5. Ministry of Health and Family Welfare, National Health Policy, Government of India, 2017. Available at http://164.100.158.44/showfile.php?lid=4275 (accessed February 2019).

6. Himani Chandna, '"Modicare" budget may have to be raised to Rs 10,000 crore to make it really work', *The Print*, 25 September 2018. Available at https://theprint.in/governance/modicare-budget-may-have-to-be-raised-to-rs-10000-crore-to-make-it-really-work/124255/ (accessed February 2019).

7. Maitri Porecha, 'Is Ayushman Bharat facing a funds squeeze?', *BusinessLine*, 29 January 2019. Available at https://www.thehindubusinessline.com/money-and-banking/is-ayushman-bharat-facing-a-funds-squeeze/article26122082.ece?utm_term=SOF&utm_content=twit (accessed February 2019).

8. S. Nandi, H. Schneider, and S. Garg, 'Assessing geographical inequity in availability of hospital services under the state-funded universal health insurance scheme in Chhattisgarh state, India, using a composite vulnerability index', *Global Health Action* 11 (1), November 2018.

9. A. Ranjan, P. Dixit, I. Mukhopadhyay, and S. Thiagarajan, 'Effectiveness of government strategies for financial protection against costs of hospitalization care in India', *BMC Public Health* 18 (1), 16 April 2018, 501.

10. Ibid.

11. S. Selvaraj, A. Karan, and I. Mukhopadhyay, 'Publicly-financed health insurance schemes in India: How effective are they in providing financial risk protection?', *Social Development Report*, 2014, Council for Social Development, New Delhi, 2015.

12. I. Chakravarthi, B. Roy, I. Mukhopadhyay, and S. Barria, 'Investing in Health: The Healthcare Industry in India', *Economic and Political Weekly* 52 (45), 11 November 2017.

13. Chetna Choudhry, '2 Gurugram Fortis doctors arrested for medical negligence', *The Times of India*, 13 April 2018. Available at https://timesofindia.indiatimes.com/city/gurgaon/2-gurugram-fortis-doctors-arrested-for-medical-negligence/articleshow/63753176.cms (accessed February 2019).

14. J. Das, Y. Aiyar, and J. Hammer, 'Unjoined dots of a scheme', *The Indian Express*, 5 October 2018. Available at https://indianexpress.com/article/opinion/columns/pradhan-mantri-jan-arogya-yojana-national-health-protection-scheme-narendra-modi-5387281/ (accessed February 2019).

15. Ila Patnaik, Shubho Roy, and Ajay Shah, 'The rise of government-funded health insurance in India', NIPFP Working Paper Series, No. 231; National Institute of Public Finance and Policy, 21 May 2018. Available at https://www.nipfp.org.in/media/medialibrary/2018/05/WP_231.pdf (accessed February 2019).

16. Indranil Mukhopadhyay, 'When Medicines Cause Misery', *Common Cause* 36 (2), April–June 2017. Available at http://www.commoncause.in/publication_details.php?id=519 (accessed February 2019).

17. S. Selvaraj, I. Mukhopadhyay, et al., 'Universal access to medicines: evidence from Rajasthan, India', *WHO South-East Asia Journal of Public Health* 3 (3), July–December 2014, 289–99.

18. Chhaya Pachauli, 'Whatever Happened to India's National Free Medicines Scheme?', *The Wire*, 27 March 2018. Available at https://thewire.in/health/whatever-happened-to-indias-national-free-medicines-scheme (accessed February 2019).

19. Jan Swasthya Abhiyan, *Draft People's Health Manifesto, 2018*, 25 September 2018. Available at http://phmindia.org/2018/09/25/draft-peoples-health-manifesto-2018/ (accessed February 2019).

eight

Big-Bang Programmes for Women's Welfare

An Evaluation

SONA MITRA

In the run-up to the 2014 General Elections, the manifesto and the election pitch of the current ruling dispensation had women's empowerment as one of its important centrepieces. Women's issues, particularly related to safety, was a central issue during the General Elections of 2014, following over a year of public outrage and protests in response to the Nirbhaya rape case in Delhi. The Bharatiya Janata Party (BJP) manifesto called women 'Nation Builders' and promised to recognise 'the important role of women in development of the society and growth of the nation', and to be committed to 'give a high priority to Women's Empowerment and welfare'. In the past four-and-a-half years, while in government, the prime minister and other leaders of the ruling party have repeatedly stressed in various forums, including campaign speeches, publicity material, *Mann ki Baat* addresses, and so on, the contributions their government has made to women's welfare and empowerment. There is a need to look at the major flagship interventions of this government, related to women, to assess how far they have actually reflected the rhetoric.

The manifesto and later pronouncements of the government are basically based on two themes, one related to securing women's right to live and right to education and the other about women's economic empowerment. In the backdrop of increasing crimes against women, ranging from violence to female infanticide and sex-selective abortions leading to the declining child sex ratio (CSR) in the country, the promise was to curb violence against women in both the domestic and public realms, saving the girl child, especially safeguarding the birth of infant girls in states with a declining CSR, strengthening the implementation of the Pre-Conception and Pre-Natal Diagnostic Techniques (PC&PNDT) Act and, finally, educating the girl child. Further, given that India has had a curious case of high rates of economic growth with declining female work participation rates, trends which came to the fore in the beginning of this decade, the pitch was to make leaders and entrepreneurs out of women. This was to be done by providing women with access to credit facilities, encouraging the formation of self-help groups (SHGs) and cooperatives, providing skilling and training facilities and increasing their employability by imparting appropriate vocational education. The campaign also promised to create several millions of new jobs, including for women.

The Union Budget of 2014–15, the first budget of the new government, launched big-bang programmes focused to achieve the above. The two major announcements in the form of programmes were *Beti Bachao, Beti Padhao* (BBBP) and a new framework for creating employment, especially self-employment (promote entrepreneurship), using the multi-sectoral approach based on the development of skills and improving access to credit. Accordingly, in the Union Budget of 2015–16, the government launched the 'Skill India' programme targeting skill development and the 'Mudra Yojana' (the Prime Minister Mudra Yojana—PMMY) for easy access to credit, especially for women, thus encouraging entrepreneurship of small and medium enterprises. The other important scheme for women that the current government pursued aggressively has been the Ujjwala programme focusing on the provision of clean cooking fuels to households.[1] The Maternity Benefits Act was amended to extend the duration of maternity leave and a scheme for providing maternity benefits, called the Pradhan Mantri Matru Vandana

Yojana (PMMVY), was also launched in 2017. While each of these sounds impressive, they need to be examined using the parameters of design, budgetary allocations and implementation in order to understand how far they have succeeded or failed in meeting their objectives. Further, while on the one hand there are all these schemes and the critiques of these schemes, the NDA-II government has also faced a lot of flak for its silence in the face of increasing violence against women, especially following the Kathua and Unnao rape cases, where the alleged perpetrators were linked to the ruling party directly or indirectly.

Beti Bachao, Beti Padhao

The BBBP scheme was initially launched in 100 districts in January 2015, from Panipat district in Haryana, a district with one of the lowest CSRs at 864, according to Census 2011. It was then gradually expanded and, in the latest budget (2018–19), the programme was extended to all 640 districts in India. The major objectives of the BBBP scheme were three-pronged: to prevent gender-based sex-selective elimination; to ensure survival and protection of the girl child; and to ensure education of the girl child. In its last phase, the programme adopted a multi-sectoral approach that included effective enforcement of the PC&PNDT Act, pre-natal/post-natal care of mothers, enrolment of girls in schools, community engagement/training/awareness generation, etc., and involved three nodal ministries, namely the Ministry of Women and Child Development (MWCD), the Ministry of Health and Family Welfare, and the Ministry of Human Resource Development.

While the government's own reports, press releases and the BBBP's website showcase several success stories of the programme, such as being able to increase the CSR in some of the major offending states like Haryana, Punjab and Rajasthan, several media reports and reports of the Comptroller and Auditor General (CAG) of India have also simultaneously highlighted the not-so-encouraging outcomes of this ambitious programme. According to CAG state reports, the scheme has not been able to achieve its objectives of improving either the CSR or the sex ratio at birth. In fact, the reports have shown that in various districts of Haryana and Punjab, the sex ratio has worsened. For example, in Panipat, Haryana, the ratio was 892 against the target of 902, but it dropped further to 881. Similar trends were reported from four districts of Punjab. Even the aim of increasing girls' enrolment in secondary schools and reversing the trends in drop-out rates of girls was left incomplete. Further, the claims of the government of increased sex ratios are questionable in the light of ground reports, highlighted in an article in *The Wire*,[2] which show that there have been several instances of underreporting in male births and exaggerated reporting in female births, thus leading to misleading figures.

While the impact on sex ratios can only be verified when independent data like the Census become available, some major gaps in programme implementation and design are already visible. A valid criticism for the BBBP scheme in its initial days was about a lack of imagination in terms of having clear guidelines for implementation. Further, underutilisation of funds was one of the major pitfalls of the programme until 2017–18 that also led to the diversion of funds to other programmes, often women-specific programmes not intended to be funded by the BBBP allocations. While the allocation of funds increased and utilisation also picked up in the last fiscal year (2017–18), it is agreed that a large-scale impact of the programme remains to be felt. Hence the amounts allocated and funds utilised under BBBP were lower in the initial years and increased in leaps and bounds successively (Figure 8.1).

However, these increases being considered a success of implementation comes with a caveat, because that would depend on what the money has been spent on. For instance, audits conducted by the CAG in Haryana found that in its first year of implementation, a 'themed gate' was built, marking the inauguration of the programme in the Panipat district of the state. Similarly, a recent report in *The Quint*[3] highlighted that from 2014–15 to 2018–19, over 56 per cent of the funds for BBBP were spent on 'media related activities' and less than 25 per cent of the funds were disbursed to districts and states. Clearly, these increased allocations towards the end of the period were more on publicity rather than for any programme implementation purposes. In addition, if we look at the important programmes implemented by the MWCD since 2014–15, it becomes evident that the imagination of the BBBP is not anything new to justify the hype created around it. This was, in fact, a mere continuation of the already existing plethora of schemes and programmes for women's empowerment, which are now being differently packaged as BBBP. Programmes such as the implementation of the PC&PNDT Act, and primary and secondary girl-child-focused education programmes (such as components in Sarva Shiksha Abhiyan and the Rashtriya Madhyamik Shiksha Abhiyan, Mahila Samakhya, National Scheme for Incentive to Girl Child for Secondary Education, construction and running of girls' hostels for students of secondary and higher secondary schools, scholarship programmes for girl children, and so on) either no longer exist separately, or are on their way to being wrapped up.

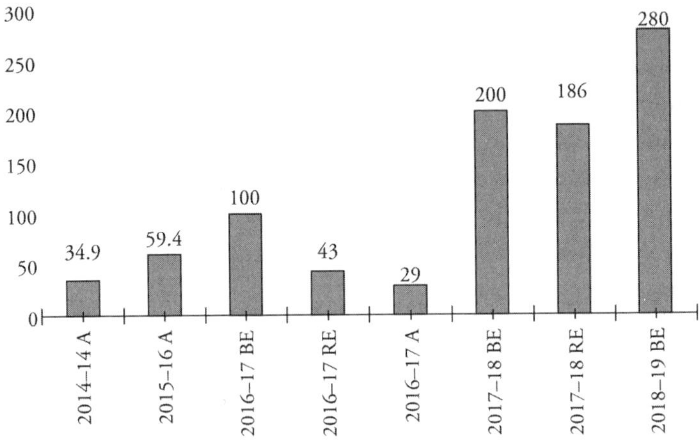

FIGURE 8.1: Funds Allocated and Utilised under BBBP (in Rs Crore)

Source: Compiled by author from Expenditure Budget Vol. I, Union Budgets, 2015–16 to 2018–19, Government of India.

For example, the Mahila Samakhya does not feature in the budgets post 2014–15. The allocations to the National Scheme for Incentive to Girl Child for Secondary Education was discontinued from 2015–16 for two years and was restarted in 2017–18, with reduced allocations from Rs 320 crore in 2017–18 (Budget Estimate, or BE) to Rs 256 crore in 2018–19 (BE). The Sarva Siksha Abhiyan and Rashtriya Madhyamik Shiksha Abhiyan are being completely funded out of the education cess with no extra amount being allocated from the government's own coffers. The gender budget statement, which reported an array of programmes under the Department of School Education and Literacy, barely reports two programmes now. These trends possibly indicate that the increased allocations to BBBP were actually at the cost of siphoning off some of the older programmes, which neither augurs well for BBBP, nor indicates any radical initiative for securing women's rights to live and get educated.

Women's Economic Empowerment: Emphasising Entrepreneurship

The newly formed government in 2014 came with a major promise of creating employment, which was undoubtedly one of the urgent requirements for an economy reeling under 'jobless growth' for almost a decade, more so in the later part of the decade. Within such joblessness, declining women's work participation rates created ripples in policy circles, and one of the major focuses of discussions revolved around women's economic empowerment and targeted employment generation for women. If we consider budgets as one of the major policy documents of the government, then the successive annual Union budgets included announcements to create employment opportunities in the economy with special emphasis on women's employment.

From the very onset of this regime, several policy announcements related to employment made it amply clear that the emphasis on increasing economic activities was not to be led by wage-employment creation, but by increasing self-employment within the economy. Thus, the thrust was on creating an enabling environment by imparting skills, facilitating access to institutional credit and encouraging small and medium entrepreneurship among the youth and women. So the existing wage employment programmes such as the Mahatma Gandhi National Rural Employment Guarantee Act (MGNREGA), which incidentally had high rates of women's participation, instead of being expanded to urban areas, were pushed to the backburners even in rural areas. Such tendencies of marginalising programmes like the MGNREGA are evident from the declining rate of allocations with each successive annual budget since 2014–15 (Table 8.1), ground reports of implementation bottlenecks such as inordinate delays in fund flows, wage payments, and so on.

Instead, a strategy of creating self-employment based on an entrepreneurship model financed by low-interest institutional credit facilities such as the PMMY loans was pushed by the government as an employment-generation mechanism for the economy. Even programmes such as the Prime Minister's Employment Generation Programme launched under the aegis of the Ministry of Micro, Small and Medium Enterprises (MSME) encouraged self-employment ventures, micro-enterprises, and mechanisms for increasing income-earning capacities of individuals rather than creating wage-employment possibilities. Women's entrepreneurship was given special attention within this framework of employment generation.

Accordingly, in its first budget in 2014–15, the government launched the mega 'Make in India' Mission that focused on providing a boost to the almost stagnant manufacturing sector, thus creating the much-needed new employment/jobs. The initiative was launched with action plans prepared for 27 sectors. The Department of Industrial Policy and Promotion coordinates action plans for 15 manufacturing sectors, while the Department of Commerce coordinates 12 service sectors.

The targets of Make in India were to attract foreign direct investment, provide ease of doing business, and thus increase investment in sectors which would, in turn, generate employment. In

TABLE 8.1: Trends in the Allocations for Important Employment-generating Programmes

(Total allocation for a ministry is given in crores, individual allocation for employment-generating programmes under that ministry is given in crores)

Ministries/Programmes	2015–16 A	2016–17 A	2017–18 RE	2018–19 BE
Ministry of MSME	2,829	3,628	8,431	8,662
1. PM's employment-generation programme (credit-based programme)	1,429	1,935	4,040	2,556
2. Entrepreneurship and skill development	200	181	153	340
Ministry of Skill Development	1,008	1,663	2,368	3,400
3. PM's Kaushal Vikas Yojana	991	1,522	2,303	3,273
Ministry of Labour and Employment	4,642	4,748	6,580	7,700
4. Jobs and Skill development (includes PM's Rozgaar Protsahan Yojana)	63	295	602	1,798
Department of Rural Development	77,369	95,069	109,042	112,403
5. MGNREGA	37,341	48,215	55,000	55,000
6. NRLM	2,514	3,158	4,350	5,750
Ministry of Housing and Urban Affairs*	-	36,946	40,754	41,765
7. NULM	269	329	349	310
Total of select employment-creating/promoting programmes (1–7)	42,807	55,635	66,797	69,027
GDP at current market price	136,82,035	151,83,709	167,84,679	187,22,302
Select employment-creating/promoting programmes as share of GDP (8 as % of GDP)	0.31	0.37	0.4	0.37

Note: *The Ministry of Housing and Poverty Alleviation was removed and a new Ministry of Housing and Urban Affairs was established in 2016–17. However, these were not mere replacements and hence, the budgetary allocations for the ministry for 2015–16 and thereafter are not comparable.

Source: Compiled by author from Expenditure Profile, Union Budget of 2018–19, Government of India.

addition, the idea of the successful implementation of Make in India was based on the effective implementation of several programmes/missions such as Skill India, Start-up India, and so on.

Thus, while Make in India did not have components directly targeting employment generation for women specifically, the Skill India initiative included specific proposals for increasing both women's participation in economic activities and increasing the employability of women. The Pradhan Mantri Kaushal Vikas Yojana, the flagship scheme instituted by The Ministry of Skill Development and Entrepreneurship (MSDE) under the Skill India programme, which was launched on 15 July 2015, witnessed more than 35 lakh people being trained in an array of skills, 50 per cent of which were imparted to women candidates. The skill development of women included training focusing on information technology (IT), textiles and clothing, beauty and wellness, healthcare, retail, and also in construction, electronics and IT hardware, financial services, and so on, to enable women's entry into newer occupations.

Further, the component of Skill India implemented by the Ministry of Rural Development focuses on the training and capacity-building of women SHGs under the Deen Dayal Antodaya Yojana in the National Rural Livelihoods Mission (NRLM), and individual training under the Deen Dayal Upadhyaya Grameen Kaushal Yojana, which is a placement-linked skill development programme. These programmes have a provision of mandatory coverage of 33 per cent women candidates in each project.

Skill India has been facilitated by access to credit under the PMMY. The PMMY was launched in 2015, encouraging women to start new ventures or create 'start-ups' using the discounted loans and thus become an engine of women's empowerment via entrepreneurship. The salient features of the PMMY inter alia include extending institutional finance by providing loans up to Rs 10 lakh for manufacturing, processing, trading, services and activities allied to agriculture, provision of Mudra card for withdrawal of working capital, refinance facility for Member Lending Institutions and credit-backing facilities. Since its inception, the government claims to have breached all limits of the target amount. While it is true that the amount of loans sanctioned is higher than what was targeted, the size of each loan is so small that it cannot be considered enough to start a business that employs other persons.

Although approximately 75 per cent of the loan amount has been provided to women for encouraging small business among them, according to an estimate in *India Today* using official data, the average of sanctioned loans under the PMMY in the last four years comes to Rs 46,530, while that of the disbursed amount is Rs 45,034.[4] A simple calculation shows that while the upper limits of loans were set at decent levels, the amount of per capita loans disbursed has, in fact, declined. For example, the total loans advanced in financial year (FY) 2018–19 (as of July 2018) stands at Rs 190,258 crore, with the total number of accounts at 98,193,283. In FY 2017–18, the number of accounts were 62,738,411, with Rs 180,035 crore loans advanced. A comparison of both years shows that while the number of accounts increased by almost 57 per cent, loans advanced increased by a meagre 6 per cent, thus indicating a per capita decline in the amount of loans advanced.

In addition, the reports of good practices brought out by the MSDE and MSME reveal that such entrepreneurship among women has led to more beauty parlours, tailoring units, tuition centres, and various other small ventures in food processing, rather than women using it for alternative/newer start-up initiatives, which may have had the potential for breaking the rigid occupational barriers which women workers persistently face in the context of Indian labour markets.

The above trends highlight some of the problems associated with the framework of pushing an entrepreneurship model based on encouraging micro and small enterprises, that is, emphasising self-employment over wage-employment programmes in the overall policy design and framework. Within such a framework, the element of women's economic empowerment faces greater challenges. Women are unable to access enough wage-employment opportunities, nor are they able to break the stereotypes associated with women's self-employment through such entrepreneurship. Instead, the trends in skilling and entrepreneurship among women continue to reinforce those occupations that are 'traditionally female', and do not usually have the ability to increase the income-earning potentials or asset ownership of women. Further, entrepreneurship with forced credit often has the tendency to push women into a cycle of indebtedness.

Addressing 'Care Work of Women': Prime Minister's Ujjwala Yojana and Maternity Benefits

In a bid to reduce the daily drudgery in a woman's life, the Pradhan Mantri Ujjwala Yojana (PMUY) was conceived to provide cleaner cooking fuels to women which would ensure 'smoke-free' kitchens and hence reduce potential health hazards for women caused due to excessive exposure to fumes produced by solid fuels, and also reduce the burden of collecting firewood.

The PMUY was launched in 2016 by the Ministry of Petroleum and Natural Gas with a target to distribute five crore liquefied petroleum gas (LPG) connections to poor women 'free of cost' by March 2019. The target has also set a bar of releasing eight crore connections by March 2020. As of 18 July 2018, nearly 4.5 crore connections were released as per the government's own estimates (Table 8.2), which indicate meeting 93 per cent of the target releases. So, in terms of achieving the targets, the scheme has performed exceedingly well. However, to assess the scheme on providing long-term 'smoke-free' kitchens for below poverty line (BPL) families, especially in rural areas, the financial provisions of the scheme also need to be assessed.

The financial provision of the programme entails that the government would provide a cost-free connection, that is, cover for Rs 1,600. However, the additional cost of the first gas stove and cylinder at about Rs 1,500 would have to be borne by the households

Table 8.2: Achievements and Funds Utilised under the PMUY

Year	Target (Rs crore)	Connections Released (Rs crore)	Allocations (Rs crore)	Fund Utilised (Rs crore)
2016–17	1.5	2	2,500	2,500
2017–18	1.5	1.56	2,500	2,251
2018–19*	2	1.17	3,200	1,642

Note: *The 'connections released' and the 'fund utilised' figures are up to 18 July 2018.

Source: Compiled by author using figures from Expenditure Profile, Union Budget document, 2018–19, and Lok Sabha unstarred question #817, 2018.

and the cost of subsequent refills to sustain the connection. Experts have pointed out the difficulties of sustaining the figures, given the increase in the price of LPG cylinders in the past two years. A study in the *Economic and Political Weekly* by Dabadge and others[5] clearly showed that in spite of the official figure of about 80 per cent of PMUY beneficiaries opting for at least one refill, the numbers of refills are far from sufficient to meet the cooking needs of the number of targeted households. A recent report in the *Indian Express*, based on a study in tribal districts in Gujarat, shows that not only are people not using their LPG connections because they cannot afford refills, but their ration cards have also now been removed from the BPL category because they have LPG connections![6] Another study commissioned by the Petroleum Planning and Analysis Cell showed that around 90 per cent of surveyed households without LPG connections in many districts of Bihar, Uttar Pradesh, and Rajasthan cited the high refill price of LPG as a barrier to using it.[7]

While the increasing price of LPG cylinders is a serious obstacle to keeping the connections alive, studies have also reported anomalies in recording and reporting data on coverage. The same study also refers to an additional access barrier with the introduction of the Direct Benefit Transfer (DBT) of LPG or Pratyaksh Hanstantrit Labh (PAHAL) Programme (Aadhaar-linked subsidy transfer), which has excluded a number of the intended beneficiaries. Several media reports have also highlighted a need for systematic methods of information dissemination in order to be able to track the actual coverage and success of the programme.

It is necessary to point out that this programme, along with its intended objectives, also has an additional component of addressing issues related to women's unpaid care work. While this aspect has not been highlighted in the claims of the government, undoubtedly this provision for access to clean fuels not only reduces the aspect of the drudgery of women's unpaid care work related to cooking with solid fuels, but also has a positive impact on reducing the time spent on cooking and collecting/gathering alternate sources of fuel. In the current context of ensuring women's economic empowerment against a backdrop of declining women's work participation rates, such reduction of the 'burden' of unpaid care has a potential to go a long way in facilitating women's access to labour markets. These also help in improving the employment rates. The scheme, therefore, has an emancipatory element in its overall disposition and, therefore, needs to be appreciated and facilitated.

However, given the current state of implementation, as pointed out, one cannot be certain about the success of this programme, unless the sustainability of the scheme is suitably established. The absence of the 'sustainability' factor becomes evident as, despite the rapid increases in the price of LPG cylinders, there is no mechanism to control the price rise.

Another announcement by this government, which also has the potential to recognise the burden of unpaid care work on women, is related to maternity entitlements. The Maternity Benefits Act was amended to increase the maternity leave period from 12 weeks to 26 weeks. While this is a welcome move, this Act only includes women in the organised sector, who are less than 10 per cent of the entire women's workforce in the country. Further, the Act lays the entire burden of payment for the maternity leave on the employer (irrespective of size of establishment), thereby disincentivising the employment of women. This Act would be more meaningful if it covered women in the informal sector and also mentioned what the government's role is in ensuring its implementation, while preventing discrimination in hiring practices.

The prime minister also announced a maternity benefit scheme giving Rs 6,000 for all pregnant and lactating women, in his new year's eve speech on 31 December 2016, soon after demonetisation. This was no new proposal and was, in fact, a legal obligation following the inclusion of such an entitlement in the National Food Security Act (NFSA), 2013. The much delayed PMMVY was launched later in 2017 in a truncated form, covering only the first live birth and giving only Rs 5,000.[8] As many have pointed out, this is in violation of the NFSA and, in fact, excludes women who are most marginalised. The budgetary allocations for this scheme have also been insufficient, as pointed out in a letter to the finance minister from 60 Indian economists before the Union Budgets of 2017–18 and 2018–19.[9]

PREVENTION OF VIOLENCE AGAINST WOMEN AND PROGRAMMES ADDRESSING SAFETY CONCERNS OF WOMEN

Against the backdrop of rising violence against women, prevention of violence and programmes dedicated to ensure redressal and safety mechanisms formed a major part of women's empowerment programmes. The policy framework of addressing violence against women and focusing on redressal and the prevention of violence is also based on a range of schemes to be implemented through the MWCD. These programmes form an important component of programmes implemented by the MWCD, apart from BBBP, the Integrated Child Development Services (ICDS) and other nutrition-related programmes.

Some of the key interventions in the redressal of violence by the Union government include helplines, one stop crisis centres, shelter homes, and compensation funds for survivors of violence. The budgetary outlays for these schemes, however, have also been much below Rs 100 crore for each scheme, which does not clearly meet the estimated requirements. For example, the one stop crisis centres or '*Sakhi*' (as renamed by the current government in 2015), supposed to facilitate women's access to an integrated range of services including medical aid, police assistance, legal aid and case management, psychosocial counselling, and temporary support services, is yet to take off as per the requirements. The current need is to have one such centre in all 640 districts of the country. However, until 2018, approvals for only 300 such centres were extended and only 170 centres became operational. This figure is way below the target achievement and speaks volumes about the lackadaisical implementation of an important redressal mechanism against the backdrop of growing violence against women, reflected in their low coverage and shortage of human resources for implementation, among other factors. If we go by the budgetary allocations, the 2018–19 budget allocated Rs 105 crore for the programme, whereas the requirement to set up functional centres across the country would be at least double the current allocations.

The other important intervention by the government related to safety of women and prevention of violence was setting up the 'Nirbhaya Fund' to adequately design programmes to this effect. Following the gruesome incident of the Delhi gang rape in December 2012, the Central government had set up this fund for ensuring the safety and protecting the dignity of women. The Nirbhaya Fund was set up with a non-lapsable corpus of Rs 1,000 crore in 2013–14. Further, an amount of Rs 1,000 crore was provided in 2014–15. For the FYs 2016–17 and 2017–18, an amount of Rs 550 crore (each FY) was provided. In the 2018–19 budget, Rs 500 crore have been provided for transfer to the Nirbhaya Fund. However, this fund has remained one of the most underutilised funds of the government due to a lack of imagination in terms of designing and implementing programmes. A recent media report indicated that until 2017, only 16 per cent of the Nirbhaya fund remained utilised.

The custodian of the Nirbhaya fund is a government-notified Empowered Committee of Officers under the Chairmanship of Secretary, Ministry of Women and Child Development. The programmes conceived under this fund related to setting up special police helplines for women, designing safe public transport and other safety mechanisms. However, it was disparate and hence, the fund was not utilised to its potential until 2018, reflected in the dire state of women's safety across the country. It is only towards the end of this government's term that, in November 2018, a detailed proposal has been forwarded to set up 1,023 Fast Track Special Courts, capacity-building and training for forensics in cases of sexual assault and strengthening of forensic laboratories under the Nirbhaya fund, and setting up surveillance mechanisms for the railway and other public transport systems. The central victim compensation funds were also increased to Rs 200 crore in Budget 2018–19.

Given this, it is clear that the effective utilisation of the fund, one of the key provisions in the Union budget for the safety of women, could have led to improvements in women's safety in the country in the past couple of years. However, with gross underutilisation of the more than Rs 3,000 crore Nirbhaya fund, it does not seem to have had any impact on the ground yet. This can be established with conviction, given the series of gruesome incidents such as the rapes in Unnao and Kathua, that marked the tenure of this government.

MWCD AND OTHER PROGRAMMES: FROM THE LENS OF BUDGETS

Apart from the above-mentioned important programmes directed at the empowerment of women, the exercise to analyse the government schemes for women also entails an examination of the other programmes implemented for women by the MWCD and a few other ministries. The gender budget statement (GBS), placed regularly every year along with the Union budget since 2004–05, provides an overview of allocations made by a number of ministries towards improving the status of women's empowerment. Despite the limitation of the GBS to only provide a budgetary lens to the government programmes, it does highlight the government's priorities and hence becomes a useful tool.

The trends in allocations towards programmes focused exclusively on women, provided by the GBS, clearly shows that in terms of spending priorities, there has not been any major change in trends between 2014–15 and 2018–19 compared to periods prior to it (Figure 8.2). The share of expenditure on women's programmes over the years has approximately stood at around 1 per cent of the total budgetary expenditure. This clearly reveals that, at least in terms of priorities accorded to women within the existing array of welfare programmes and schemes, there has been a mere reshuffling of allocations between individual programmes and have not exactly prioritised women per se.

Similar trends are revealed by allocations to the MWCD (Figure 8.3), which is the nodal ministry for implementing important programmes for women including BBBP and those related to improving the status of nutrition and safety of women, prevention of violence against women and a few others.[10] These trends necessarily

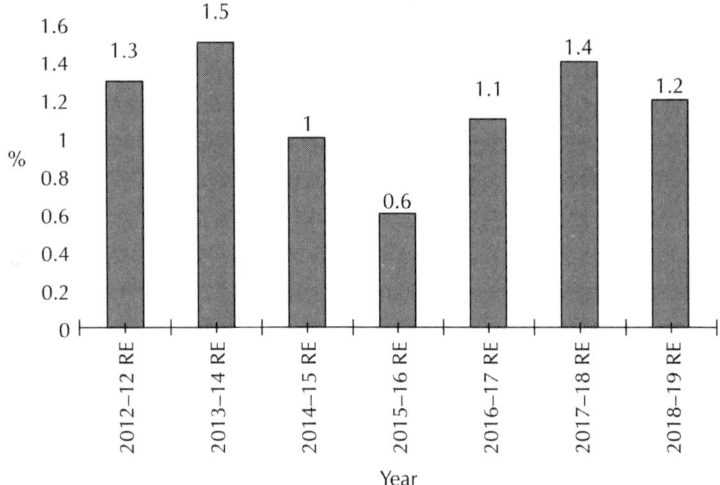

FIGURE 8.2: Share of Expenditure for Schemes Exclusively for Women to Total Budgetary Expenditures (%)

Note: RE = Revised Estimate.

Source: Compiled by author from Statement 13, Expenditure Budget, Union Budgets, 2013–14 to 2018–19, Government of India.

indicate that while women were pitched as 'national leaders', there has not been any radical transformation to the approach that already existed.

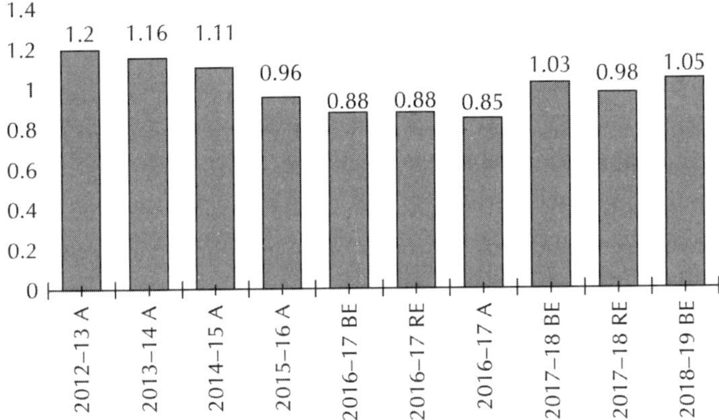

FIGURE 8.3: Allocations to MWCD as Proportion of Total Expenditure (%)

Note: A = Actuals; BE = Budget Estimates.

Source: Adapted from 'Of Hits and Misses: Analysis of Union Budget 2018–19', Centre for Budget and Governance Accountability, New Delhi. Available at http://www.cbgaindia.org/wp-content/uploads/2018/02/Of-Hits-and-Misses-An-Analysis-of-Union-Budget-2018-19-2.pdf (accessed February 2019).

It is evident that, despite the promises made, this government has shown a lack of a holistic approach towards women's empowerment. A number of mechanisms that were in place to work towards such a policy framework have also been undermined in recent years. Gender Responsive Budgeting (GRB) as a tool was introduced with some dynamism, but its implementation has now slackened.

This is also because of the absence of any planning body within the governmental system that can provide a proper situation analysis followed by suitable planning and budgetary allocations. While the high-level committee on the status of women submitted a detailed report in 2015, which is an excellent situation assessment, the follow-up to that has been filled with ad hoc measures. At this juncture, the importance of not only a planning body, but also of the erstwhile Working Group of Feminist Economists (WGFE), formed in the 11th Plan period, needs to be reiterated. The WGFE was instrumental in the overall gendering of the 12th Plan document, thus providing extremely useful guiding material for the process of GRB. The effective designs of certain programmes for women during the 12th Plan period were a consequence of such an approach.

The priorities accorded to women's empowerment by this government clearly show the lack of political will in actually implementing the same and hence, the ground realities, despite having a few good programmes in place, does not reflect any improvement in women's situation in the country. The failures in these programmes have also to be seen in the larger context of women being adversely affected by both the economic policies of the present regime, where there is no generation of decent employment opportunities, and the increasing violence in society, which also has a disproportionately greater impact on women's lives.

Notes and References

1. Though there are problems associated with identifying a programme for providing clean fuels for cooking exclusively for women, on the grounds of institutionalising gender stereotypes, since the government conceptualises and publicises the programme as such, the analysis, for the time being, also treats it similarly in the chapter.

2. Wamika Kapur, 'Why the *Beti Bachao Beti Padhao* Scheme Has Failed on Several Counts', *The Wire*, 4 May 2017. Available at https://thewire.in/education/beti-bachao-beti-padhao-scheme-failed (accessed February 2019).

3. Aditya Menon, 'Truth of "Beti Bachao Beti Padhao": 56% Funds Spent on Publicity', *The Quint*, 21 January 2019. Available at https://www.thequint.com/news/india/truth-of-beti-bachao-beti-padhao-funds-spent-on-publicity (accessed February 2019).

4. Prabhash K. Dutta, 'Mudra Yojana is a Mission or Mess? 5-Point Fact Checker', *India Today*, 19 September 2018. Available at https://www.

indiatoday.in/india/story/mudra-yojana-is-a-mission-or-mess-5-point-fact-checker-1244538-2018-05-29 (accessed January 2019).

5. Ashwini Dabadge, Ashok Sreenivas, and Ann Josey, 'What has the Pradhan Mantri Ujjwala Yojana Achieved so Far?', *Economic and Political Weekly* 53 (20), May 2018, 69–75.

6. Syed Khalique Ahmed, 'Women from Tribal Villages "Lose" BPL Status after Getting Ujjwala LPG', *The Indian Express*, 24 January 2019. Available at https://indianexpress.com/article/india/women-from-tribal-villages-lose-bpl-status-after-getting-ujjwala-lpg-5553174/ (accessed January 2019).

7. Dabadge et al., 'What has the Pradhan Mantri Ujjwala Yojana Achieved so Far?'.

8. Rashme Sehgal, '2.6 Crore Live Births a Year, and Modi's Maternity Scheme Reached Less than a Lakh Women in 2017', *The Wire*, 14 February 2018. Available at https://thewire.in/government/2-6-crore-live-births-a-year-and-modis-maternity-scheme-reached-less-than-a-lakh-women-in-2017 (accessed February 2019); and Dipa Sinha, 'Modi Government's Maternity Scheme has Conditions that Defeats its Purpose', *NDTV Every Life Counts*, 22 September 2017. Available at https://everylifecounts.ndtv.com/modi-governments-maternity-scheme-conditions-defeats-purpose-16742 (accessed January 2019).

9. The Wire Staff, 'Economists Write to Jaitley, Seek Increase in Pension, Maternity Benefits in Next Budget', *The Wire*, 20 December 2017. Available at https://thewire.in/economy/economists-write-jaitley-seek-increase-pension-maternity-benefits-next-budget (accessed January 2019).

10. Some of the other major programmes under the MWCD for improving the overall status of women would be the ICDS, PMMVY, Scheme for Empowerment of Adolescent Girls, National Crèche Scheme, one stop crisis centres, *Swadhar Greh* and Women's Helpline.

nine

Samajik Nyay and *Samajik Samrasata?*

Amit Thorat

Before the 2014 elections, many warned the public at large of the choice that lay in front of them. Should the Indian people vote for a person, under whose watch (as Chief Minister of Gujarat) one of the worst religious riots between Hindus and Muslims took place in 2002? These riots have been described by scholars as state-sponsored terrorism and ethnic cleansing, which saw anywhere between 1,000 to 2,000 people being killed, based on varying sources.[1]

Should Indians overlook the political tenure that saw mass killings and accept the promise of economic prosperity? Or should they take a moral and ethical stand and vote accordingly? If the Indian people decided to vote in favour of personal prospective economic gains, then they would have, in a sense, accepted the questionable moral and ethical illegitimacy of a regime under whose watch members of a minority community were viewed as lesser humans and which fuelled communal fires for electoral political gains.

While the Special Investigating Team appointed by the Supreme Court of India cleared Narendra Modi in 2012 of collusion in the violence, it needs to be seen whether he will be cleared of the accusation that he did not fulfil the promises he made to the Indian people, especially the minority communities, such as the Scheduled Castes (SCs, also referred to as dalits) and Muslims, as stated in the Bharatiya Janata Party's (BJP) manifesto for the 2014 elections.

Manifesto Claims

The section on 'Social Justice and Empowerment' of the SCs, Scheduled Tribes (STs), Other Backward Classes (OBCs), and the other weaker sections in the 2014 BJP manifesto begins by saying, 'The BJP is committed to bridge the gap (between SCs, STs, OBCs & OTHs), following the principles of *Samajik Nyay* (social justice) and *Samajik Samrasata* (social harmony)'.[2]

Anyone reading these lines in 2014 might have been moved by the use of the words 'Samajik Nyay' and 'Samajik Samrasata', and would have probably equated these printed words with the notions of natural justice and harmony with which we as humans are born. Despite good intentions, the true nature and understanding of justice and harmony as perceived by the party has clearly emerged only now, in hindsight, after four years. Another line from the manifesto reads, 'We will accord highest priority to ensuring their security, especially the prevention of atrocities against SCs & STs'. Let us evaluate this claim against the reality of the situation of the dalits and their experience in the past four years.

The dalit people bear the burden of thousands of years of oppression and have only recently started to voice their concerns and to develop a sense of human, social, and economic rights, especially under the guidance and leadership of B. R. Ambedkar, who not only attempted to change their lot, but also did his best to emancipate a nation steeped in tradition and religious dogma, via constitutional provisions. While dalits across the country face exclusion, discrimination, abuse, humiliation, and violence, and have been doing so since Independence, it takes an atrocity of a certain kind to shake the foundation and wake the social consciousness of an oppressed group that internalises most of the atrocities and violence as the norm.

The public abuse, beating, and humiliation of four dalits from a family of seven in a village called Mota Samadhiyala, of Una taluka in Gujarat, was one such incident. On 11 July 2016, just two years after the BJP's nation-wide cow protection campaign, a dalit family of seven received a call from Bediya village, informing them that a cow had died and needed to be removed. The family bought the dead cow and a few of its members were removing its skin, a job forced onto dalits for centuries, when they were approached by *gau rakshaks* (protectors of cows). The dalits were accused of having killed the cow before skinning it. Four dalits were rounded up, badly beaten, tied to the back of a car, and paraded in the city. A video of this was shot and circulated. This video went viral and sent shockwaves across the collective consciousness of Hindus and angered the dalit community like never before.

Dalits were not the only ones who faced the wrath of the rakshaks, who viewed Muslims also as posing a threat. Between 2010 and 2017, of all the violence that was meted out around cow protection, Muslims were the target in 52 per cent of the cases and accounted for 84 per cent of the 25 people killed across 60 incidents, based on a content analysis of English media by IndiaSpend. As much as 97 per cent of these attacks were reported after the NDA-II government came to power. These attacks were reported from 19 of 29 Indian states, with Uttar Pradesh (10), Haryana (9), Gujarat (6), Karnataka (6), Madhya Pradesh (4), Delhi (4), and Rajasthan (4) reporting the highest number of cases.

Incidences of severe brutality against the dalits are not new. The Khairlanji village massacre, in Bhandara district of the state of Maharashtra, where four members of a dalit family were beaten, paraded naked, and then brutally killed, by none other than their fellow villagers from an upper caste (OBC) in 2006, was much more severe in its macabre violence, hate, and inhumanness than the Una incident.

The Khairlanji incident, however, is more a reflection of the social discord, competition, and wariness of the OBC community towards dalits, as the latter were shunning their caste-linked traditional work and, through education and reservation, attempting social and economic mobility. It was reported that the dalit family in Khairlanji not only owned land, but also refused to allow the construction of a road through it, which was the tipping point for the backlash of the village against them.

The Una incident was more a reflection of the social ethos that emerged from political sanction based essentially on religious dictates around cow protectionism and a ban on beef eating. So is the rise of self-styled gau rakshak groups, their rounding up of people—largely dalits and Muslims—whom they suspected of hurting the cow, and of dispensing public justice in the form of public lynching, beatings, and murder. This sort of social policing and punishment dispensation meted out by upper-caste vigilante groups derives from Hindu texts such as the *Manu Smriti*. This text prescribes what type of punishment should be dispensed for any action that violates the prescribed Hindu social norm or code. These punishments are for all Hindus, from brahmins at the top to the untouchables right at the bottom. However, the nature of the punishments prescribed for dalits are particularly cruel, macabre, and sadistic in their intent and conception.

For instance, according to the *Manu Smriti*,[3] if a dalit overhears the enunciation of the sacred Vedic verses even by accident, molten glass should be poured into her/his ears and if s/he enunciates the Vedic verses, the tongue should be cut out. In a similar vein, it prescribes an entire range of other punishments—verbal abuse, threats, intimidation, humiliation, forcing people to ingest human urine and excreta. Physical punishment would include beating, flogging, lynching, abduction, mutilation, cutting of body parts, murder, burning, etc. Community-level punishment would include social and economic boycott, setting fire to houses, property and fields, looting and rioting, etc. Sexual violence against the women of the community would include parading them naked, molestation, sexual assault, rape, etc.

While individual and community-based atrocities have been the reality of dalits since ancient times, this particular kind of public violence meted out by self-styled, community-based outfits such as the gau rakshaks, that too in public, is a new and disturbing development. This was recognised as such by the dalit community and led to mass protests across the country in response to the Una incident. While society is seen as backward and slow to shed its religious and superstitious beliefs, the State was always seen as the upholder and dispenser of human rights and law enshrined in the Constitution. This fundamental idea has changed and those in power are now being seen as tacit supporters and believers of Vedic Law, rather than constitutional law. This has happened for the first time in such a blatant manner in the conscious memory of independent India.

Figures on Caste-based Atrocities

Let us then look at what has happened since 2014 in terms of incidences of caste-based atrocities against the dalits. Table 9.1 shows the number of cases of crimes against the SCs and also those registered under the Prevention of Atrocities (PoA) Act. While between 2014 and 2016 the total number of cases of crime against the SCs has risen only by 1 per cent and those under the PoA Act fallen by 11 per cent, we find that the numbers have risen for the states of Gujarat, Haryana, Madhya Pradesh, and Odisha under both types of cases. Except for Odisha, all the remaining states had a BJP-led government. The political environment seems to have become conducive to the carrying out of caste crimes and portends a disturbing trend.

TABLE 9.1: Crimes against SCs Total and those Registered under the PoA Act in Major States, 2011–16

States	Under POA			Overall Crimes Committed			PoA% Change	Total % Change
	2014	2015	2016	2014	2015	2016	2014–16	2014–16
Andhra Pradesh	2,104	2,263	1,889	2,113	2,263	2,335	–10	11
Bihar	7,874	6,293	5,448	7,886	6,367	5,701	–31	–28

(Contd)

Table 9.1 (Contd)

States	Under POA			Overall Crimes Committed			PoA% Change	Total % Change
	2014	*2015*	*2016*	*2014*	*2015*	*2016*	*2014–16*	*2014–16*
Chhattisgarh	359	216	243	359	216	243	−32	−32
Gujarat	1,075	1,009	1,156	1,094	1,010	1,322	8	21
Haryana	444	510	604	475	510	639	36	35
Himachal Pradesh	113	91	15	119	94	116	−87	−3
Jharkhand	903	736	18	903	736	525	−98	−42
Karnataka	1,865	1,841	429	1,865	1,852	1,869	−77	0
Kerala	712	695	721	712	696	810	1	14
Madhya Pradesh	3,294	3,546	4,918	3,294	3,546	4,922	49	49
Maharashtra	1,763	1,795	1,518	1,768	1,804	1,750	−14	−1
Odisha	1,657	1,821	1,796	1,657	1,823	1,796	8	8
Punjab	123	147	91	123	147	132	−26	7
Rajasthan	6,734	5,911	5,028	6,735	5,911	5,134	−25	−24
Tamil Nadu	1,486	1,735	1,205	1,494	1,736	1,291	−19	−14
Telangana	1,427	1,292	1,101	1,427	1,293	1,529	−23	7
Uttar Pradesh	8,066	8,357	9,361	8,066	8,357	10,426	16	29
Uttarakhand	60	80	36	60	80	65	−40	8
W. Bengal	130	150	93	130	150	119	−28	−8
All India	40,300	38,564	35,692	40,300	38,613	40,743	−11	1

Note: State-wise figures have only been provided for some major states, whereas the totals are for all-India figures and, therefore, not totals of the figures given in the corresponding columns above.

Source: National Crime Record Bureau 2017.[4]

Higher Education

The BJP manifesto also claims, 'Steps will be taken to create an enabling ecosystem of equal opportunity—for education, health and livelihood'.[5]

Let us consider education, for instance, and higher education in particular. Higher education is a space that is rarefied and has been captured by the elite historically, and has traditionally been reserved for the upper castes in India. The provision of constitutionally mandated reservations in public education institutions after Independence was the only way the low castes, who were excluded from education as they did not have a right to education according to the Hindu shastras or sacred texts, could find access to higher education. The dalits realised that education was the key for escaping their lot and finding a place in a more egalitarian and just society, especially after Ambedkar demonstrated how it could be done and called his sisters and brothers to 'educate, agitate and organize'.[6]

While access to higher education is still difficult, once access is attained, issues of discrimination are common and not new. Students have been known to succumb to these discriminatory practices in colleges and institutions (by faculty and administration alike), and found it easier to end their lives rather than face continued humiliation and discrimination. However, two incidents of suicide, one by Rohith Vemula at the University of Hyderabad in July 2016, and the other by Muthukrishnan Jeevanantham, in March 2017, at Jawaharlal Nehru University (JNU), led to widespread public and dalit outrage, protests, and demonstrations by students across the country.

To understand the nature, extent, and severity of the discrimination faced not only by students enrolled in institutions of higher education but also the faculty who belonged to minority communities, a joint project organised by the author and collaborators at University College London, the School of African and Oriental Studies (SOAS), and the University of Edinburgh conducted multiple, day-long, focused group discussions with students from five or six universities and colleges, and also separate focused group discussions with faculty members. An attempt was made to bring in as much diversity as possible in the groups by getting students and faculty across gender, caste, religion, ethnicity, sexual orientation (both physical and social), etc.

Since the final results of the study, which was funded by the British Academy (International Partnership and Mobility Scheme—IPM 2016) and titled 'Discrimination in Higher Education in India' are still to be published, without going into the details of our findings, we can safely say that, from our interactions with students, we found that at every step of the process of accessing higher education—that is, from the interview process for selection and admission process, to classroom interaction with faculty, out-of-class interactions with administrative staff and fellow students on the campus, to final grading and evaluation—students from communities such as SCs, STs, and OBCs face innumerable hurdles and identity-based harassment and discrimination.

While this kind of behaviour is usually meted out to the students by faculty members, administrative staff, or fellow students, even teachers from these communities were not spared harassment, bullying, and discrimination through the collusion of other staff members and those in the administration. The list of examples of how this is actualised in various aspects and spheres of university life is the subject of an entire paper (currently underway). However, suffice it to say here that the Ministry of Human Resource Development (MHRD) and the University Grants Commission (UGC) have not instilled confidence in the student and the teaching community.

The decision to withdraw reservations in faculty promotions, to reduce the number of seats under reservation by taking a department rather than college[7] or university as a unit, the ending of concessions in entrance exams marks for SC, ST, and OBC students, making the viva the final selection criterion (while students have been demanding that viva should either be entirely done away with or given a weightage of not more than 10 per cent), the course-wide reduction in intake of students, transferring of seats meant to be offered to SC, ST, and OBC students to general category students (117 in JNU, for instance)—all belie the promise made in the 2014 election manifesto.

Rather than ensuring improved access of minority community students to higher education, by increasing the number of seats offered, giving concessions in entrance exam cut-off criteria, offering financial assistance, putting in place institutional mechanisms to sensitise non-minority students, faculty, and staff to the harmful individual, social, and cultural repercussions of discrimination at places of higher education, the present dispensation has worked in exactly the opposite direction and, in doing so, revealed an entirely different intention from what was promised in the manifesto.

Prevalent Mindsets

The BJP manifesto further promises, 'BJP is committed to the eradication of untouchability at all levels'.

In 2011–12, a pan-India survey called the India Human Development Survey (IHDS)[8] was jointly undertaken by the National Council of Applied Economic Research (NCAER) in New Delhi and the Department of Sociology (quantitative) at the University of Maryland, Washington state, USA. Amongst the thousands of questions that were enumerated, it asked two questions of the slightly more than 42,000 survey households across all states and union territories of India (except Andaman and Nicobar Islands and Lakshadweep). First, '(d)oes any member of your family practice untouchability?' If the answer was 'yes', the response was recorded. In case the response was 'no', then a subsequent question was asked: 'Would it be all right for a scheduled caste person to enter your kitchen or use your utensils?'

A working paper[9] analysing the responses to these two questions shows that 30 per cent of rural and 20 per cent of urban India accepted practising untouchability. These estimates, based on face-to-face interviews with the respondents, are most likely severe underestimates as people, when asked questions of this nature that are sensitive, embarrassing and, in a manner, confessional, tend to either refuse to answer the question or give a politically correct answer.

Either way, that nearly 30 per cent of India admits to practising untouchability was in itself shocking in today's day and age. It made headlines in *The Indian Express*[10] and led to widespread discussion and debate in both the print and digital media. The findings also came out later as a small opinion piece.[11]

Our analysis went on to further disaggregate the households that admitted to practising untouchability. Figure 9.1 shows the break-up by social groups. It finds that 52 per cent of brahmins agreed that they practise untouchability, not surprisingly the highest for any social group. Rather interestingly, they were followed by the OBCs at 33 per cent, out-scoring the forward castes that came at 24 per cent, and probably reflects the increasing sense of discontent with the upward mobility of the SCs. Also surprising is the finding that the SC, ST, and the 'other'[12] groups have fallen prey to, and now display traits identified with the process of 'sanskritisation'[13] and imitate the behaviour of the upper castes.

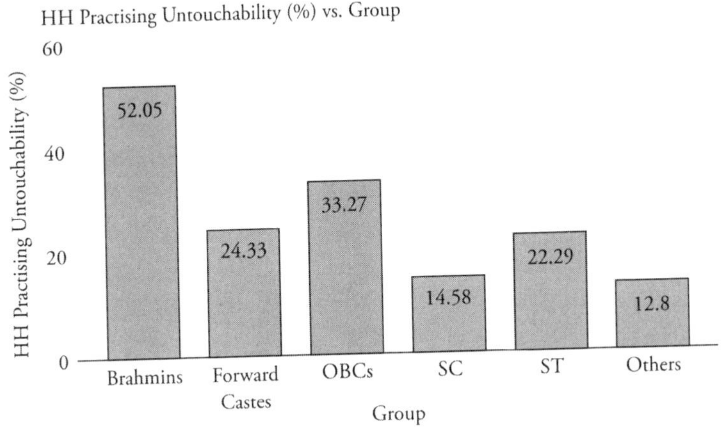

FIGURE 9.1: Households Practising Untouchability (%), Social Groups, All India

Source: Crime in India, 2016, National Crime Record Bureau, Ministry of Home Affairs.[14]

While the study findings were for the year 2011–12, a question about untouchability, based on these findings, was asked in the Lok Sabha[15] by Sri Jayadev Galla to the BJP's Minister of Social Justice and Empowerment and was answered on 3 March 2015. The official response recorded with respect to the parent institutes that conducted the survey, in reply to the ministry's request for details, is that 'the [NCAER] report is not published'. While that might be true, the NCAER (including the author and project principal investigator) had sent a two–three page note, not once but twice, indicating that we stand by the results. The minister did not use this in his response to the question, nor did he make it known.

In 2016, a first-of-its-kind representative telephonic survey called Social Attitudes Research for India (SARI) was undertaken by research in compassionate economics (r.i.c.e) and JNU.[16] The first round of the survey covered the two states of Uttar Pradesh and Rajasthan, and the metro cities of New Delhi and Mumbai. The survey made telephonic calls to a large number of people in these four places, large enough for the sample to be statistically representative of the entire population in these states and cities, and asked, amongst others, the same two questions on untouchability that the IHDS survey mentioned above had (Table 9.2). The results were published in an *EPW* paper.[17]

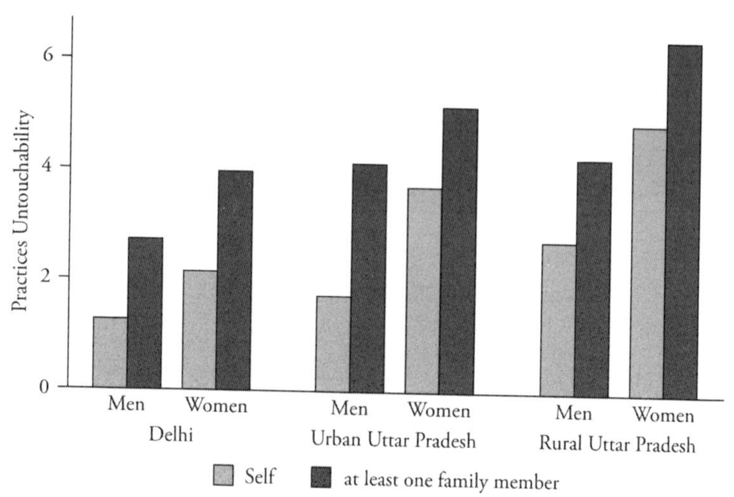

FIGURE 9.2: Gender and Regional Divide on Practising Untouchability

Source: Author's calculations based on the India Human Development Survey, 2011.

Also, the questions were asked for at least one family member practising untouchability, and if the respondent himself or herself practised the same. The responses for New Delhi, and rural and urban Uttar Pradesh, can be seen in Figure 9.2.

The survey gives us several important insights. One, the incidences of the practice of untouchability are very high, anywhere from 62 per cent in rural Uttar Pradesh to 11 per cent in New Delhi. Women report the practice of untouchability more than men. These are startling and disturbing results. These estimates are also much higher than the ones we saw earlier from the IHDS survey, where

TABLE 9.2: Percentage of Non-Dalit Hindus who say they Practise Untouchability

Respondent's Sex	Female	Male	Predominantly Female	Predominantly Female[I]	Female	Male
Untouchability Practised by:	family or self	family or self	family or self	family or self	self	self
Rural Rajasthan	66	50	50	68	54	34
Rural Uttar Pradesh	64	43	46	56	48	28
Urban Rajasthan	50	33	44	47	31	15
Urban Uttar Pradesh	48	42	40	51	35	18
Delhi	39	27	12	20	21	12
Mumbai	n/a	21	5	5	n/a	10

Note: The estimates in columns (1–3) use the question: 'In your household, do some members practice untouchability?' In column (4), a household is counted as practising untouchability if the respondent answered 'yes' to that question or to the question: 'Would there be a problem if someone who is from a Scheduled Caste entered your kitchen or used your utensils?' In columns (1–2), if a respondent did not understand the question, the surveyor explained: 'There are many meanings of "untouchability", one meaning is that some people think that it is not good to sit down and eat with Dalit/Harijan people'. SARI respondents who answered 'yes' to the question of whether some members of their household practised untouchability were additionally asked: 'Do you yourself practise untouchability?' Columns (5) and (6) record answers to that question.

Source: Compiled by author from Coffey, et al. 2018; IHDS 2011; SARI 2016.

about 27 per cent of Indians on average admitted to practising untouchability. Comparable estimates for Uttar Pradesh and New Delhi based on IHDS data (Table 9.3) are 44 per cent and 16 per cent, respectively, which are lower than the SARI estimates.

TABLE 9.3: Share of Population Admitted to Practising Untouchability, 2011

States	% Pop. Practising Untouchability	States	% Pop. Practising Untouchability
Madhya Pradesh	51	Haryana	23
Rajasthan	49	Punjab	23
Himachal Pradesh	49	Tamil Nadu	20
Chhattisgarh	47	Jammu and Kashmir	19
Bihar	46	Jharkhand	17
Uttarakhand	46	Delhi	16
Uttar Pradesh	44	Andhra Pradesh	10
Orissa	43	Northeast	6
Assam	33	Maharashtra and Goa	3
Karnataka	32	Kerala	1
Gujarat	31	West Bengal	1

Source: India Human Development Survey, 2011.

One reason for the higher estimates from the SARI survey is that it was a telephonic survey and people were more comfortable answering these sensitive and potentially embarrassing questions on untouchability, in a situation in which they did not have to face an interviewer unlike the IHDS, and therefore were probably more forthcoming. The purpose here is not to compare the two survey results, as they are not strictly comparable, but to indicate that the practice is widespread, whether we accept it or turn a blind eye to it and tell ourselves that these are social norms and practices from the past.

My question is: What has the BJP government done in the past four years after it made a promise to work towards addressing the practice of untouchability; to take on the above-mentioned estimates of the basic 'mindset and beliefs' of society and its inhuman manifestation; to make attempts to change social attitudes through political will; or to follow up on its own party statements with concrete action condemning these practices?

VERDICT

On the account of providing an enabling environment for the progress of the minorities, on furthering their education and working on finding ways and remedies to change the notions of 'purity and pollution' prevalent in society, not only did the BJP government fail miserably, but it also took conscious steps and initiatives to dilute or remove existing provisions for the benefit of the minorities, such as the weakening of the PoA act, reducing reservation in universities for minority faculty, reducing the number of seats offered, and increasing the qualifying marks for entrance exams for SC, ST, and OBC students, among many other obvious acts that amount to overt exclusion and discrimination as a State policy. The words printed in the BJP 2014 manifesto, it now seems, were mere words, as the actions and performance of the government prove beyond doubt. The people of India would perhaps do well to be wary of the promises, intentions, and the anti-minority and anti-dalit agenda of the party in power.

NOTES AND REFERENCES

1. Asghar Ali Engineer (ed.), *The Gujarat Carnage* (Hyderabad: Orient BlackSwan, 2003).

2. BJP, *Election Manifesto 2014*. Available at file://localhost/BJP, 2014 Elections Manifesto (accessed February 2019).

3. Manu VIII, 270, 271, 272, 374.

4. National Crime Records Bureau, *Crime in India 2016 Report*, Ministry of Home Affairs, 2017. Available at http://ncrb.gov.in/StatPublications/CII/CII2016/pdfs/NEWPDFs/Crime%20in%20India%20-%202016%20Complete%20PDF%20291117.pdf (accessed February 2019).

5. BJP, *Election Manifesto 2014*. Available at https://www.bjp.org/images/pdf_2014/full_manifesto_english_07.04.2014.pdf (accessed February 2019).

6. See https://drambedkarbooks.com/2012/06/26/dr-ambedkars-final-words-of-advice/ (accessed February 2019).

7. In April 2017, the Allahabad High Court, on a petition filed by a BHU faculty member, had ruled in favour of the plaintiff and struck down UGC guidelines that treated the whole university as a unit for providing reservations. After popular opposition to the ruling from the teaching community and coalition party members, the Central government brought in two petitions, one by the UGC and another by the MHRD in the Supreme Court, hoping it would reverse the Allahabad High Court's earlier ruling. But it seems that owing to poor preparation and a lack of genuine intention, the petitions were rejected by the Supreme Court on 22 January 2019. This can be seen as indicative of the present government's lack of belief in the Constitution and the provisions instituted by it for the minorities, as also the lack of a desire on the part of the judiciary to understand the depth and gravity of these provisions and their far-reaching consequences.

8. The India Human Development Survey (IHDS) is a nationally representative, multi-topic survey of 41,554 households in 1,503 villages and 971 urban neighbourhoods across India. The first round of interviews was completed in 2004–05; data is publicly available through ICPSR. A second round of IHDS re-interviewed most of these households in 2011–12 (N=42,152) and data for same can be found at https://www.icpsr.umich.edu/icpsrweb/DSDR/studies/36151 (accessed January 2019).

9. Amit Thorat and Omkar Joshi, *The Continuing Practice of Untouchability in India: Patterns and Mitigating Influences*, India Human Development Survey Working Paper No. 2015-2, 2015. Available at https://ihds.umd.edu/sites/ihds.umd.edu/files/publications/papers/ThoratJoshi3.pdf (accessed January 2019).

10. Seema Chishti, 'Biggest Caste Survey: One in Four Indians Admit to Practising Untouchability', *The Indian Express*, 29 November 2014. Available at https://indianexpress.com/article/india/india-others/one-in-four-indians-admit-to-practising-untouchability-biggest-caste-survey/ (accessed January 2019).

11. Amit Thorat, 'Mapping Exclusion', *The Indian Express*, 3 December 2014. Available at https://indianexpress.com/article/opinion/editorials/mapping-exclusion/ (accessed January 2019).

12. Here, the category 'others' represents all those households that did not identify themselves as any of the following categories: brahmin, forward caste, SC, ST or OBC. So, in effect, they either did not know what category they belonged to or were unwilling to share that information.

13. M. N. Srinivas talks about the idea of sanskritisation. He writes:

The caste system is far from a rigid system in which the position of each component caste is fixed for all time. Movement has always been possible, and especially in the *middle regions of the hierarchy*. A caste was able, in a generation or two, to rise to a higher position in the hierarchy by adopting vegetarianism and teetotalism, and by Sanskritising its ritual and pantheon. In short, it took over, as far as possible, the customs, rites, and beliefs of the Brahmins, and adoption of the Brahminic way of life by a low caste seems to have been frequent, though theoretically forbidden. This process has been called 'Sanskritisation' in this book. (emphasis added)

M. N. Srinivas, *Religion and Society among the Coorgs of South India* (London: Asia Publishing House, 1965).

14. Available at http://ncrb.gov.in/StatPublications/CII/CII2016/pdfs/ NEWPDFs/Crime in India - 2016 Complete PDF 291117.pdf (accessed February 2019).

15. Vijay Sampla, *Answer to Unstarred Question no. 1204 by Jayadev Galla* (3 March 2015). Available at http://164.100.47.194/Loksabha/Questions/ QResult15.aspx?qref=12500&lsno=16 (accessed January 2019).

16. D. Coffey, P. Hathi, N. Khurana, and A. Thorat, 'Explicit Prejudice', *Economic and Political Weekly* 53 (1), 2018, 46–54.

17. Ibid.

ten

Environmental Policies Delinked from *Aam Aadmi*

Is the Mask of Environmentalism Falling?

Shouvik Chakraborty

Introduction

Climate scientists have pressed the panic button. They are warning that time is running out. A recent study published by the *Proceedings of the National Academy of Sciences* shows that if immediate actions are not taken, the earth will permanently change into a 'Hothouse Earth', beyond which any efforts made to reverse these developments will prove futile because that threshold limit will have been crossed.[1] What is the timeframe? The most recent Intergovernmental Panel on Climate Change (IPCC) report suggests that we, as humankind, might have just over a decade left to limit global warming. However, this is only possible if there are rapid, far-reaching and unprecedented changes in all aspects of our lifestyles, especially those of the affluent in our societies. And that is because, as the IPCC report shows, there is more than a 95 per cent probability that human activities are responsible for warming the planet and climate change. In order to stabilise the temperature to no or limited overshoot of 1.5 degrees Celsius (C), total global emissions will need to fall by 45 per cent by 2030 and reach net zero by 2050. If these targets are not met, tropical countries like India are likely to be most negatively affected because of their low altitudes and pre-existing high temperatures.

Although India's per capita emission levels are low, it is, currently, after China and the USA, the third largest greenhouse gas emitter in the world. While these other two countries have reduced their emission levels, India's greenhouse gas emissions rose by an alarming 4.7 per cent in 2016, notwithstanding the commitment to the Paris Climate Agreement. According to the most recent updated World Health Organization (WHO) Global Ambient Air Quality Database, 14 Indian cities were among the 15 most polluted cities in the world in 2016. Kanpur tops the list as the most polluted city in the world with average yearly $PM_{2.5}$ level[2] at 173 µg/m^3 in 2016, which is 17 times higher than the safe limits set by the WHO. Issues related to the environment and ecology affect ordinary people the most. Energy usage in India is skewed in favour of the rich, though the negative impacts from the emissions of such energy usage disproportionately affect the poor, who have limited resources with which to shield themselves from the pollutants.

The negative impacts of pollution on health are now well-documented. According to the United Nations (UN), around 7 million people die each year globally from exposure to polluted air, both indoor and outdoor. Inhaling polluted air can damage brain tissue and undermine cognitive development in young children, with long-term implications for their overall health and development. During the recent episode of severe air pollution in the city of New Delhi in November 2017, doctors declared it a 'public health emergency'. No wonder the crisis has indeed reached a state of emergency. Nevertheless, the question remains whether the National Democratic Alliance (NDA) government led by Prime Minister Narendra Modi has handled this emergency with the urgency and significance that a crisis demands.

Advocating for the government, the Union Environment Minister Harsh Vardhan recently declared that India is expected to surpass the commitments that it had made three years ago in the Paris Climate Pact well ahead of time. This is a welcome development, as India is expected from the pact not only to lower its emission intensity of the gross domestic product by 33–35 per cent from 2005 levels by 2030, but also raise the share of renewable sources. However, there are other indicators that show that India is not doing all that well as far as the environment is concerned. According to the Environment Performance Index (EPI), India ranked 155 among 178 countries in 2014—the year the NDA-II assumed power—and slipped to 177 (out of 180 countries) in 2018.[3] Only three countries—the Democratic Republic of Congo, Bangladesh and Burundi—performed worse than India. These results show that India's performance in environment-related issues under this government has not only failed to maintain the status quo, but has actually deteriorated to a significant extent.

The results of the EPI study were vehemently denied by some ministers of the Bharatiya Janata Party (BJP), stating that these results were arbitrarily determined. However, the environmentalists in India who have been working at the grassroots level were not surprised by these findings. In a *New York Times* report,[4] they alleged that from the moment it was elected to power, the NDA-II government started watering down the existing environmental regulations under the guise of 'ease of doing business'. The government, they said, moved with remarkable haste to clear away even the minimal regulatory frameworks currently in place, in order to facilitate the industrial, military, mining and power projects that had earlier been withheld by the United Progressive Alliance (UPA) government.

The recent news of ecological and environmental injustice pouring in from all over the country only points to the callous attitude of the government on these issues. One such example is the recent death of G. D. Aggarwal, who was on a 111-day fast-unto-death protest to protect and restore the Ganges river. In his last letter to Prime Minister Modi in August 2018, Aggarwal wrote, 'But in the past four years all actions undertaken by your Government have not at all been gainful to Ganga and in her place, gains are to be seen only for the corporate sector and several business houses.'[5] Reports in the media suggest that Modi never responded to this letter. Interestingly, in June 2009, Aggarwal was able get a hydropower project on the

Bhagirathi river cancelled through a similar hunger strike, when Manmohan Singh was the prime minister of India.

Unfortunately, the general level of awareness among Indians on environment-related issues like climate change is low. A recent analysis published in the scientific journal *Nature Climate Change* shows that more than 65 per cent of respondents in India had never heard of the term climate change.[6] However, it is also a historical fact that India, in the past, had successful ecological and environmental movements like the *Chipko* and Silent Valley movements, and the *Narmada Bachao Andolan*, to name just a few. In that tradition, there have been some episodes of successful environmental movements in recent years, and the resistance is growing.

According to the *Environment Justice Atlas* (an international database), India is home to the *largest* number of environmental conflicts globally at the stunning figure of 279, which includes environmental disputes, conflicts over forest land, and scarcities of essential resources like water and fresh air. On 28 May 2018, Tamil Nadu ordered the shutdown of the Sterlite copper plant, which residents alleged had been responsible for significant environmental damage, including air pollution and groundwater contamination. During this movement, at least 13 people were killed when the police fired at a large crowd of protesters. The capital city, New Delhi, recently had a movement against the cutting of more than 16,000 trees in the guise of a development project. As reported widely, the Delhi High Court stalled this government-owned National Buildings Construction Corporation project, which was sanctioned by the Union ministry in November 2017. In response to the increasing air pollution in Delhi and the inaction of the government, social movements and resistances are gaining strength across the city.

The NDA-II Government's Approach to Environment and Ecology

The NDA-II government made some significant policy changes that degraded the environment in India.

First, the government decided to dilute the rules in the Forest Rights Act and Forest Conservation Act, which mostly affects the natural resource-rich states. These states are, traditionally, home to a substantial section of the tribal population in India. The Compensatory Afforestation Fund Act of 2016 was intended to regulate how an existing collection of Rs 50,000 crore, collected since 2006, and the future annual flows of Rs 6,000 crore were to be used by forest officials on afforestation, plantations and other wildlife conservation-related activities without the prior consent of the forest dwellers. From compulsory consent to no consultation, these new rules have betrayed the rights of the tribal peoples, whose resistance is growing all over the country to defend their rights under the Forest Regulation Acts. The dilution of these rights of the adivasis unleashed the powerful forest bureaucracy to grow plantations on their traditional lands without prior consent, or even consultation, in many cases. Such easing, in turn, also strengthened the hands of the big industrial houses, which are now exempt, to a large extent, from having to acquire the consent of local *gram sabhas* or settling the issue of tribal rights in order to expand their mining projects. One such example is the NDA-II government's environmental clearance to Hindustan Copper Ltd to expand mining in Jharkhand state, which, according to estimates made by *Bloomberg*, will cost the Indian economy around Rs 3.75 trillion per year in ecological damage.

Second, with the passage of the Coal Mines (Special Provision) Act, 2015 and the Mines and Minerals (Development and Regulation) Amendment Act, 2015, the expansion of domestic coal usage for the generation of power has only worsened the existing problems of pollution. Coal is a cheap fuel. However, it is also the dirtiest one. According to the United States Energy Information Agency, the carbon dioxide emissions from coal are 100 mmt per quads (million metric tonnes per one quad of energy), which is almost double the emissions from natural gas at 56.1 mmt per quads, and also much higher than the emissions from petroleum at 68.7 mmt per quads of energy. A study by the Delhi-based Centre for Science and Environment shows that Indian coal-fired thermal power plants heavily utilise resources like land, water and, of course, coal, and are therefore considered the most inefficient and polluting thermal power plants in the world. The study also finds that more than 75 per cent of such plants do not comply with governmental regulations.[7]

Third, the erosion of the Environmental Impact Assessment (EIA), a tool under the Environment (Protection) Act intended to regulate construction projects, had a damaging impact on the environment, especially at a time when construction activity is one of the major contributors to environmental degradation and global warming. The EIA is a crucial measure of responsible environmental governance and a determining factor for maintaining the balance between the people, environment and industry. It assesses factors such as pollution load, transport load, sewage load, the source of sand for a project and, therefore, estimates the overall impact of a construction project on the environment. Amended in December 2016, the NDA-II government removed from the EIA the requirements for any environmental clearance to building constructions covering a built-up area between 20,000m^2 to 150,000m^2, and these clearances will henceforth be issued in an integrated manner along with the building permission under Model Building Bye Laws. This amendment means that there will be no further requirement for any consent or clearance from regulatory bodies of the State Pollution Control Board under the Water (Prevention and Control of Pollution) Act of 1974 and the Air (Prevention and Control of Pollution) Act of 1981. The changes also entailed that building constructions with an area of less than 20,000m^2 will self-assess and self-declare without any evaluation from the state-level EIA. Such dilutions in regulations made the problem of air pollution even worse.

Fourth, in April 2016, under the direction of and in collaboration with the Ministry of Environment, Forestry and Climate Change (MoEFCC), the Central Pollution Control Board (CPCB) revised the Comprehensive Environmental Pollution Index (CEPI).[8] A survey done in 2009 in 17 states of India identified 43 industrial clusters out of 88 as Critically Polluted Areas (CPAs) and the other 32 areas as Severely Polluted Areas (SPAs). Following that survey, on 13 January 2010, the UPA government imposed a round of moratoriums on further expansion of industrial projects in those critically polluted industrial areas. However, with measures taken to improve the environmental health of these areas, the UPA government subsequently removed most of these areas from the list. It finally identified eight industrial clusters where the moratorium remained: Ghaziabad (Uttar Pradesh), Panipat (Haryana), Singrauli (Uttar Pradesh), Vapi (Gujarat), Indore (Madhya Pradesh), Jharsuguda (Odisha), Ludhiana (Punjab) and Patancheru-Ballaram (Andhra Pradesh).[9] Upon assuming power, the NDA-II government gave industrial clearance in all these areas pending review of the CEPI index. The revised and updated CEPI index is alleged by environmentalists in India to be a more relaxed version of the previous one. The CPCB has argued that due to the lack of data, the revised version left out the essential criteria of the potential impact of pollution on human health and eco-geological features. This necessarily signifies that potentially affected populations in a cluster and assessment of health impacts will no longer be considered factors in this newly constructed CEPI index. Not surprisingly, environmentalists in India argued that these diluted environmental norms were designed to give more leeway to the industrial projects, which could, in the near future, severely affect the millions of people living in and around these industrial clusters.

One can, however, argue that such a dismal portrayal of this government may not be a fair analysis. Modi has received the 'Champions of the Earth' award, which is the highest honour bestowed by the United Nations Environment Programme. This award, which he shared with Emmanuel Macron, the current President of France, was in recognition of the policy leadership category for their pioneering work in championing the International Solar Alliance, and Modi's pledge to eliminate all single-use plastic in India by 2022. In a party document released in August 2018, the BJP has portrayed Modi as a champion of the global movement against climate change. His government has claimed that the flagship programme of Ujjwala Yojana provided liquefied petroleum gas (LPG) connections to more than five crore households covering 715 districts in India, which, to a substantial extent, has eradicated the problem of household air pollution. The river connectivity project under Modi has also received much attention in the media. A marginal increase in forest cover has been highlighted as a significant achievement by the MoEFCC. The mainstream media are extensively discussing these success stories. In the next section, we shall discuss all of these issues, and evaluate the extent of these successes.

Evaluating the 'Successful' Environmental Programmes of the NDA-II Government

Expansion of Renewable Energy

Addressing the plenary session of the World Environment Day celebration on 5 June 2018, Modi stated,

> We are engaged in a massive push towards renewable energy generation. We have targeted generation of 175 gigawatts [GW] of solar and wind energy by 2022. We are already the fifth largest producer of solar energy in the world. Not only this, we are also the sixth largest producer of renewable energy.

The expansion of renewable energy like solar and wind is a welcome policy direction. There are benefits to expanding these energy resources, not only from the perspective of the environment, but also the economic benefits of generating more employment opportunities. Nevertheless, the question remains whether the NDA-II government has put forth enough effort to take advantage of the extremely favourable cost conditions in the field of renewable energy, which include solar photovoltaic (PVs) and onshore winds now being at cost parity with fossil fuels. The levelised costs of electricity from renewable energy sources have declined at a rapid pace, especially for PVs (Figures 10.1a, 10.1b).[10]

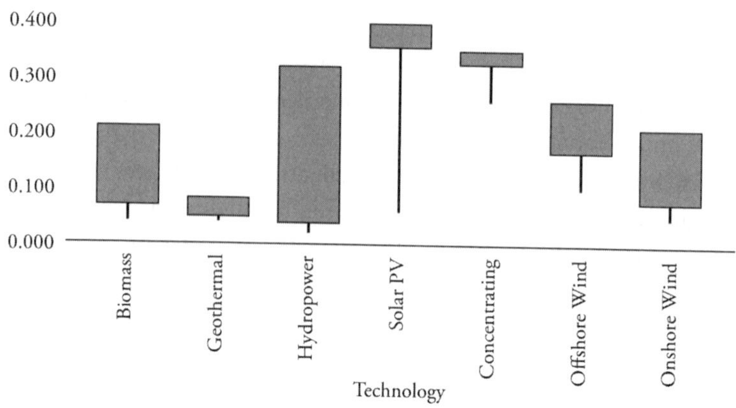

FIGURE 10.1A: Global Levelised Cost of Electricity from Utility-scale Renewable Power-generation Technologies in 2010

Note: Figures on Y-axis are in 2016 USD/kwh.

Source: Author's construction based on International Renewable Energy Agency (IRENA) Renewable Energy Cost Database. Available at https://www.irena.org/ourwork/Knowledge-Data-Statistics/Data-Statistics/Costs/LCOE-2010-2017 (accessed February 2019).

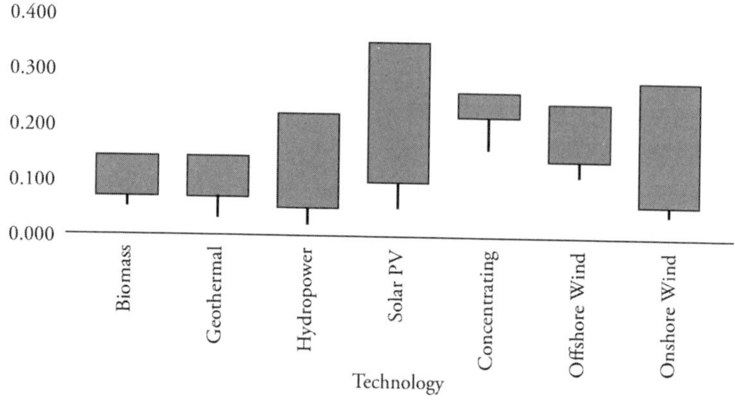

FIGURE 10.1B: Global Levelised Cost of Electricity from Utility-scale Renewable Power-generation Technologies in 2017

Note: Figures on Y-axis are in 2016 USD/kwh.

Source: Author's construction based on IRENA Renewable Energy Cost Database. Available at https://www.irena.org/ourwork/Knowledge-Data-Statistics/Data-Statistics/Costs/LCOE-2010-2017 (accessed February 2019).

Taking advantage of these lower costs, other developing economies like China and advanced countries like the USA, Germany and Japan have performed much better than India in renewable energy generation. According to the IRENA database, China and Brazil currently rank as the first and third largest producers of renewable energy. China is way ahead of India in its expansion of renewable energy. Their performance in terms of solar energy is worth a closer look, particularly since the Indian government highlights it as a significant success story. In 2017, China had an installed capacity of 131 GW, while India has an installed capacity of 18 GW. According to the IRENA database, over the period 2014–17, China increased its installed capacity in solar energy by 105.5 GW, while India increased its capacity by only 14.3 GW—a mere one-seventh of the former. A comparison with other countries like the USA and Japan shows that they installed almost twice the amount of solar capacity over this period compared to India (Figure 10.2).

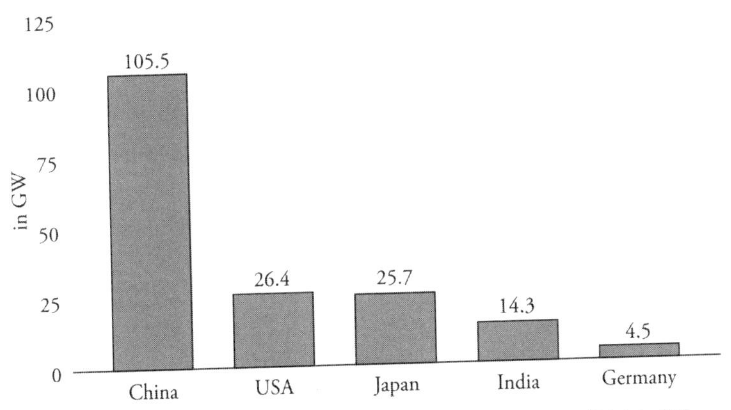

FIGURE 10.2: Additions in Installed Solar Capacity (2014–17)

Source: Author's construction based on IRENA Trends in Renewable Energy Capacity and Generation Database. Available at https://www.irena.org/ourwork/Knowledge-Data-Statistics/Data-Statistics/Capacity-and-Generation/Statistics-Time-Series (accessed February 2019).

This story also holds for the overall expansion of the renewable energy capacity of these countries. Over the same period, India added 33.3 GW of capacity in the form of renewable energy sources, while China added 207.2 GW of renewable energy capacity, or approximately six times. It shows, as reflected in Figures 10.3a and 10.3b, that while China has been hugely successful in taking advantage of the reduced costs of renewable energy, India's efforts have been moderate. The USA, which currently has a president who denies climate change and discourages the use of renewable energy, also installed more renewable energy compared to India. Despite the reductions in costs due to global technological advancement in the field of renewable energy, the NDA-II government was unable to reap these benefits to their full extent. Moreover, these potential benefits are slowly being eroded. The recent imposition of a safeguard duty on imported PV cells by this government and the ongoing depreciation of the Indian rupee vis-à-vis the US dollar have already lessened, to a substantial extent, some of these cost advantages. If the government is concerned enough about the deteriorating environmental health in India, there is an immediate need to spend more on research and development of renewable energy sources, to support their expansion, and limit the expansion of fossil fuels, especially coal.

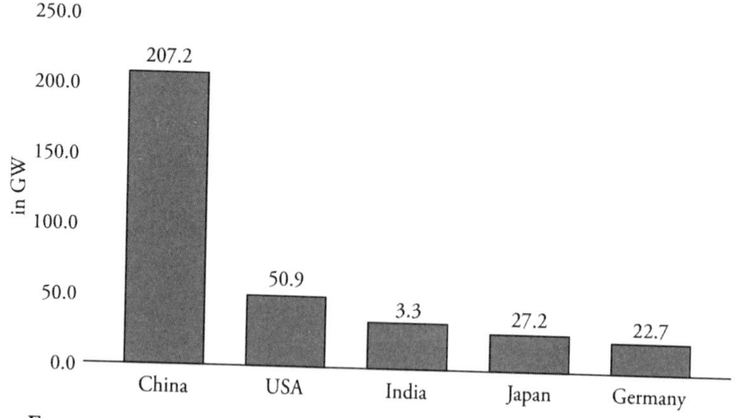

FIGURE 10.3A: Additions to Installed Renewable Energy Capacity

Source: Author's construction based on IRENA Trends in Renewable Energy Capacity and Generation Database. Available at https://www.irena.org/ourwork/Knowledge-Data-Statistics/Data-Statistics/Capacity-and-Generation/Statistics-Time-Series (accessed February 2019).

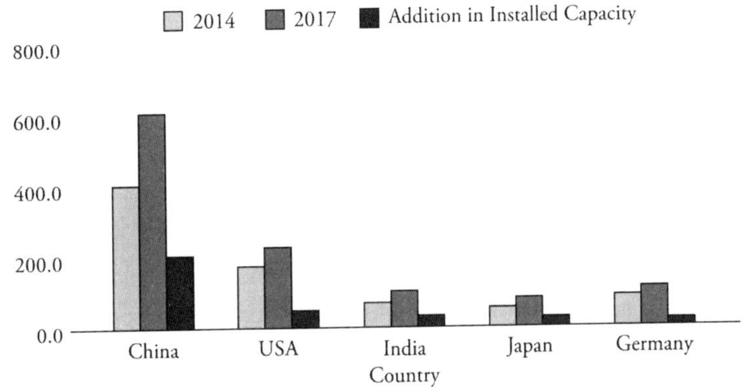

FIGURE 10.3B: Installed Renewable Energy Capacity (GW)

Source: Author's construction based on IRENA Trends in Renewable Energy Capacity and Generation Database. Available at https://www.irena.org/ourwork/Knowledge-Data-Statistics/Data-Statistics/Capacity-and-Generation/Statistics-Time-Series (accessed February 2019).

The current reality, however, is very different from that ideal scenario. One of the primary objectives for advocating the use of renewable energy sources is to limit, and finally eliminate, the use of fossil fuels, especially coal. However, according to a recent report published by the Centre for Financial Accountability in June 2018, the financing of coal-fired power plants continues in India, with public-sector banks financing a substantial chunk of it.[11] This report found that 12 coal-fired power plants with a combined capacity of 17 GW obtained loans of Rs 60,767 crore out of a total lending of Rs 83,680 crore disbursed by the banks to 72 energy projects reviewed in that report. The remaining 60 renewable energy projects with a combined capacity of 4.5 GW mobilised only Rs 22,913 crore. The report also adds that eight out of the top 10 lenders to these coal-fired power plants are public-sector banks. Most of the coal-fired power plants were existing projects, while the renewable ones were predominantly the newer ones needing more financial assistance to start up those projects. This apparent favouring of coal-fired power plants is very problematic; if the use of coal continues to expand, as it has done under this government, then even with the use of renewable energy sources, the increasing emission levels cannot be controlled.

Pradhan Mantri Ujjwala Yojana

The Pradhan Mantri Ujjwala Yojana (PMUY), launched in 2016 to provide LPG connections, was also supposed to help the environment as it would serve to replace the traditional cooking fuels like kerosene, cow dung and solid biomass, which are primarily responsible for household air pollution, especially in rural areas. This scheme is a good initiative taken by this government, and a step in the right direction. The initial success of the programme is evident from the PMUY's website as more than 5 crore connections have already been disbursed, and the target and scope of the scheme have been revised to disburse more than 8 crore connections by March 2020.

Despite this government's claims of the initial success of this programme, as seen in Chapter 8 (this volume), there are some serious concerns related to how successful it has been in meeting its objectives.

As of 1 July 2018, the data reported by the Ministry of Petroleum and Natural Gas states that around 4.5 crore households have subscription vouchers for LPG connections under the PMUY scheme. However, these subscription numbers are themselves unreliable. For instance, in that same report, it appears that there are a few states where the number of such subscribers with active domestic connection exceeds the total number of estimated households in those states.[12]

As mentioned in the earlier chapter, while there is a substantial increase in the number of customers with LPG connections due to the PMUY scheme, the data shows that there has not been any significant growth in the consumption of LPG cylinders. According to the Centre for Monitoring Indian Economy (CMIE) database, Figure 10.4 shows that there is substantial growth in the number of LPG customers from 9.4 per cent in 2014–15 to 16.2 per cent in 2016–17. However, the same data reveals that the annual growth in the LPG consumption decreased from 10.5 per cent to 9.8 per cent over the same period.

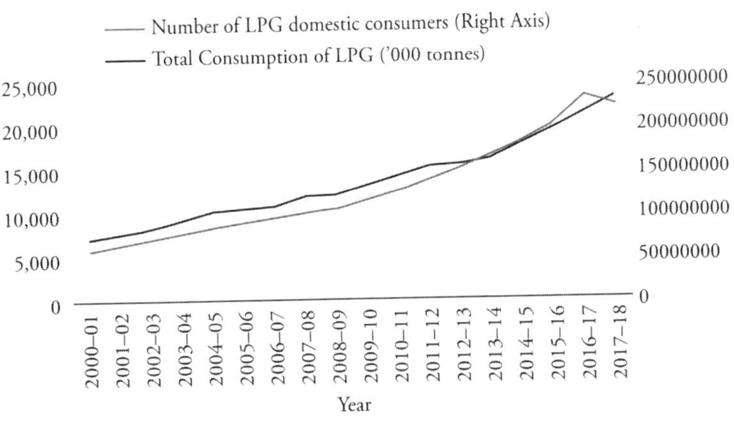

FIGURE 10.4: Consumption of LPG

Source: Author's construction based on CMIE database.

The primary reason for the failure of this programme is its pricing structure. Under this programme, a below poverty line (BPL) household is entitled to a cooking stove or hot plate and the first LPG cylinder, and is not responsible for any overhead payments at the time of subscription. The typical cost of the stove and the first LPG cylinder, which is approximately around Rs 1,500–1,600, is extended as an interest-free loan to these beneficiaries through the dealers and distributors of LPG. This loan is expected to be recovered in the form of equal monthly instalments by selling unsubsidised refills to these subscribers. The usual subsidy on an LPG cylinder is in the range of Rs 250–300 per cylinder. So, oil companies like Indian Oil, Bharat Petroleum and Hindustan Petroleum are expecting to recover this loan once these subscribers of the programme return to buy five to six refills at the unsubsidised rate. For a BPL family, paying these exorbitantly high unsubsidised prices for their LPG cylinders is a chimera. For instance, in May 2016, the average price of an unsubsidised LPG refill cylinder was around Rs 554 in Kolkata, which then rose to Rs 781.5 as on 8 August 2018.[13]

The BPL household, in all probability, will choose to use the other cheaper cooking fuels like kerosene or coal or firewood (which is almost freely available) rather than pay such a hefty price for the refill of an LPG cylinder.

Recent news reports suggest that these state-owned oil companies are now deferring the payments of these instalments for a certain period to motivate the use of LPG cylinders again, though it appears that this would only lead to the postponement of the current problem.[14] Meanwhile, some media reports suggest that oil marketing companies are making provisions for the possible projected losses due to this PMUY programme.

Rural Electrification

The other flagship programme of providing clean energy in the form of electricity to households in India received much attention in the media when the government claimed that '100 per cent village electrification' had been achieved. On 28 April 2018, Modi tweeted this success story, declaring, 'I am delighted that every single village of India now has access to electricity.' Two important things need to be mentioned here. One, the definition of village electrification in India is very narrow; according to the revised definition issued in February 2004, a village would be considered electrified if necessary infrastructures such as power transformers are available in the inhabited locality and the Dalit hamlets (where they exist), ensuring that electricity reaches public places, and to at least 10 per cent of the total number of households. If evaluated by this definition, then the performances of the previous UPA-I and UPA-II governments are actually far better than that of the NDA-II government. Figures 10.5a and 10.5b show that the annual average number of villages electrified in India under the UPA-I regime was almost double compared to that of the NDA-II government. Thus, it can be argued that the credit for achieving '100 per cent village electrification' should, in fact, go to the earlier governments which started the process of electrifying villages much earlier, and at a faster pace.

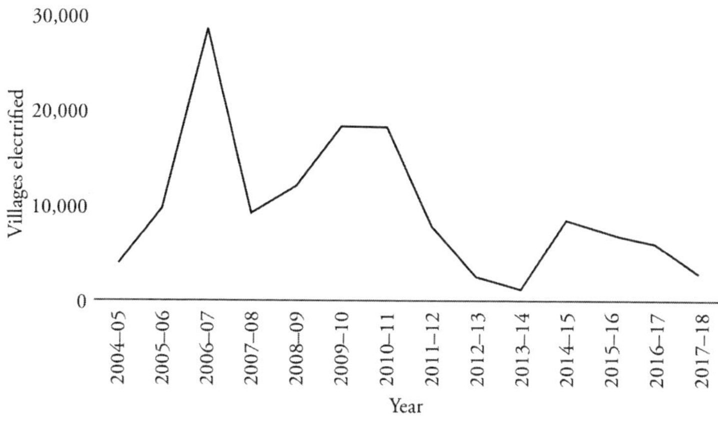

FIGURE 10.5A: Year-wise Villages Electrified

Source: Author's construction based on Annual Report, Ministry of Power, Government of India, various issues.

Tenure	Annual Average Village Electrification
NDA-II	6,110
UPA-II (2009–14)	9,680
UPA-I (2004–09)	12,753

FIGURE 10.5B: Annual Average Number of Villages Electrified, 2004–18

Source: Author's construction based on Annual Report, Ministry of Power, Government of India, various issues.

Two, it is clear that the achievement of 100 per cent rural electrification does not, in any way, signify that all households in India have access to electricity. The claim of 'total electrification' is far from reality. The Saubhagya scheme of this government was essentially launched to achieve that very purpose. According to the government's website, as of 8 November 2018, more than 11 million households still need to be electrified. Once these households are connected to the grid, the more important task is to ensure that these households receive a reliable and affordable supply of electricity on a sustained basis. Blackouts in the villages are very common. According to a study by the Council on Energy, Environment and Water, in the state of Odisha, almost 64 per cent of households experienced two or more days of 24-hour blackouts in a month, while 31 per cent experienced three or more days of low voltage supply. These are a stark reality in Indian villages. Hence, the celebrations of success and the media hype over the '100 per cent rural electrification' are premature and have garnered a great deal of publicity.

Water Pollution and River Connectivity

A significant promise made in the election manifesto of the BJP in 2014 was to prevent the pollution of rivers and to ensure the cleanliness, purity and uninterrupted flow of the rivers, especially the river Ganges. A massive 'Clean Rivers Programme' was promised to be launched across the country driven by people's participation to achieve these objectives. When the NDA-II government came to power in 2014, a flagship programme, Namami Ganga, was launched with a budget of Rs 20,000 crore, to be spent over the period 2015–20 to clean the polluted waters.

However, statistics show a very different reality. According to the CPCB, as evident from Figure 10.6, the number of polluted river stretches increased under NDA-II from 302 in 2015 to 351 in 2018. The condition of the Ganges is much worse. According to a petition filed by *The Wire* under the Right to Information (RTI) Act, this government has released only Rs 5,523 crore, a fraction of the promised sum, for cleaning the Ganga, and Rs 3,867 crore has already been spent on it.[15] However, these spendings did not lead to any cleaning of the Ganga, and as the Green Tribunal recently ruled, 'not a single drop of the Ganga has been cleaned so far.'[16] According to some scholars, since the clean Ganga mission has been in place for more than 40 years, the problems associated with this programme were well-known, and therefore also the possible solutions to those problems. However, the Namami Ganga project 'continued to languish in lethargy and inertia. The main issues got lost in specious technicalities, flagrant violation of laws, ubiquitous corruption, and absence of coordination between the Centre and States.'[17]

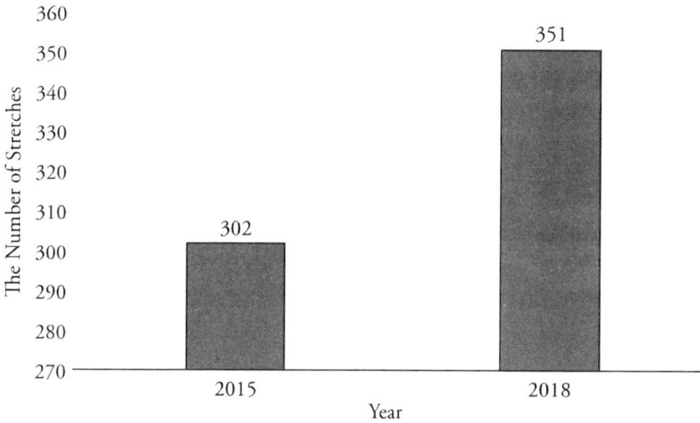

FIGURE 10.6: The Number of Polluted River Stretches in India, 2015 and 2018

Source: Author's construction based on Central Pollution Control Board, MoEFCC.

On a similar note, the project to interlink rivers is an example of a costly proposal with substantial adverse impacts on land, forests, biodiversity, rivers, and the people who are dependent on it for their livelihoods. On 30 March 2018, Modi made a strong case for interlinking of rivers, arguing that the mission of this programme is to ensure greater equity of water distribution by enhancing the availability of water in drought-prone areas by diverting it from areas that have surplus water. This project is intended to be a significant programme involving the construction of around 15,000 km of new canals and 3,000 big and small dams and storage facilities. Environmentalists argue that such construction would eventually lead to massive deforestation, which would further reduce the ability of the earth to absorb carbon dioxide and to adapt to the threats of climate change. The Ken–Betwa river project is a glaring example of such deforestation efforts, which plans to clear out 6.5 per cent of the forest reserve. It threatens about 200 square km of the Panna tiger reserve, further endangers the gharial species and with it, the Ken River and large parts of the Bundelkhand area. Even the Central Water Commission was reluctant to give the go-ahead for this project, although the project was finally approved on 25 May 2017 by the environment ministry.[18] The need of the hour is proper management of groundwater in India through local-level harvesting and conservation of rainfall. According to these experts, it is difficult to define 'surplus' water, as every drop has some ecological role to play. In their 2004 article on interlinking of rivers, the authors Bandopadhyay and Perveen conclude that 'hydraulic equity at the national level does not mean undertaking projects for transfer of water at public expense, from better water-endowed river basins to dry areas for inefficient and commercial use through socially and economically wasteful projects not approved through open professional assessments.'[19]

The Forestry and Ecology under the NDA-II Government

In the recently published *State of Forest Report 2017*, the government celebrated the success story of India's tree and forest cover, registering an increase of 6,600 square km or 0.94 per cent of the total forest-covered area in two years since 2015.[20] This development certainly appears to be positive. However, caution needs to be exercised while interpreting this data, since the number of districts covered to evaluate the forest area in the 2017 report is 633, while the earlier reports based on Census 2001 covered only 589 districts. The other parameters observed since 2014 raise further doubts about these statistics. According to *The New York Times*, under the NDA-II government, the percentage of industrial projects approved in wildlife habitats has gone up significantly from 45.5 per cent to 73.3 per cent.[21] The quick sanction of these big development projects, which were previously rejected by the UPA-II government due to the projected negative impacts on the ecology and environment, has threatened the existence of the wildlife in their natural habitats and disrupted the ecological balance. It is also reported that, within the first three months of assuming office, the NDA-II government approved 33 out of 41 proposals, diverting over 70 square km of forest land to other uses.

This approach to development goes hand-in-hand with the various reconstitutions of the governing bodies and dilution of environmental laws undertaken by the NDA-II government. Immediately after coming to power in the central government, the MoEFCC led an affidavit in the Supreme Court on 22 July 2014 to reconstitute the National Board for Wildlife. Although environmentalists cited various reasons to register their protest against this move, from favouritism to the lack of expertise among the members of the board, no changes were made. Meanwhile, some of the critical provisions in the wildlife and environmental regulation laws like the Wildlife Protection Act of 1972, the Forest (Conservation) Act of 1980, and the Environment (Protection) Act of 1986 were being diluted. Prerna Bindra, a wildlife conservationist who has been in the forefront of the battle to conserve India's wildlife, alleged in her book, *The Vanishing: India's Wildlife Crisis*, that developmental projects that fail to account for environmental costs have led to an 'ecocide', threatening ecological and environmental security.[22] The recent killing of the tigress, Avni, captures this reality to a large extent.

Conclusion

Since coming to power in 2014, the NDA-II government has been active in environment- and ecology-related issues. However, all these activities have one thing in common—their underlying policies are skewed in favour of the private corporate sector and large business houses, not only in terms of the further relaxing of environmental regulations in order to ease the growth of those businesses, but also to facilitate further accumulation under the guise of environmental governance. The environmental and ecological policies formulated by any government across the globe should be intended to protect the masses, or the common person, who are the worst sufferers. The government does not appear focused on this goal. The environmentalists in India have been accusing the current government of not just proposing extensive changes which are themselves detrimental to the environment, but also of implementing those changes in an undemocratic manner. The current government is proposing and amending rules without any public consultations, and yet claims to be protecting the interests of the public. This attitude is precisely the reason why its flagship programmes and schemes are turning out to be ultimately unsuccessful. For example, schemes like PMUY, though well-intended, are beginning to fail because the intricacies of the programmes are complicated and have little connection with the ground reality.

In India, where a majority of households burn collected firewood and biomass, asking those households to pay almost Rs 700–800 per month for cooking fuel is a reflection of how disconnected the government is from the masses. Similarly, the NDA-II government had to do away with the National Clean Energy Fund, and the levy and collection of a cess on water due to the implementation of the Goods and Services Tax (GST), which is raising serious concerns among environmentalists about the future environmental health of India. It is no wonder that there is so much resistance across India on environmental and ecological issues. Such resistance ultimately reflects the discontent the people feel against the current administration and its policies.

Notes and References

1. Will Steffen, Johan Rockstrom, Katherine Richardson, et al., 'Trajectories of the Earth System in the Anthropocene', *Proceedings of the National Academy of Sciences* 115 (33), 2018, 8252–59. Available at http://www.pnas.org/content/115/33/8252 (accessed February 2019).

2. Environmentalists and policymakers across the globe use measurements of fine particulate matter ($PM_{2.5}$) to estimate the level of air pollution and to understand the health impacts of such pollution. The WHO considers an annual mean of 10 $\mu g/m^3$ (micrograms per cubic metre of air) to be a safe limit.

3. The 2018 EPI ranks 180 countries on 24 performance indicators across 10 issue categories covering environmental health and ecosystem vitality.

These metrics provide a gauge at a national scale of how close countries are to established environmental policy goals. The EPI thus offers a scorecard that highlights leaders and laggards in environmental performance, gives insight on best practices, and provides guidance for countries that aspire to be leaders in sustainability.

4. Jeffrey Gettleman, Kai Schultz, and Hari Kumar, 'Environmentalists Ask: Is India's Government Making Bad Air Worse?', *The New York Times*, 8 December 2017. Available at https://www.nytimes.com/2017/12/08/world/asia/india-pollution-modi.html (accessed February 2019).

5. *The Wire*, 11 October 2018. Available at https://thewire.in/rights/read-gd-agarwal-final-letter-narendra-modi-saving-ganga (accessed February 2019).

6. Tien Ming Lee, Ezra M. Markowitz, Peter D. Howe, et al., 'Predictors of Public Climate Change Awareness and Risk Perception around the World', *Nature Climate Change* 5 (11), July 2015, 1014–20.

7. Centre for Science and Environment, 21 February 2015. Available at https://www.cseindia.org/indias-first-ever-environmental-rating-of-coal-based-power-plants-finds-the-sectors-performance-to-be-way-below-global-benchmarks-5685 (accessed February 2019).

8. CEPI is an index value with a range from zero to 100, in which CPAs are those with a score of 70 and above, and those between 60 and 70 are classified as SPAs.

9. These areas have been named in a news report published in *Business Standard* on 19 July 2014.

10. Levelised cost of electricity is often cited as a convenient summary measure of the overall competitiveness of different generating technologies. It represents the per-megawatt hour cost (in discounted real dollars) of building and operating a generating plant over an assumed financial life and duty cycle.

11. Centre for Financial Accountability, 24 June 2018. Available at http://www.cenfa.org/coal/psbs-back-coal-whereas-private-owned-renewables/ (accessed February 2019).

12. The subscription coverage for some states like Delhi, Punjab and Goa stands at 126.2 per cent, 129.4 per cent and 138.1 per cent, respectively. Since there is no disaggregated district-level data, it becomes difficult to verify the numbers reported by the distributors in these reports.

13. Ravi Nair, 'Modi's Gas for the Poor Scheme Marred by Data Inflation, Poor Implementation', *The Wire*, 11 August 2018. Available at

https://thewire.in/government/pradhan-mantri-ujjwala-yojana-separating-fact-from-fiction (accessed February 2019).

14. *The Times of India*, 24 March 2018. Available at https://www.timesnownews.com/business-economy/economy/article/ujjwala-scheme-payment-deferment-loan-relief-for-poor-households-under-plan/210748 (accessed February 2019).

15. Dheeraj Mishra, 'Almost Rs 4,000 Crore Spent, but the Ganga is More Polluted under Modi's Watch', *The Wire*, 20 October 2018. Available at https://thewire.in/environment/ganga-pollution-narendra-modi-increased (accessed February 2019).

These numbers are cited from this article.

16. 'Not a drop of the Ganga has been cleaned: NGT', *The Hindu*, 7 February 2017. Available at https://www.thehindu.com/news/cities/Delhi/Not-a-drop-of-the-Ganga-has-been-cleaned-NGT/article17205902.ece (accessed February 2019).

17. Raghu Dayal, 'Modi's Tryst with Clean Ganga', *The Hindu Business Line*, 29 August 2018. Available at https://www.thehindubusinessline.com/opinion/modis-tryst-with-clean-ganga/article24812047.ece (accessed February 2019).

The quote has been cited from this article.

18. Himanshu Thakkar, 'Do We Really Need Interlinking of Rivers?', *The Mint*, 20 September 2017. Available at https://www.livemint.com/Opinion/VwhUEH5UUYava6GZISa1zH/Do-we-really-need-interlinking-of-rivers.html (accessed February 2019).

This discussion has benefitted from this article.

19. Jayanta Bandopadhyay and Shama Perveen, 'Interlinking of Rivers in India: Assessing the Justifications', *Economic and Political Weekly* 39 (50), 2004, 5307–16.

20. The data has been cited from *State of Forest Report*, various issues.

21. This data is reported from Gettleman et al., 'Environmentalists Ask'.

22. Prerna Bindra, *The Vanishing: India's Wildlife Crisis* (New Delhi: Viking, 2017).

Part III

Governance

Suit-Boot ki Sarkar and its 'Battle' against Corruption

Roshan Kishore

Introduction

The narrative around corruption in India is, in some ways, amusing. The 2G Spectrum allocation became the biggest scam under the second United Progressive Alliance (UPA-II) government. The Congress and its allies paid heavily for it politically. Anti-corruption was a prominent plank in the Bharatiya Janata Party's (BJP) 2014 campaign led by Narendra Modi. Yet, the Supreme Court acquitted all the accused in the 2G case, where the prosecutor was the Central Bureau of Investigation (CBI), which reports to the Central government. So, was there no corruption, or did the present government fail to build a strong case?

The biggest step against corruption undertaken by this government has been demonetisation. While announcing its implementation on 8 November 2016, the prime minister went on record in listing three primary objectives of the policy: purging illegal wealth in cash; destroying fake currency in the economy; and weakening terrorist activities by disrupting their cash flows. Within a few months, it was clear that most of the money in circulation had come back to the banks, instances of fake currency were being reported more frequently, and the situation in the Kashmir valley had deteriorated. Did we, then, achieve any advance in the battle against corruption?

To be sure, the government claims success in both instances. Re-auctioning of the spectrum generated windfall revenues for the exchequer. The money trail from returned deposits after demonetisation will help to increase the tax base in the economy, or so we are told. It is not very difficult to find people on either side of the political spectrum, who can argue *ad nauseam* about the good and bad, or corrupt and non-corrupt motivations behind such policies. Moreover, it is not very difficult to find cynics who will dismiss such commentary as part of the ongoing political banter.

The purpose of this chapter is not to argue that the current government is more/less corrupt than its predecessor, although this government has had its own share of controversies related to corruption, such as the alleged irregularities in the Rafale deal or in Jay Shah's business investments. What it will try and argue instead is that the political economy of the narrative around corruption has changed fundamentally under the present dispensation compared to what it was, not just under the previous government, but from long before Narendra Modi became the prime minister in 2014.

INITIAL SETBACKS FOR THE NDA-II GOVERNMENT

A little political digression is useful here. The BJP's massive 2014 win was followed by more election victories after the Lok Sabha polls. The BJP formed governments in Haryana, Maharashtra, and Jharkhand in the same year. However, this was to change in 2015. Despite having won all seven seats in the 2014 Lok Sabha polls in the national capital, the BJP suffered a humiliating defeat at the hands of the Aam Aadmi Party (AAP) in the 2015 assembly polls held in Delhi. The AAP won a whopping 67 out of 70 seats, while the BJP won just three. The defeat was symbolic in the perception battle on corruption because the BJP had named Kiran Bedi, a retired Indian Police Service (IPS) officer and an estranged comrade of Arvind Kejriwal from the Lokpal movement, as its prospective chief ministerial candidate in the state. Bedi herself lost the election.

As is always the case after a big political defeat, the media did not spare the BJP, including its top leadership, after the Delhi poll results. One of the recurring themes was caricature around a suit which the prime minister had worn to a formal reception hosted for then US President Barack Obama, which had Narendra Damodardas Modi woven into the fabric. The BJP's opponents used the imagery to portray the party and its stalwart leader as almost vulgar in the brazen display of power and wealth. That the caricatures hurt the BJP was evident from the fact that the suit was auctioned within less than a month of the prime minister having worn it. One of the most stringent criticisms of the government on this issue came from the Congress (then in waiting) president Rahul Gandhi, who called the Modi government a *suit-boot ki sarkar*. While the literal translation of the phrase is a government of the well-dressed, what it implied was that this was a government of the rich and privileged. The charge had a political context as well. The government had brought in an ordinance to change the Land Acquisition Bill, which diluted the critical provisions of the UPA-era law and weakened the bargaining power of farmers whose land was being acquired. Not only did Narendra Modi sell his suit, but he also withdrew these controversial amendments. This was a decisive victory for the Opposition vis-à-vis a government which had got a historic majority just a year before.

Later in the year, the BJP suffered a big defeat at the hands of a grand alliance of the Janata Dal (United) (JD[U]), the Rashtriya Janata Dal (RJD), and the Congress in the critical state of Bihar. The defeat had a significant bearing on the political narrative around corruption, because Lalu Prasad Yadav, the RJD's most prominent leader, had been disqualified from even fighting elections on corruption charges. Because the JD(U) had been a long-time partner of the BJP in Bihar and the Congress had a marginal presence in the state, it was the RJD which was seen as the main adversary of the BJP. The Delhi and Bihar results were big blows to the efficacy of the BJP's anti-corruption politics. In one state, it lost a fight between figureheads who were peers in an important anti-corruption movement. In another, people voted for a 'corrupt' politician and rejected the BJP. The Bihar election results were announced on 8 November 2015. Exactly a year later, on 8 November 2016, the Modi government announced demonetisation.

THE PREMISE OF DEMONETISATION: SCHADENFREUDE, NOT ECONOMICS

One did not have to wait for the Reserve Bank of India (RBI) to declare details of currency notes which had come back to the banking system to call the economic bluff of demonetisation. The policy was aimed at punishing those who earned black money by making their cash stocks of unaccounted wealth unusable. The prime minister himself articulated this in clear terms while making a speech in Japan.[1] Anybody who understands the basic concept of stocks and flows in economics will know that such expectations are flawed. There cannot be a one-to-one extrapolation between the ratio of junked cash to total cash in circulation and the scheme's effect on black income. Here is an example to explain this: Suppose a property developer sells a flat worth Rs 1 crore to a person. He can declare the entire amount to the tax authorities and pay tax on it. Or, he could offer a deal to the buyer that he would sell the flat for Rs 90 lakh, but take Rs 30 lakh in unaccounted cash, and the official value of the flat would be declared at Rs 60 lakh. The seller would lose Rs 10 lakh in value, but save Rs 40 lakh in taxable income. The Rs 30 lakh in cash would then become a part of what can be termed black income in that particular year. Let us assume that the seller makes one such deal every month. In that case, he would have made Rs 3.3 crore in 2016 (Rs 30 lakh each between January and November). If all of this money has been kept in Rs 500 or Rs 1,000 notes, he would be in trouble. However, that is extremely unlikely.

First of all, cash is not the only option to store unaccounted wealth. A 2012 report prepared by the National Institute of Financial Management on unaccounted income found that cash was the least preferred option for storing unaccounted wealth. It is also not necessary that unaccounted income should be held as wealth. For example, the seller described above could be using his monthly stream of Rs 30 lakh in unaccounted earnings to pay wages to his construction workers. In that case, he would have successfully re-routed Rs 3 crore of black income to the construction workers and would only risk losing the Rs 30 lakh which are the proceeds of November. The damage to the seller is thus partial and temporary. He can possibly defer payments to his labour contractors. Once new currency notes begin re-circulating in the economy, he can use them to pay off his debts and wash away his sins in the vast informal network of the Indian economy. If the total value of cash in circulation in Rs 500 and Rs 1,000 notes was Rs 3,000 crore, and our flat seller were to junk Rs 30 lakh of cash in hand, it would be incorrect to assume that the magnitude of black income was only 0.01 per cent, since the total unaccounted income of the seller is Rs 3.3 crore, which comes to 0.11 per cent. If the cash junked was double the amount, one would arrive at a different estimate of black money for the same amount of unaccounted income.

The short point is that, at best, demonetisation would only be a small and temporary problem for those who earn unaccounted incomes. Subsequent developments were to vindicate—both statistically and anecdotally—these claims, which were made by many other commentators and academicians as well. More than 99 per cent of the scrapped currency notes came back into the banking system. This meant that there were no windfall gains from demonetisation. Even claims of a significant expansion of the tax base do not look very robust as tax-buoyancy—percentage increase in taxes per unit increase in income—actually went down between 2016–17 and 2017–18.[2] The usual income tax raids, and search and seizures during elections have continued to unearth substantial amounts of cash deposits in new notes even after demonetisation. This shows that even the limited use of cash as unaccounted income (Rs 30 lakh in our example above) continues to enjoy a free run in the Indian economy. So, let alone sounding a death knell for the black economy, demonetisation did not even manage to check the use of unaccounted cash.

What needs to be kept in mind is that demonetisation inflicted huge collateral damage on the Indian economy. Economic activity, especially in the informal sector, was severely crippled due to the scarcity of cash, which serves as the most significant medium of exchange. It is the poor who paid the highest price for this disruption, as their dependence on the informal economy is much more than that of the rich and privileged. Yet, the BJP achieved a decisive victory in the Uttar Pradesh elections in early 2017, and it had not paid any big political price for the miseries it inflicted during demonetisation until the middle of 2018. To be sure, it did suffer a decline in seats in the 2017 Gujarat Assembly elections and fell short of a majority in the 2018 Karnataka elections, despite having won a majority of Lok Sabha seats in the state in the 2014 elections. The BJP has also lost key elections in the Hindi-belt states of Rajasthan, Madhya Pradesh, and Chhattisgarh, held at the end of 2018. Although the side-effects of demonetisation, via a slump in the rural economy, seem to be catching up with the BJP, the party continues to champion demonetisation even now. There is more to this political behaviour than just obduracy.

Demonetisation was premised on creating a fake rich–poor polarisation by trying to portray that while the poor were indeed suffering from the policy, the rich were suffering even more. The prime minister's repeated rhetoric about how he had made influential and elite people his enemies due to demonetisation is robust proof of this strategy. The BJP's political campaign sold this policy in the larger package of the government's pro-poor agenda, which included welfare schemes such as Ujjwala Yojana (which gave a one-time subsidy on LPG connections to the poor) and the MUDRA yojana (which was, in effect, merely a rechristened version of already existing loan schemes of public-sector banks). In other words, it appears that this was part of a concerted effort to rid the government of the *suit-boot ki sarkar* tag, which had damaged its political prospects in the previous year.

The fact that no political party saw the game plan in the implementation of demonetisation allowed the BJP to stay with a coherent political narrative on the ground. The Opposition's reactions ranged from pointing out that demonetisation led to a reduction of a few percentage points in India's gross domestic product (GDP) growth—which nobody on the ground explicitly relates to—or calling it an outright scam, without any proof of money trail so far. To be sure, the task was not an easy one. One of the first side-effects of demonetisation was a sharp crash in the prices of fruits and vegetables, which destroyed farm incomes. Yet, no political party took a categorical position on the issue, lest they were labelled pro-price rise. Ironically, all this occurred at a time when both the government and the RBI were continuously trying to shift the goalposts on the objectives and rules of demonetisation. So while the government never won the intellectual battle on demonetisation—Gita Gopinath, the newly appointed chief economist of the International Monetary Fund (IMF) had said that no serious economist would justify the policy—it did not even face a serious challenge in the political battle.

The polarising power of demonetisation was evident to this author when he was travelling in Karnataka before the 2018 assembly elections. Reactions to demonetisation were starkly different among Hindu and Muslim respondents, with the former dismissing the short-term pain and the latter making a big deal of it.[3] What it suggested was that a section of the electorate was willing to forget the pains of demonetisation in order to make sure that the BJP's Hindutva politics did not suffer. Shadow-boxing with fictitious powerful holders of black money and complementing this with already existing polarising strategies allowed this government to make sure that the battle on corruption was now being fought on the BJP's terms. Leaders like Arvind Kejriwal and Lalu Yadav were not being allowed to shape it in their favour. It was the optics, rather than the results of the battle being fought, which mattered. While the BJP gained, the informal sector of the economy suffered heavily. More pain was in store for this sector in the days to come.

GOODS AND SERVICES TAX: PRO-BUSINESS FOR WHOM?

The Goods and Services Tax (GST) had been in the making for many years. It was an idea first conceived under the UPA government, and the BJP, including the prime minister, who was then the chief minister of Gujarat, opposed it. The impasse continued under the NDA-II government too. However, there was a political consensus, and GST was rolled out with much fanfare—a special session of Parliament was held at midnight—on 1 July 2017. The biggest economic justification for GST is that it streamlines taxation on economic activities across the length and breadth of the country. There are no multiple rates across states, which could potentially distort economic incentives. Also, tax incidence works on value-added approach via an input credit system. This means that if a company making kurtas buys fabric from another seller, it can claim a refund of the taxes paid by the fabric seller from its tax liabilities. So, there is an incentive to declare the expenses incurred at each step of the production chain. The latter aspect in an economy like India has an important side effect.

There is no wall which separates production networks across formal and informal enterprises in India. Many of the informal enterprises are competitive, not because of higher productivity, but because they could afford to do businesses without having to pay any taxes. If taxes became a part of their unit costs, already small mark-ups would have gone negative. While there is a degree of tax evasion involved here, such enterprises were also an essential source of income and employment in the economy. This has changed after the implementation of GST. A big firm which was already under the tax net would like to use input tax credits while purchasing inputs or outsourcing work. Even if the small firm were entitled to exemption from GST due to its turnover being below a certain threshold, its compliance costs are bound to increase significantly. An example can explain this. Let us suppose the kurta company discussed above used to buy fabric from a group of weavers in a village who were not a part of the tax net earlier. In the post-GST phase, the company would not get any input tax credit if it continues buying from the villagers who are not a part of the tax net. This means it is losing money it could have saved in tax credits. One could argue that the weavers in the village need not worry about paying GST because their annual turnover would be below the threshold level. However, even to be able to claim that, they would have to invest a certain amount of money in getting the requisite documents. The short point is, GST has increased the economic burden on small firms in the Indian economy. The hiatus between the reality and optics of such a policy is the same as demonetisation. The government has always sold GST as a pro-business and anti-corruption move. The point is, even a criticism of the GST along class lines (it is bad for the small businessman) is bound to get labelled as a defence of corruption.

What is ironic is the fact that as elections come closer, GST seems to have neither prevented corruption, nor boosted tax collections. The interim Union Budget for 2019–20 has admitted that there has been a huge shortfall in GST collections.

A *Business Standard* story by Nitin Sethi and Ishan Bakshi, published a day before the meeting of the GST Council held in January 2019, explained how the new tax had given birth to inter-state cartels which were carrying out tax evasion by creating fictitious firms to fake input tax credits.[4] As has been explained above, this method exploits the provision that allows companies to claim tax refund for input purchases from other firms. It is another matter that subsequent investigation has found that the so-called sellers existed only on paper. The authors reported that the total tax evasion under GST had already crossed Rs 15,000 crore.

These facts highlight the bravado involved in the government's claims that GST would prove to be a game changer in terms of revenue mobilisation and prevention of tax evasion. Instead of accepting its mistakes, the government, however, seems to be tweaking the GST structure—both in terms of tax rates and compliance rules—to provide relief to small businesses. Given the fact that the government was determined not to accept these demands when they were made by the Opposition, the question that needs to be asked is whether the GST will be used by the dominant party in India (the GST Council includes both the Central and state governments) to provide strategic relief just before elections while maintaining a disproportionate burden on small businesses in the normal course. If the answer is yes, it can be said that GST has increased the smaller entrepreneur's economic vulnerabilities under the garb of preventing corruption and tax reform.

ELECTORAL BONDS: DISGUISING QUID PRO QUO WITH BIG BUSINESS

That political parties in power get more funds than those in opposition is common knowledge in India. Yet, the sheer magnitude of the BJP's lead in terms of incomes vis-à-vis opposition parties after it captured power in 2014 has been baffling. Statistics compiled by the election and political party watchdog, Association for Democratic Reforms, speak for themselves (Figure 11.1).[5] By 2016–17, the BJP's income had become more than four times that of the Congress, a lead which the Congress did not enjoy vis-à-vis the BJP when it was in power. What is even more remarkable is the fact that in terms of donations worth more than Rs 20,000—often taken as a proxy for corporate donations—the BJP was getting 12 times more money than the Congress. To be sure, a part of the growing asymmetry between the BJP's and Congress's economic fortunes is probably also a result of the latter's diminishing political graph across the country. Yet, it is difficult to deny that the surge in the BJP's income, primarily from donations worth more than Rs 20,000, is symptomatic of an unprecedented level of backing from big business for the present regime. It is only fair to question what sort of a quid pro quo must have come with such financial backing from big business for a political party.

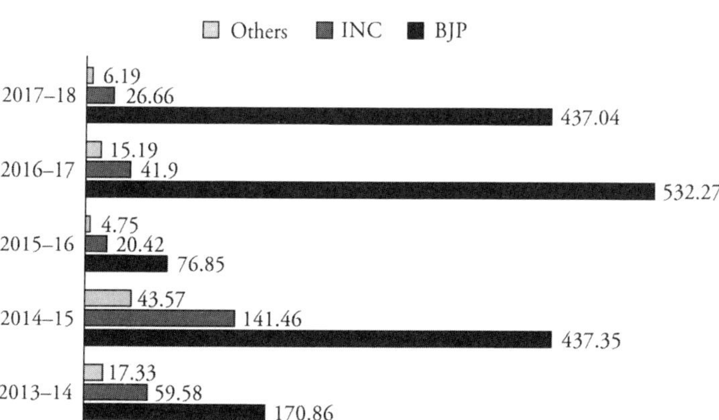

FIGURE 11.1: BJP's Income Surges Ahead of Others

Note: All figures in Rs crore.

Source: Adapted by author from Association for Democratic Reforms data.[5]

At least on the face of it, the corporate world has strict rules about conflict of interest. Insider trading is not allowed in stock markets. One of India's most celebrated corporate leaders, Chanda Kochhar, had to resign as the chairperson of ICICI Bank because her husband had financial dealings with a company, the co-partner of which received a big loan from Kochhar's bank. It is both shocking and ironic that no such red flags exist in the world where business interacts with politics in India. To put it crudely, we have no way of finding out whether a company has made a financial contribution to a political party and, at the same time, whether it has received some favour from the government being run by the same party. To be sure, political funding has never been very transparent in India. The bulk of the incomes declared by political parties is shown as having come from 'cash donations' below the threshold at which income tax details of the donor have to be declared. Even the declared donations often came from political funding trusts, which had many business houses as their members. However, the current NDA-II government has made an important contribution to the opacity around political funding in the country.

While presenting the Union Budget for 2017–18, Finance Minister Arun Jaitley introduced the provision of electoral bonds as part of his efforts to 'cleanse the system of funding of political parties' in the country. The stated objective was yet again at odds with the actual effect of the scheme on the ground. Milan Vaishnav, a senior fellow at Carnegie Endowment for International Peace in Washington, D.C., and author of *When Crime Pays: Money and Muscle in Indian Politics*, described this in an article in *The Indian Express*:

> The twist is that the donor neither needs to disclose it has purchased the bonds nor must it identify the recipient party. The political party in question will need to report it has received bonds, but it too does not have to disclose the donor's identity ... to declare electoral bonds a major victory in the effort to improve transparency in political funding is farcical. There is, by design, nothing transparent about the scheme. In fact, the stated goal is to protect the anonymity of donors by giving them an avenue to contribute without revealing their identity (which corporates, fearful of retaliation by parties to whom they have not given, especially prize).[6]

Readers would probably be irked by the fact that a chapter on corruption under the NDA-II government has not even mentioned the Rafale controversy so far. Let us imagine, for a moment, how the political narrative would have evolved if it were to be known that companies such as Anil Ambani's Reliance and many others who were given lucrative contracts or policy concessions by the government had made donations to the BJP via electoral bonds. However, such information has been made secret by the law passed by the current government.

The Fight against Corruption: Surgical Strikes on the Poor, Soft Gloves for the Rich

The discussion so far has tried to highlight the political economy divide in how this government has shaped its anti-corruption battle.

The poor were used as cannon fodder during demonetisation, which ironically was used to get votes from the same class. The back-to-back implementation of demonetisation and GST administered twin shocks to the entire informal economy in India. The relative pain was much smaller for big business. In fact, it will not be wrong to say that big business gained at the cost of the informal economy. Add to this the fact that it has never been more comfortable for the big and mighty to take and return favours, thanks to even more opaque rules of political funding.

Those who tried to question the sacrificing of the informal economy in the name of so-called anti-corruption and reform measures were either ignored or dismissed as siding with the corrupt. No opposition party has made any serious efforts to demand a roll-back of policies such as electoral bonds or to ask for greater transparency in India's political funding system. Part of the reason why this has not been done could be that almost all political parties in India use unscrupulous means to fund their activities, especially during elections. The Opposition's angst could be more about why the BJP is getting so much money rather than worry about the institutionalisation of opaque funding methods, which encourages conflicts of interest at the highest levels. It is not surprising, therefore, that the prime minister feels confident enough to say that he is not scared of appearing with big industrialists, and enterprises such as Paytm and Jio do not hesitate to put the prime minister's pictures in their newspaper advertisements.

The public discourse on corruption in India has converted itself into an apolitical and vacuous shouting match on television screens. In class terms, the tables have turned, actually. The UPA implemented a scheme such as the National Rural Employment Guarantee Act (NREGA). The public distribution system is one of the bigger legacies of the welfare state character of India. There is no denying the fact that there was and continues to be corruption in the working of these schemes. What is also true, however, is the fact that these schemes also provided a big boost to the living standards of the poorest of the poor. Even if it came at the cost of allowing a patron–client network of corrupt bureaucracy and contractors, pre-NDA-II India invested in policies which were pro-poor.

India after NDA-II thinks otherwise. In an abstract world, there is nothing wrong in encouraging the use of digital transactions to reduce black money and asking everyone to deposit their cash in banks to generate a money trail. This is what the government's defence of demonetisation has been after its claims of purging black money stocks fell flat. However, in a country where millions of people still work in the informal sector, such an anti-corruption policy also meant inflicting a body blow to the incomes and livelihoods of the poor and the downtrodden. The recently leaked findings of the National Sample Survey Organisation (NSSO) report on employment show that the unemployment rate in India reached a 45-year high in 2017–18, the period immediately after demonetisation and GST. In absolute terms, India saw a destruction of 18 million jobs between 2011–12 and 2017–18. The fact that the government has announced direct income transfers for farmers and income-tax rebates to the small income-tax payer is a clear acknowledgement of the hit to the incomes of the poor and non-rich in the Indian economy. However, all this was a small price to pay in the eyes of the government, which was keen to reinvent its political narrative.

Unless the political opposition to the BJP recognises this fundamental change, it will not be very successful in countering the individual appeal and, dare one say, notions of the unquestionable integrity of the prime minister in political battles. The present regime wants to de-class and de-politicise the narrative around corruption. And its motivations for doing this are not to eradicate corruption, but to make redundant and trivialise the class opposition to its policies. That is why opponents of demonetisation were being termed anti-national by the BJP.[7]

Notes and References

1. Available at https://www.youtube.com/watch?v=IlJmGEQ1MB0 (accessed January 2019).

2. Roshan Kishore, 'Did Windfall Gain from Cheap Oil Encourage Modi Govt to Take Fiscal Gambles', *Hindustan Times*, 30 January 2018. Available at https://www.hindustantimes.com/india-news/did-windfall-gain-from-cheap-oil-encourage-modi-govt-to-take-fiscal-gambles/story-jEyO5LeX5WLWN5nu2bocwL.html (accessed January 2019).

The data cited is from this article.

3. Roshan Kishore, 'Karnataka Elections: Hindutva could be BJP's Insurance against Anger over Demonetisation', *Hindustan Times*, 12 May 2018. Available at https://www.hindustantimes.com/analysis/hindutva-could-be-bjp-s-insurance-against-anger-over-demonetisation-in-karnataka/story-fjW4NcoyHZb5J25CGWfM6J.html (accessed January 2019).

This discussion appeared in this particular article.

4. Nitin Sethi and Ishan Bakshi, 'How "Briefcase" Companies are Defrauding the GST System of Thousands of Crores', *The Wire*, 9 January 2019. Available at https://thewire.in/business/briefcase-companies-tax-evasion-gst-crores (accessed January 2019).

5. Roshan Kishore, 'BJP Got Rs 532 cr in Donations above Rs 20K, more than 12 Times of Congress: ADR', *Hindustan Times*, 30 May 2018. Available at https://www.hindustantimes.com/india-news/bjp-got-rs-532-cr-in-grants-above-rs-20k-more-than-12-times-of-congress-adr/story-a3ZgRCN3KmmmziS48DXE7H.html (accessed January 2019).

6. Milan Vaishnav, 'Electoral Bonds Prize Anonymity, You Won't Know Who's Bought Them', *The Indian Express*, 8 January 2018. Available at https://indianexpress.com/article/opinion/electoral-bonds-prize-anonymity-you-wont-know-whos-bought-them-5015810/ (accessed January 2019).

7. Surendra P. Gangan, 'Those Opposing Demonetisation Anti-national: Maharashtra CM Devendra Fadnavis', *Hindustan Times*, 22 November 2016. Available at https://www.hindustantimes.com/mumbai-news/those-opposing-demonetisation-anti-national-maharashtra-cm-devendra-fadnavis/story-GnzwQDV5eitcBVVtJbSEnK.html (accessed January 2019).

twelve

Aadhaa(r) *Adhura* Welfare
A Critical Assessment

Anmol Somanchi[1]

The Narendra Modi-led National Democratic Alliance (NDA) came to power in 2014 on two key planks: *vikas* (development) and anti-corruption. Positioning himself as a reformer who would enhance State efficiency and fix India's welfare system, governance reform was a key component of Modi's vision for *Achhe Din* (prosperous days). Over the past four years, a bedrock of this reform agenda has been the vigorous integration of Aadhaar with the whole gamut of welfare programmes and government services. In many ways, Aadhaar has become ubiquitous today. Yet, in the lead up to the elections, Aadhaar was one of the many Congress-bred demons that the Bharatiya Janata Party (BJP) promised to tame. The prime ministerial candidate Narendra Modi rallied against the Aadhaar project, calling it 'public loot' and a 'political gimmick'.[2] When the Modi-led NDA was elected to power, all signs suggested that Aadhaar's fate was sealed. However, in a manner characteristic of many of its subsequent 'U-turns', the NDA-II government reversed its stance entirely on the matter.

As the government's tenure comes to an end, the benefits from Aadhaar largely remain unclear, while there is plenty of evidence that it is resulting in the exclusion of deserving beneficiaries from their entitlements. Yet, the government has persisted in insisting on it for various schemes and programmes. Further, the government has refused to release any useful data to assess whether Aadhaar has led to any real 'savings' in fiscal spending. Instead, the government (including the prime minister and the finance minister) has preferred to reiterate claims that have been discredited.[3] It is now increasingly clear that Aadhaar makes it possible to reduce government budgets on welfare schemes, irrespective of how these reductions happen, and not to provide persons with access to basic services.

This chapter assesses the impact of Aadhaar on major welfare programmes during the NDA-II government's tenure. The first section discusses the two broad arguments made in favour of linking Aadhaar to welfare—inclusion and efficiency—and shows how they are not entirely valid. The second section provides a survey of the evidence relating to Aadhaar's effects on the Public Distribution System (PDS), the Mahatma Gandhi National Rural Employment Guarantee Act (MGNREGA), and Social Security Pensions. The third section briefly discusses the reliability of Aadhaar, especially its role in facilitating fraud, following which the chapter is concluded.

Aadhaar: Little Scope, Exaggerated Hope

Since its inception, Aadhaar was projected as a magic bullet to fix the 'leaky' welfare system in India. We were told that by linking Aadhaar to welfare programmes, 'ghosts and fakes' would be deleted, middlemen eliminated, and corruption would finally be plugged. This powerful narrative was readily accepted by the public and allowed the Aadhaar project to scale up at a rapid pace. As Aadhaar began to be linked to various welfare initiatives, massive figures of savings began to be quoted. These were at the core of the government's case in the long-drawn Supreme Court cases challenging the validity of the project. This 'welfare façade' of Aadhaar, as Reetika Khera calls it, was intensely promoted in public discourse, while the serious privacy and surveillance issues surrounding it were strongly suppressed, if not dismissed outright.[4]

The case made for linking Aadhaar to welfare can be categorised broadly into the 'inclusion' and 'efficiency' arguments. A critical examination of both these arguments, however, reveals that they rest on weak ground.[5]

Inclusion

Aadhaar was projected as a universal digital Identity (ID) that would empower millions of citizens excluded from welfare programmes due to the lack of an official ID and allow them to access social security benefits. To enrol for an Aadhaar, residents must submit two existing IDs and to accommodate those who did not have any official ID, an 'introducer' system was put in place: a person without any ID proof could apply for an Aadhaar if an existing Aadhaar holder could testify for them. One would imagine the introducer system to be highly popular if the claims of persons having no official IDs were true. However, in response to a Right to Information (RTI) query in 2015, the Unique Identification Authority of India (UIDAI) revealed that only 0.03 per cent of all Aadhaar numbers were enrolled through this system. In other words, 99.97 per cent of Aadhaar holders already had two existing documents at the time of enrolment, and hence, were not excluded due to the lack of an ID proof.

In the context of welfare, it is also worth noting that the mere possession of an Aadhaar does not guarantee inclusion. To be entitled to benefits, individuals must meet the eligibility criteria of the respective scheme as set by the government. For instance, to receive old-age pension in Jharkhand, an individual must be 60 years or older and have an income less than Rs 7,500 per annum. Therefore, Aadhaar linking and authentication has now become an added hurdle that beneficiaries must pass before they can access their legal entitlements.

The other crucial 'inclusive' promise of Aadhaar was that it would foster financial inclusion by facilitating easier access to financial institutions and services, primarily the banking system, as Aadhaar was conceived as the crucial Know-Your-Customer (KYC) document that peopled lacked. The lack of the KYC is only one of the many barriers to accessing financial services, including other supply side constraints like weak penetration of bank branches, inappropriate financial instruments, and high costs of servicing new customers. Therefore, whether this lack is the key barrier is a moot question. The parallel roll-out of the Pradhan Mantri Jan Dhan Yojna (PMJDY), which led to the opening of Aadhaar-linked zero balance accounts, has surely increased the proportion of Indians with a bank account. What is not clear is how much of this should be attributed to Aadhaar and whether this was not possible in the absence of Aadhaar. Based on a three-state survey, the State of Aadhaar Report (SOAR) 2017–18 estimates that almost 90 per cent of those who opened a bank account using Aadhaar already had a valid proof-of-identity document at the time of Aadhaar enrolment.[6]

Of late, another claim doing the rounds, especially after the Supreme Court disallowed the use of Aadhaar authentication by private companies, is that the electronic-KYC facility of Aadhaar would reduce the verification costs associated with the paper-based KYC, and thus bring down the costs of servicing new customers, especially in rural areas where the marginal cost is high. In theory, this does make sense. But here again, SOAR provides two interesting findings, which raise questions over such potential benefits. First, only 12–13 per cent of respondents in Rajasthan and Andhra Pradesh who opened a bank account in the past three years used the e-KYC facility.[7] Second, no significant difference was found when comparing the time taken to open a bank account between users of the e-KYC and the traditional KYC.

Rather than inclusion, Aadhaar has systemically led to exclusion at multiple levels. First, the lack of an Aadhaar number entirely disqualifies an individual from even applying for welfare benefits. Second, the process of linking the number with the respective database of the welfare scheme and bank account (in the case of bank payments) is not trivial. In addition to manual errors, mismatch in details like name and age between Aadhaar and administrative databases can lead to exclusions and delay. Last, it is now clear that

Aadhaar authentication is far from reliable. Evidence from various surveys and ground reports from across the country suggest that a significant minority of beneficiaries face authentication failures, of which a large share leads to exclusion from welfare benefits.[8]

Efficiency

While 'inclusion' was one aspect of Aadhaar's welfare façade, the other was the claim that it would be a 'game-changer' for welfare by bringing an end to corruption. This belief was held not just by the government, but also by a whole range of actors including reputed academics, policy think tanks, and political commentators. This line of argument has taken various forms, but the crux of it is that Aadhaar would allow the government to remove duplicates and fakes from beneficiary lists, enable Direct Benefit Transfers (DBTs), prevent identity theft by using biometric authentication, and provide an intensive digital trail to monitor implementation. Put together, Aadhaar was to empower citizens by enhancing State capacity and increasing the efficiency of welfare delivery. But close to a decade after Aadhaar's inception, the experience has been rather sobering.

The potential benefits of Aadhaar in plugging leakages is best understood by looking at the various sources of corruption in welfare programmes and by evaluating the role Aadhaar can play in plugging such corruption. These frauds primarily take three forms:

(i) Identity Fraud: 'Fake' or 'duplicate' beneficiaries receive benefits;

(ii) Quantity Fraud: Beneficiaries do not receive their full entitlements; and

(iii) Eligibility Fraud: Ineligible persons receive benefits.

Linking Aadhaar to welfare programmes can help plug Identity Fraud and clean up the beneficiary lists of welfare programmes; however, this has no role to play in identifying Quantity or Eligibility Fraud. Without establishing any credible evidence on the contribution of each of these frauds to total corruption, the notion that Identity Fraud is the culprit has been created. As a result, the citizen has been portrayed as the prime corrupt actor, and State functionaries have been left out of the equation. Recent evidence (discussed further) reveals how unfair this notion is.

It is often claimed that Aadhaar has allowed the government to implement DBT, which basically means the transfer of wages, subsidies, pensions, scholarships, etc., directly from the government into the bank accounts of beneficiaries. But the government had already been doing this long before Aadhaar came into the picture. With the MGNREGA, for instance, wages have been directly transferred to workers' bank accounts since 2011–12 using the National Electronic Fund Transfer (NEFT) system. It was the same with pension payments in various states. The added value of the Aadhaar-enabled Payments System (AePS) over the existing NEFT is questionable. Instead, AePS has brought with it a whole new set of issues related to the fragile payment systems.[9]

In the same vein, it is true that Aadhaar can allow 'portability' of benefits by providing a credible authentication system. For example, a person will be able to receive grain at any PDS shop in the state, and not just the one at which they are officially registered. This will be especially beneficial for the migrant population. However, this is possible even with a smart card system. Additionally, the exclusive discussion on authentication systems obscures the fact that allowing portability of benefits will require the government to put in place a highly sophisticated supply management system to allow ration shops to account for unexpected demand. Aadhaar cannot help much with this, which probably explains why portability has hardly been introduced anywhere.

A reliable digital trail of transactions is essential for the effective implementation of welfare programmes. Besides allowing the government to closely monitor implementation, it is also expected to increase accountability by enabling public scrutiny. The digitisation of muster rolls and PDS records, for instance, was an important step in this direction. The pace of digitisation, however, has been chequered across states. Aadhaar being made mandatory has surely been a catalyst in this process. Take the case of Jharkhand. Starting with eight districts in August 2016, the government digitised the entire PDS with a large majority of ration shops now being enabled with a Point of Sale (PoS) machine with the mandatory Aadhaar-based Biometric Authentication (ABBA). This, however, as we will see, has come at a cost: that coercive Aadhaar seeding, serious exclusion issues, and increased transaction costs. The experience of states like Chhattisgarh and Tamil Nadu, which digitised their PDS even before Aadhaar, point to the fact that such levels of digital sophistication can be achieved by using more reliable and less disruptive technologies.[10] Smart cards, for instance, can generate the same digital trail as Aadhaar without relying on fragile technologies like biometric authentication, the internet, and remote servers.

It can be argued that in some ways, Aadhaar has hampered efficiency in welfare delivery. Aadhaar can lead to what Khera calls the 'displacement' effect—the exclusive focus on Aadhaar (and implicitly on Identity Fraud) distracts administrative focus from other crucial reforms like making application processes more accessible, enforcing a grievance redressal system, reducing payment delays, and curbing bribes and other forms of Quantity Fraud.[11] Importantly, the Aadhaar system has brought with it a high level of centralisation. For instance, despite wanting to help, a ration dealer cannot do much for a genuine beneficiary in the case of authentication failures. The starkest manifestation of this over-centralisation is the recent spate of 25 starvation deaths directly or indirectly attributable to Aadhaar-related exclusions.[12]

The government has put forth various savings figures attributable to Aadhaar based on deletions of 'fake' or 'ghost' beneficiaries; the latest figure is Rs 90,000 crore, while until last year, it was Rs 57,000 crore. These figures, however, can easily be discredited using other sources of government data like RTI responses and responses to questions in Parliament.[13] First, deletions made even before Aadhaar was implemented are counted. With Liquefied Petroleum Gas (LPG), for instance, a large share of the reported Aadhaar-based deletions happened from simple list-based deletions prior to Aadhaar. Second, deletions made for reasons entirely unrelated to Aadhaar, such as death, migration, and voluntary surrender are also attributed to Aadhaar. Third, expenditure reductions resulting from the exclusion of genuine beneficiaries are projected as valuable Aadhaar-enabled savings. For instance, a survey of all deleted pensioners in Khunti town in Jharkhand revealed that close to 35 per cent of all deletions were found to be alive and genuine beneficiaries.[14] Despite various attempts by the public and civil society, the government has refused to release any credible data or methodology to justify these numbers. Another widely cited figure was the one put forth by the World Bank in its *World Development Report 2016*, claiming that Aadhaar could lead to annual savings to the tune of USD 11 billion. Drèze and Khera, however, demonstrate how untenable assumptions and post-hoc calculations were used to arrive at these numbers.[15]

SURVEY OF EVIDENCE

This section presents the available evidence from surveys, ground reports, RTIs, and responses in Parliament to assess Aadhaar's impact on welfare programmes like the PDS, the MGNREGA, and pensions.[16]

Aadhaar and the PDS: Pain without Gain

The past five years or so have seen various state governments mandate ABBA to receive grain entitlements from the PDS every month. By April 2018, more than 80 per cent of the 23.27 crore total ration cards were seeded with Aadhaar numbers, and around 60 per cent of the 5.27 lakh ration shops were installed with Aadhaar-enabled electronic-PoS (e-PoS) devices.[17]

The successful working of ABBA, however, rests on a set of fragile technologies (see Figure 12.1). To begin with, at least one member of the household must link their Aadhaar number to the household ration card. All ration cards not linked to Aadhaar (irrespective of the underlying reasons) are deemed 'fake' and deleted from the list.

The cornerstone of the ABBA system is the PoS machine, installed at each ration shop, which stores the data for all registered ration cards and authenticates a beneficiary by matching their fingerprints with the data stored in the Aadhaar database.

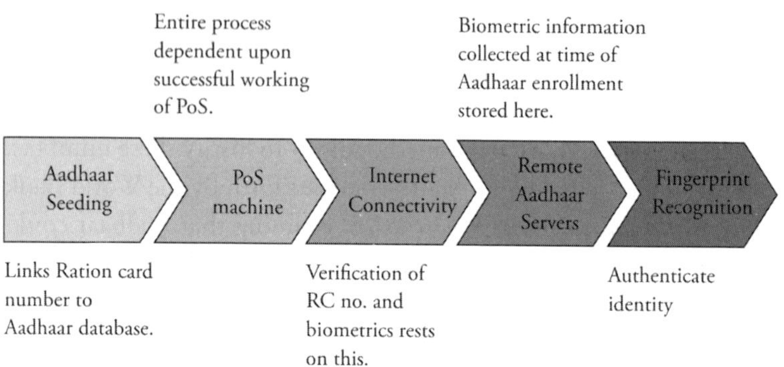

FIGURE 12.1: How ABBA in PDS Works

Source: Created by the author, based on the text of J. Drèze, 'Dark Clouds over the PDS', *The Hindu*, 10 September 2016.

While it is claimed that ABBA has transformed the PDS, all available evidence suggests that Aadhaar has done little to curb existing forms of corruption. Instead, it has led to serious issues of exclusion, disruptions, and increased transaction costs.

The primary form of fraud that Aadhaar can curb is Identity Fraud—ghosts, fakes, and duplicates on the PDS lists. Narendra Modi claimed in the Lok Sabha in 2017 that Aadhaar led to the discovery of nearly four crore 'fake' ration cards. Subsequent RTIs by civil society revealed that the government had no data to back this claim, and neither was the claim correct; the figure was 'retroactively' revised to 2.33 crores.[18] By refusing to release relevant data, the government has made it extremely difficult to assess Aadhaar's contribution to these deletions, which could be for various reasons. However, it is clear that Identity Fraud does not appear to be a serious issue, especially after the clean-up of the PDS lists that occurred with the roll-out of the National Food Security Act, 2013.

Responses by the government to questions in Parliament suggest that a large share of the 2.33 crore deleted ration cards was due to reasons like ineligibility, which are not attributable to Aadhaar.[19] In fact, a state-wise and year-wise breakdown of the deletions reveals that a large share of these deletions occurred before Aadhaar seeding even began in the respective states.[20] A Randomised Controlled Trial (RCT) in Jharkhand by researchers at the Abdul Latif Jameel Poverty Action Lab (J-PAL) found 'essentially no ghost PDS beneficiaries'.[21] In Odisha, government data suggests that Aadhaar was responsible for only 4 per cent of the total deletions made between November 2015 and November 2017, which accounts for less than even 1 per cent of total ration cards in the state.

The main form of corruption in the PDS is not Identity Fraud; instead, it is Quantity Fraud—dealers give beneficiaries less than their entitlement. For instance, instead of giving a household 35 kilograms (kgs) of rice, a dealer only gives them 30 kgs and diverts the rest to the open market. A survey of 900 households in Jharkhand (henceforth the 'Jharkhand-PDS Survey') found that on an average, a household was receiving 93 per cent of its entitlements (conditional upon successful transaction).[22] While this reflects a massive improvement for Jharkhand compared to some years ago, it also shows that Quantity Fraud continues unabated even after ABBA has been made mandatory. The proportion of entitlements being received was identical between sample villages where ABBA was mandatory and where it was not. Other reports find similar results.[23] This is not surprising, given that Aadhaar does nothing to improve the power dynamics between the dealer and the beneficiary. If anything, it skews it in favour of the dealer since only the dealers are aware of the frequently changing rules around Aadhaar and are the ones who direct the beneficiaries through the technological process.

Evidence from various sources suggests that the breakdown of the technological system is leading to the exclusion of beneficiaries. Of the various failure points, two are worth highlighting. First, the entire authentication process relies heavily on stable internet connectivity, which is a serious infrastructure constraint, not only in rural India, but in parts of cities as well. Second, biometric authentication has proved to be far less reliable than initially claimed, especially for the most vulnerable, such as the elderly and manual workers, whose fingerprints have worn out due to age and/or rough manual work. While some of these are cases of temporary failure, there are a few households who face authentication failures repeatedly month after month. Despite certain safeguards like the One-Time Password (OTP) facility being in place, frequent ground reports suggest that the denial of rations is widespread.[24]

The Jharkhand-PDS Survey, which surveyed households that had not transacted in the previous month (non-transacting households), found that in villages where ABBA was mandatory (online villages), close to 13 per cent of such households reported having no 'PoS-able' members—one whose Aadhaar number was seeded and was able to pass the biometric authentication. Often, they were smaller households, elderly couples, or widows, for whom the PDS was a crucial source of security. A fifth of the non-transacting households reported that no PoS-able member was available to collect grains at the time of distribution. This is especially a problem for households where some members temporarily migrate to nearby areas in search of work. About 10 per cent of the households reported that the PoS system did not work; this includes breakdown of the PoS machine, connectivity issues, biometric failures, and error messages. Unstable and erratic internet connectivity was found to be a major issue, with even light rain leading to disruption. Biometric authentication was also a serious issue, a problem, as already stated, that was especially common for manual workers and the elderly. Collectively, these Aadhaar-related issues were reported by close to half the non-transacting households in online villages. Government data suggested that the overall proportion of non-transacting households in the sample online villages in May 2017 was 21 per cent. Extrapolating from the survey, this means that almost 10 per cent of households in online villages were excluded from the PDS due to these issues. In comparison, the overall proportion of non-transacting households in sample offline villages was found to be 4 per cent, of which a much smaller proportion was owing to Aadhaar.

While the government has consistently stated that no person would be deprived of benefits due to Aadhaar, reports of exclusion have continually poured in from various parts of the country. SOAR reports that close to two million households in three states (Andhra Pradesh, Rajasthan, and West Bengal) were excluded from the PDS because of Aadhaar.

Besides outright exclusion, ABBA has also increased transaction costs for households. In cases of authentication failure or technological breakdown, households either wait at the ration shop for extended periods in anticipation of restored connectivity or make additional trips at a later date. The Jharkhand-PDS Survey found that in comparison to offline villages, households in online villages had to, on an average, make half an additional trip and spend 30 per cent more time to receive the grain to which they are entitled. In fact, even among transacting households, 50 per cent reported at least one Aadhaar-related issue. SOAR reports that 40–60 per cent of households in Andhra Pradesh and Rajasthan had to make more than one attempt to successfully authenticate and 2–3 per cent had to make more than three attempts.

While linking Aadhaar with ration cards could help with ration card management, there are hardly any benefits that come with monthly biometric authentication. Instead, for the elderly and the disabled, it has meant that they cannot ask a relative or a neighbour to collect the grain on their behalf, and must personally go to the ration shop every month. Given the mounting evidence on the damaging effects of Aadhaar, it is high time the government reconsiders Aadhaar's role in the PDS.

Dampening the MGNREGA's Demand

The MGNREGA, enacted in 2005, provides a crucial safety net by legally entitling all rural households to 100 days of guaranteed employment every year, especially during periods of rural distress. Households are to be paid within 15 days of work completion as per the pre-defined MGNREGA wage rates. These wage rates generally tend to provide a wage floor in rural areas. Given the labour-intensive nature of the work provided, the MGNREGA has been found to be fairly successful at self-targeting poor households.

During the early days of the MGNREGA, corruption was quite rampant. A main feature of this was Identity Fraud in the form of inflating worker lists (known as muster rolls) by introducing 'ghost' workers. Since wages were paid in cash to workers by the same local officials generating these muster rolls, the excess wages were pocketed by the officials. The digitisation of muster rolls and the transfer of wages directly to bank accounts (which started in 2007–08) led to Identity Fraud being curtailed to a large extent. The bank payment of wages, however, brought with it a persistent issue of payment delays. Further, other forms of corruption (workers forced to receive less than the wages officially credited) continued unabated.

As the integration of Aadhaar with the MGNREGA began, it became clear that the main 'intervention' that came with it was that these payments were made to Aadhaar-linked bank accounts through the AePS instead of the NEFT. The key form of fraud that this was expected to plug was Identity Fraud. In response to an RTI filed by Jean Drèze, the government's own data revealed that of the 94 lakh total job cards deleted in 2016–17, only 12.6 per cent pertained to cases of 'fakes' and 'duplicates'. The rest pertained to other reasons like migration, voluntary surrender, etc., for which Aadhaar could not have played any role. In addition to plugging Identity Fraud, it was claimed that the AePS would make the wage disbursal process more 'efficient'. Yet, till date the benefits resulting from the transition are entirely unclear.

One study by the J-PAL in Andhra Pradesh, based on an randomised control trial (RCT), documents the reduction in corruption through the introduction of biometric-based smart cards. These results are often attributed to Aadhaar, despite the fact that they were based on a system of smart cards unrelated to Aadhaar. Another study by researchers at the Digital Identity Research Initiative (DIRI), the Indian School of Business (ISB), causally claimed that the introduction of Aadhaar leads to increased demand and the allocation of MGNREGA works during periods of drought. These results were, however, found to be based on a gross misunderstanding of the MGNREGA, a set of incorrect assumptions, and a very weak causal mechanism.[25]

Wage payment delays, which have been an issue since bank payments were instituted, have remained very high even after the introduction of Aadhaar.[26] The AePS has brought with it new issues relating to rejected payments, diverted payments, and locked payments.[27] In a similar vein, the SOAR report states that the government's own data suggests that 12 per cent beneficiaries faced authentication failure. Of the surveyed beneficiaries who had used ABBA to withdraw wages, 2.5 per cent reported being unable to do so.

As Jean Drèze has noted, the frequent revisions to the payment system and the constant move in the direction of ever-increasing sophistication is causing the beneficiaries much hardship.[28] The negative effects on demand resulting from the persistent wage payment delays and the added layers of complications related to Aadhaar could have disastrous effects for the MGNREGA, which, by design, is meant to be demand-driven.

Aadhaar and Pension: Denial and Disruptions

Under the National Social Assistance Programme (NSAP), the elderly, widows, and disabled living in poor economic conditions are entitled to monthly social security pensions. These are essentially targeted unconditional cash transfers. Given that the recipients are some of the most vulnerable persons in society, these pensions provide an important source of dignity and economic security.

While these pension schemes are ridden with implementation challenges, such as a complex and opaque selection process and irregular payments, recent research suggests that pensions are performing well in crucial respects—they are targeted progressively,[29] increase consumption and lower poverty,[30] and are highly valued by the recipients.[31] Importantly, there does not appear to be a significant issue of Identity Fraud.[32]

In recent years, many states have made it mandatory for pensioners to link their Aadhaar numbers with the administrative pension lists as well as with bank accounts. It is worth noting that as with the MGNREGA, the primary change that came with Aadhaar was the shift from the NEFT to the AePS. As with other welfare programmes, frequent ground reports have suggested that this has led to exclusion. Analysing the data from the Andhra Pradesh pensions portal, Jain, Khera, and Patibandla estimate that between April 2017 and February 2018, ABBA failed for 6–10 per cent of the beneficiaries each month.[33] Despite having an override in place, the authors report that about 20,000 of the 37.4 lakh total pensioners in the state are excluded every month. Early ground reports from Rajasthan suggested that thousands of alive and genuine pensioners who had failed to link their Aadhaar for various reasons were struck off from pension lists and declared dead.[34] Similar reports of denial have poured in from other states, including Uttarkhand, Jharkhand, Chhattisgarh, Uttar Pradesh (UP), and Andhra Pradesh. In Jharkhand, there have been instances of starvation deaths where pensions were denied or diverted due to Aadhaar-related factors.

In September 2017, the Jharkhand government claimed that Aadhaar seeding had resulted in the deletion of close to three lakh 'fake' pensioners in 2016–17, leading to savings to the tune of Rs 200 crore. Despite attributing these large savings figures to Aadhaar, the government has declined to release any data backing such claims. Soon after this announcement, we conducted a survey in one town (Khunti) to assess Aadhaar's role in these deletions.[35] Contrary to government claims, we found that as upper bounds, only 27 per cent of these deletions were fakes or duplicates; this works out to about 3 per cent of the total pensioners in Khunti town. This further suggests that Identity Fraud in pensions is limited. In fact, the largest share of respondents (35 per cent) reported Aadhaar-related issues resulting in exclusion. Reasons included faulty Aadhaar seeding, inability of the elderly and the disabled to make repeated trips to submit documents, and a general lack of awareness about Aadhaar-related procedures. Some of these persons were able to subsequently get their pensions to resume after making repeated trips to the bank and block offices, but even for them, the 'arrears' were not paid. Not only has the Jharkhand government refused to acknowledge these issues, but it also projects these exclusions and disruptions as valuable Aadhaar-enabled savings.

As it turns out, the government's own data suggests that Identity Fraud is not a serious problem. As was the case with the PDS and the MGNREGA, RTI applications filed by independent researchers reveal that 94 per cent of all deletions pertained to routine and legitimate reasons like death, migration, etc. Only 6 per cent could be cases of Identity Fraud that Aadhaar could have identified.[36]

While the government has continued to assure the public, the Parliament, and the Supreme Court that individuals would not be denied benefits, this is not what is seen on the ground. The denial of the meagre pension amounts of highly vulnerable persons is a grave travesty of justice.

The Myth of Aadhaar Reliability

The Government of India and the UIDAI have repeatedly argued that Aadhaar is the most trusted form of identification. Often, claims are made that by linking Aadhaar to Subscriber Identification Module (SIM) cards and bank accounts, terrorism and banking fraud would be stopped. Such claims stem from the belief that Aadhaar is more reliable than other forms of identification (like Permanent Account Number [PAN] cards, voter IDs, etc.), which can be easily faked, forged, and duplicated. This is important because it is this supposed reliability of Aadhaar that underpins its ability to clean up welfare lists and enable governance reform.

However, emerging evidence raises important questions over the reliability of Aadhaar. In the absence of any official data on the same, I compiled a database of Aadhaar-enabled frauds reported in the English media, which points to the fact that, contrary to the claims of eliminating fraud, Aadhaar has, in fact, enabled a long list of frauds—illegal land transfers, procuring passports, getting loans, casting votes, obtaining other IDs, siphoning off ration grains, etc.[37] In May 2018, the total number of frauds stood at 164.[38] More recent revision pegs the fraud count at around 300. This number is quite surely an underestimate of the true extent of fraud for two main reasons: (i) presumably only a fraction of fraud is caught and hence gets reported; and (ii) the database only relies on the English media, therefore not accounting for cases reported in the regional media (but not in the English media).

The methods involved in these cases varied; the two most common were Aadhaar numbers being issued based on fake or forged documents, and details like name and photograph being forged using rudimentary editing techniques and printers. There continue to be a few instances of Aadhaar enrolment operators misusing their credentials to generate unauthorised Aadhaar numbers.[39] These cases are especially striking since Identity Fraud is precisely what Aadhaar was supposed to put an end to. There have also been a few notable cases of Aadhaar-enabled scams in the PDS of UP and Jharkhand, where local officials and PDS dealers have colluded and exploited loopholes in the Aadhaar system to siphon away large quantities of grains.[40] This compilation of frauds highlights that the paper-based Aadhaar 'card' is highly susceptible to being faked or forged. Yet, today, the Aadhaar 'card' is widely used as an ID for various purposes. Further, it appears that UIDAI does not seem to have a good way of weeding out fake documents at the enrolment stage, as stated by a UIDAI official himself.[41] Both of these issues were noted by the Calcutta High Court in a recent judgment.[42] These are worrying signs for the reliability of Aadhaar.

Conclusion

Technology can surely be a tool of inclusion and empowerment, but Aadhaar's experience with welfare programmes highlights that this is possible only when the technological design is user-friendly and stable, and is rolled out and implemented in a cautious manner. As the NDA-II government's current tenure comes to an end, it is clear that just like *Achhe Din,* the Aadhaar 'revolution' is far from near. But given the publicity machinery deployed by the government and the UIDAI, one would be tempted to believe that Aadhaar has done wonders by empowering the citizen. In reality, as the evidence shows, Aadhaar is an example of 'how-not-to' design public policy. Without doing any serious damage to corruption, Aadhar has led to the exclusion and disempowerment of often the most vulnerable citizens. A recent survey of 325 households from a Particularly Vulnerable Tribal Group (PVTG) in Jharkhand revealed that more than 40 per cent of the households had faced some form of exclusion due to Aadhaar—ration cards cancelled, discontinued pensions, refusal of school admissions, etc.[43]

Despite mounting evidence of technological failures at various points in the system, it is unfortunate that the Supreme Court did not critically examine the government's assertions about Aadhaar's role in welfare. As a consequence, ironically, Aadhaar remains mandatory for welfare, where it has tangibly caused the most serious damage.

Notes and References

1. The author would like to thank Reetika Khera and Rob Sampson for their thoughtful comments on an earlier draft of this chapter.

2. 'Nandan Nilekani's Aadhaar project a political gimmick with no vision: Narendra Modi', *Economic Times*, 9 April 2014. Available at https://economictimes.indiatimes.com/news/politics-and-nation/nandan-nilekanis-aadhaar-project-a-political-gimmick-with-no-vision-narendra-modi/articleshow/33469354.cms (accessed February 2019).

3. World Bank, *World Development Report 2016* (Washington, D.C.: World Bank, 2016); J. Drèze and R. Khera, 'Aadhaar's $11-bn Question: The Numbers being Touted by Govt have No Solid Basis', *Economic Times*, 8 February 2018.

4. R. Khera, 'Introduction', in R. Khera (ed.), *Dissent on Aadhaar: Big Data Meets Big Brother* (New Delhi: Orient BlackSwan, 2019), 4.

5. For an early discussion of Aadhaar's role in welfare, see R. Khera, 'The UID Project and Welfare Schemes', *Economic and Political Weekly* 46 (9), 2011, 38–43.

6. R. Abraham, E. Bennett, R. Bhusal, et al., 'State of Aadhaar Report 2017–18', IDinsight, 2018.

7. The proportion was higher for West Bengal at 26 per cent.

8. '20 lakh people from 3 states denied ration due to #Aadhaar; Savings claim also doubtful: Report', MoneyLife Digital Team, 18 May 2018. Available at https://www.moneylife.in/article/20-lakh-people-from-3-states-denied-ration-due-to-aadhaar-savings-claims-also-doubtful-report/54087.html (accessed February 2019).

9. For a discussion on the pervasive effects of the AePS in the MGNREGA and pension payment systems in Jharkhand, see J. Drèze, 'Done by Aadhaar', *The Telegraph*, 30 August 2018.

10. For a discussion on these 'smarter' alternatives to Aadhaar, see R. Khera, 'Smarter than Aadhaar: Government's Insistence on Disruptive Option is Bewildering', *Business Standard*, 14 March 2018.

11. R. Khera, 'Impact of Aadhaar on Welfare Programmes', *Economic and Political Weekly* 50 (16), 2017, 68.

12. The Wire Staff, 'Of 42 "Hunger-Related" Deaths Since 2017, 25 "Linked to Aadhaar Issues"', *The Wire*, 21 September 2018.

13. Ibid.

14. R. Malhotra and A. Somanchi, 'Pension Tension: Aadhaar and Social Assistance in Jharkhand', *Economic and Political Weekly* 53 (36), 2018, 35.

15. Drèze and Khera, 'Aadhaar's $11-bn Question'.

16. For a comprehensive assessment, see Khera, 'Impact of Aadhaar on Welfare Programmes'.

17. Government of India, 'Lok Sabha Unstarred Question No 5786', 2018. Available at http://164.100.47.190/loksabhaquestions/annex/14/AU5786.pdf.

18. G. V. Bhatnagar, 'Did Modi Mislead Parliament on the Number of Fake Ration Cards that Aadhaar Had Exposed?', *The Wire*, 9 August 2017.

19. Khera, 'Impact of Aadhaar on Welfare Programmes'.

20. Government of India, 'Lok Sabha Starred Question No. 93', 2016. Available at http://164.100.47.190/loksabhaquestions/annex/10/AS93.pdf

21. K. Muralidharan, P. Neihaus, and S. Sukhtankar, 'Balancing the Costs and Benefits of Aadhaar', *LiveMint*, 6 March 2018.

22. J. Drèze, N. Khalid, R. Khera, et al., 'Aadhaar and Food Security in Jharkhand: Pain without Gain', *Economic and Political Weekly* 50 (16), 2017, 55.

23. For Jharkhand, see Muralidharan, et al., 'Balancing the Costs and Benefits of Aadhaar'; for Gujarat, see A. Yadav, 'Can Biometrics Stop the Theft of Food Rations? No, Shows Gujarat', *Scroll.in*, 17 December 2016; for Rajasthan, see R. Khera, 'Four Videos That Show Why Rajasthan Needs to Desperately Fix Its Public Distribution System', *Scroll.in*, 9 March 2017.

24. 'Denial of food ration due to #Aadhaar significant: Report', IANS, 17 May 2018. Available at https://www.moneylife.in/article/denial-of-food-ration-due-to-aadhaar-significant-report/54077.html (accessed February 2019).

25. S. Dhorajiwala and R. Narayanan, 'An Imaginary Friend', *The Indian Express*, 1 November 2018.

26. R. Narayanan, S. Dhorajiwala, and R. Golani, 'Analysis of Payment Delays and Delay Compensation in NREGA—Findings across Ten States for Financial Year 2017–18', Azim Premji University, Working Paper, 2. Available at https://azimpremjiuniversity.edu.in/SitePages/pdf/PaymentDelayAnalysisWorkingPaper-2018.pdf.

27. J. Drèze, 'Hollowing Out a Promise', *The Indian Express*, 13 July 2018.

28. Ibid.

29. P. Dutta, R. Murgai, and S. Howes, 'Small but Effective: India's Targeted Unconditional Cash Transfers', *Economic and Political Weekly* 52 (25), 2010, 66.

30. Neeraj Kaushal, 'How Public Pension Affects Elderly Labour Supply and Well-being: Evidence from India', *World Development* 56, 2014, 214–25.

31. S. Chopra and J. Pudussery, 'Social Security Pensions in India: An Assessment', *Economic and Political Weekly* 49 (19), 2012, 73.

32. J. Drèze and R. Khera, 'Recent Social Security Initiatives in India', *World Development* 98 (C), 2017, 555–72.

33. A. Jain, R. Khera, and V. Patibandla, 'Does IT Work? Information Technology (IT) in Welfare in India', Working Paper, 2019.

34. A. Yadav, 'Rajasthan's Living Dead: Thousands of Pensioners without Aadhaar or Bank Accounts Struck Off Lists', *Scroll.in*, 6 August 2016.

35. Malhotra and Somanchi, 'Pension Tension'.

36. I. Sabhikhi, 'How have Social Security Pensions Progressed over the Past Five Years?', Centre for Budget and Governance Accountability, 2018.

37. A. Somanchi, 'Aadhaar Fraud is Not Only Real, But is Worth More Closely Examining', *The Wire*, 3 May 2018.

38. A. Saldanha, '164 Aadhaar-Related Frauds Reported Since 2011, Most in 2018: New Database', IndiaSpend, 23 May 2018. Available at https://www.indiaspend.com/164-aadhaar-related-frauds-reported-since-2011-most-in-2018-new-database-81967/.

39. A. Arora and V. Kumar, 'SBI Alleges Aadhaar Data Misuse, UIDAI Rubbishes Charge', *The Times of India*, 29 January 2019.

40. For UP, see R. Dua, 'Aadhaar Data "Edited" to Pilfer Public Distribution System Ration in UP', *The Times of India*, 26 August 2018; for Jharkhand, see D. Sarkar, 'PDS Scam Busted: 7 Dealers and SIM Card Seller in Police Net', *Hindustan Times*, 31 December 2018.

41. R. K. Rajasekaran, 'Aadhaar Racket: 2 Accused Involved in Enrolment Project', *The Times of India*, 22 October 2018.

42. A. Kini, 'Calcutta HC Questions Non-Verification of Declarations Made During Aadhaar Enrollment', *Live Law*, 5 January 2019. Available at https://www.livelaw.in/news-updates/non-verification-of-declarations-aadhaar-enrollment-141897.

43. J. Drèze, 'Invisible People: Aadhaar Versus Particularly Vulnerable Tribal Groups', *The Telegraph*, 24 December 2018.

thirteen

The NDA-II Government's Foreign and Security Policy

A Critical Assessment

Happymon Jacob

Introduction

Notwithstanding the sound and fury surrounding the Narendra Modi-led Bharatiya Janata Party (BJP) government's foreign policy over the past four years, a close examination of India's foreign policy since 2014 would show that it has been a major disappointment. In the past four-and-a-half years, New Delhi has failed to find a détente with China, its relationship with Pakistan has nosedived, its neighbourhood policy has been an unprecedented failure, and the NDA-II government's national security management has been subpar. The NDA-II government's foreign policy has also been greatly influenced by its Right-wing cultural nationalist agenda. In an effort to pursue a pro-US foreign policy, both to be a junior partner of the greatest military power and because of its ideological affinity with the US foreign policy discourse on 'Islamic' terror, India has drifted away from its old allies. But even more importantly, the government has exhibited a clear inability to ideate on India's foreign policy and strategic trajectories; and when it tried, it ended up rupturing the country's foreign policy traditions.

This chapter will expand these arguments. To do so, I divide the chapter into six sections. I will begin with a discussion on how ideological/cultural predilections have trumped the country's national interests during the NDA-II government's tenure. The second section attempts to analyse the government's ability to balance India's relationship with the great powers in the international system. The third section discusses how the government has gone about (mis)managing India's national security. Section four deals with India's relationship with one of its key neighbours, Pakistan. The two subsequent sections deal with an assessment of the BJP government's China policy, and how it fared vis-à-vis the neighbourhood.

IDEOLOGY TRUMPS POLICY

A cursory glance at the NDA-II government's foreign policy shows that there is an ideological desire to distance itself from the past—broadly Nehruvian—intellectual structures of India's foreign policy, and to replace the normative underpinnings of India's foreign policy with an emphasis on aggression and political Hinduism.

Prime Minister Modi's official visits abroad have often been steeped in Hindu religious symbolism. Clad in saffron attire, wearing a rudraksh garland and sandal paste smeared on his forehead, the religious symbolism of Modi's visit to the Pashupatinath temple during his first visit to Nepal in 2014 was spectacular, if not prime ministerial. However, the development of a potential Hindu religious plank in Indo-Nepal relations, a key piece in the Sangh Parivar's long-cherished dream, was sabotaged by the events thereafter, including India's 'unofficial' economic blockade of Nepal in 2015. Similarly, when Modi visited Abu Dhabi in 2015, the United Arab Emirates (UAE) government announced the allocation of land for the UAE capital's first Hindu temple. The Ministry of External Affairs (MEA) tweeted, 'A long wait for the Indian community ends. On the occasion of PM's visit, UAE Govt decides to allot land for building a temple in Abu Dhabi',[1] with Modi following up with a similar tweet.

These tweets were not in keeping with the secular traditions of India's foreign policy engagements.

Yet another example is the manner in which New Delhi has gone way beyond the legitimate exercise of engaging the Indian diaspora to enthusiastically promoting overseas Hindutva/Sangh outfits for ideological ends, couched in sophisticated foreign policy showbiz. The outright enlisting of Rashtriya Swayamsevak Sangh (RSS)-affiliated organisations, such as the Overseas Friends of BJP (OFBJP) and the Hindu Swayamsevak Sangh (HSS), for the government's foreign policy pursuits and other official purposes can only be termed as attempts at saffronising our secular foreign policy. Several events in the prime minister's official visits, as well as official functions of the Indian State abroad, are organised by HSS/RSS/OFBJP activists, in collaboration with the Ministry of External Affairs (MEA) and the Indian Embassy. While these activists are indeed members of the Indian diaspora, they only represent one fragment of it, and that too, a communal one.

New Delhi's new refugee policy is also seemingly premised on a religious orientation. In January 2018, the Central government informed the Supreme Court, 'We don't want India to become a refugee capital', even as the Border Security Force (BSF) had been pushing back Rohingya refugees from the eastern borders.[2] Its approach to the Rohingya crisis (that is, its refusal to admit people fleeing for their lives into the country, or to ask Myanmar to address the human rights violations against its Rohingya population) is informed by religious considerations.

The BJP's 2014 election manifesto was unequivocal in stating that 'India shall remain a natural home for persecuted Hindus and they shall be welcome to seek refuge here.'[3] The party followed up on its promise when it came to power by proposing the controversial Citizenship (Amendment) Bill, 2016, to amend the country's citizenship laws, suggesting that Hindus, Sikhs, Jains, Parsis, and Christians entering India from Afghanistan, Bangladesh, and Pakistan not be considered 'illegal immigrants'—no word on Muslims here! While on the one hand, this appeases the communal vote banks in mainland India, the move also could potentially enhance the BJP's electoral fortunes in the north-eastern borderlands on the other, since the proposed law could alter the voter demographics in the region to the BJP's advantage. To get a more complete picture, this should be read together with the recently passed Enemy Property (Amendment and Validation) Bill, 2016, which could potentially dispossess many Muslim families of their inherited property.

Great Power Balancing that Went Awry

While on the one side the BJP-led government's narrow and skewed religious–nationalist agenda has dominated its foreign policy, on the other, it has not been adept at balancing the various poles in the global system, as would be expected of a mature power.

Despite the NDA-II government's early efforts to maintain a fine balance between India's relations with Iran on the one hand and with the US, Israel, and Saudi Arabia on the other, the policy has not been successful, especially due to its unwillingness to go against Washington's desires. In fact, India's grand plans of accessing Central Asia via Iran continue to be frustrated with the return of American sanctions against Iran.[4] India also had to abandon the Iran–Pakistan–India pipeline in 2008 due to US sanctions against Iran. US President Donald Trump's decision to withdraw from the Joint Comprehensive Plan of Action (JCPOA), popularly called the Iran nuclear deal, is also bound to have serious implications for the international system, and for India. A more unstable West Asia would automatically mean more difficult choices for New Delhi. More conflict in the region would adversely impact the welfare and safety of Indian expatriates in West Asia, leading to a sharp decline in the remittances they send home, and an assured hike in oil prices. Low crude oil prices had given India the much-needed economic cushion in the past few years—and that phase has now ended. We can recall how the US war on Iraq had a debilitating impact on Indian workers and the West Asian remittances.

Given that there is little consensus around Trump's withdrawal from the JCPOA, several of the dissenting parties might look for ways to thwart US efforts towards isolating Iran. Such efforts, especially those led by China and Russia, both parties to the JCPOA, would have implications for the Southern Asian region as well. If indeed China manages to bring together a group of regional powers, including Russia, Iran, Pakistan, and interested others to counter Washington's influence in the region, New Delhi might find itself in a corner.

India–US Relations

The most recent India–US 2+2 meeting in September 2018 appeared to be a singularly one-sided affair with Washington calling the shots, and New Delhi trying to wriggle out of US pressure without much success. For instance, the US not only insisted that India should bring down its oil imports from Iran to 'zero' in deference to the restrictions imposed by its unilateral withdrawal from the Iran nuclear deal, but also recommended that India buy American oil to make up the deficit. US oil exports to India have more than doubled in the past year, thanks to fears about US sanctions, thereby helping a booming domestic crude oil industry. Notably, at the meeting, the Indian side did not manage to get a waiver for importing Iranian crude oil.

Second, Washington seeks to impose the punitive provisions of a US federal law called Countering America's Adversaries Through Sanctions Act (CAATSA) on countries dealing with the Russian defence and intelligence sectors, making it difficult for India to buy the much-needed S-400 missile system. Given that close to 60 per cent of India's weapons systems originate from Russia, this would be a huge setback. Again, it is clear that the US would like India to buy its weapons instead.

India has recently signed the Communications Compatibility and Security Agreement (COMCASA) and the Logistics Exchange Memorandum of Agreement (LEMOA) with the US in 2016, and a third, the Basic Exchange and Cooperation Agreement for Geo-spatial Cooperation (BECA), is yet to be negotiated. These agreements are considered to be 'foundational' for a viable India–US military relationship. The argument in favour of signing these is that they will facilitate access to advanced defence systems. In the absence of the COMCASA and the attendant high-tech equipment, the interoperability between the Indian and US forces would be severely hampered.

By signing the COMCASA and by agreeing to reduce the purchase of Russian weapons systems (in line with the CAATSA), India has implicitly accepted the extraterritorial application of US law on itself. Although the original End-Use Monitoring Agreement (EUMA) was agreed between India and the US in 2009, New Delhi has now taken the application of US federal law on India to a completely new level. EUMA had reportedly ensured that US inspectors would stay away from Indian bases. There are several such concerns which cannot be answered, given that the India-specific COMCASA is not a public document, and therefore we do not know the scope of the agreement.

A related concern is whether the installation of US communication systems would compromise the secrecy of Indian military communication systems. Most importantly, it might be useful to debate the utility of such India–US agreements since, at the end of the day, the two countries are not likely to be deployed alongside each other in a conflict situation. The argument here is not that India should not make use of American assistance in strengthening its national security, but that there should be more clarity on what it entails.

Even though the 'Joint Statement on the Inaugural India–US 2+2 Ministerial Dialogue' did not explicitly mention China, the section on the Indo-Pacific region implicitly referred to it. There is no denying the fact that the 'China threat' is one of the major talking points between Washington and New Delhi today. While China is indeed a challenge, there is only so much that India–US cooperation can do to address this challenge for India.

China is not a time-tested friend of New Delhi, but Russia is. By forging a historically unprecedented partnership with the US, the NDA-II government has alienated Moscow (driving it in turn towards Islamabad and Beijing), prompting Beijing to up the ante against India in the neighbourhood, and frustrated India's possible land access to Central Asia via Iran and Afghanistan.

NATIONAL SECURITY IN THE DOLDRUMS

National security management under the BJP-led National Democratic Alliance (NDA) regime can be best described as the management of systemic inefficiency, with the institutional and ideational foundations of the country's national security architecture having become weaker since the new government took charge in 2014.

In fact, strengthening national security was one of the major electoral planks the BJP used in the run-up to the 2014 parliamentary elections. In its 2014 election manifesto, the party promised to reform the National Security Council (NSC), revamp the intelligence-gathering system, ensure greater participation of the armed forces in decision-making processes, and revise and update India's nuclear doctrine. A factual analysis shows that the NDA-II government's performance on each of these stated goals has been grossly incompetent. There has been no attempt so far to reform or strengthen the country's national security institutions, articulate a much-needed grand strategic approach to national security, and legislate on important national security matters. Despite all its pre-election rhetoric on national security and the grandstanding on securing and strengthening the nation, the BJP government's approach to national security was less than satisfactory.

Modi's presidential style hampered key institutions of national security management, which traditionally functioned on the basis of regular deliberations, briefings, and constant assessment of threat scenarios by experts, both internal and external. For instance, the

NSC, comprising the members of the Cabinet Committee on Security (CCS) and the National Security Advisor (NSA), hardly ever meets to take stock of the security environment. The National Security Advisory Board (NSAB), initially set up by the Vajpayee government to seek 'outside expertise' on strategic matters, is today a space for retired officials. With deliberative mechanisms such as the NSAB and NSC not functioning as they were set up to, the country's national security management is virtually a 'two-man' show based out of the Prime Minister's Office (PMO). As a result, there is little fresh thinking within the government or perspective planning on the country's national security or defence.

In terms of the nuclear strategy as well, despite a number of doctrinal inadequacies that need to be addressed and corrected, the government is showing little interest. The Manmohan Singh government had created a highly specialised Strategy Programme Staff 'to work on a perspective plan for India's nuclear deterrent in accordance with a 10-year cycle'.[5] There are legitimate concerns today about the mandate of this body, and how empowered it is to deliberate, strategise, and engage in strategic nuclear planning. The more India's nuclear strategy remains unarticulated, the less political control there will be.

This issue about the political control of nuclear forces becomes even more worrying with the arrival of India's first nuclear-powered ballistic missile submarine (SSBN) with nuclear-tipped missiles. Not only would the SSBN have no warhead control by civilians (that is, Bhabha Atomic Research Centre [BARC] scientists), but its captain would also be under the Strategic Forces Command, an organisation manned by military officers. Also, given that the warhead would be pre-mated with the canisterised missiles in the SSBN, the SSBN captain would have the authority to launch nuclear missiles on orders from the political authority. However, is there a foolproof Permissive Action Links system in place to ensure that an unauthorised use does not take place? There needs to be more clarity on such issues.

The intelligence agencies, that is, the Intelligence Bureau (IB) and the Research and Analysis Wing (RAW), which collect and process raw intelligence and provide policy inputs to the government, are short-staffed at every level. The agencies clearly need a lot more trained personnel today than ever before due to the complexity of challenges and threats that the country faces. These organisations, in short, face a number of challenges today in terms of a shortage of sophisticated equipment, inadequate training and staffing, and promotion and career prospects for non-Indian Police Service officers. However, nothing has been done by the NDA-II government to fulfil their promise to 'completely revamp the intelligence gathering system by modernising the intelligence department'.[6]

Another key post-26/11 institution that is in trouble today is the National Intelligence Grid (NATGRID). Created to function as a metadata intelligence grid by networking multiple datasets available with various agencies, the NATGRID is neither fully operational nor given adequate importance—it did not even have a full-time chief for a considerable period after the NDA-II government took over, indicating how the government preferred to deal with it.

India spends close to USD 50 billion annually on defence and yet there are serious concerns about the level of our defence preparedness. Notwithstanding the feel-good rhetoric about the Indian Army's readiness to fight a 'two-and-a-half front war', India might be ill-equipped to fight the wars of the modern age. One reason for this lies in our almost non-functional higher defence organisation. The demand for reforms in India's higher defence management is a long standing one and has been recommended by the Kargil Review Committee (1999), the Group of Ministers' (GoM) report (2000), and the Naresh Chandra Task Force (2012). One key recommendation of these reports has been to create the post of the Chief of Defence Staff as a single, authoritative source of military advice to the government, which was never seriously considered by this government.

Today, India's defence policy is on auto-pilot with hardly any political oversight or vision. There is little conversation between the armed forces and the political class, and even less conversation among the various arms of the forces. Besides setting up or revamping bureaucratic committees, there is little talk about serious defence reforms in the country. One of the most critical lacunae in our defence management is the absence of 'jointness' in the Indian armed forces. Our doctrines, command structures, force deployments, and defence acquisition continue as though each arm is going to fight a future war on its own.

Indeed, a number of Parliamentary Standing Committee reports have also expressly supported the need for military coordination. Even the key post of military advisor in the National Security Council Secretariat (NSCS) remains vacant. In 2018, the government did set up the Defence Planning Committee (DPC) and also decided to revive the Strategic Policy Group (SPG) within the overall NSC system. However, the government seems to mistakenly think that by having the NSA as chair, the SPG and DPC will take care of the fundamental problems in the country's higher defence sector. The post of the NSA is not legally mandated, and one might rightly wonder how an unelected and retired official with no parliamentary accountability has come to occupy such a crucial position in the country's national security decision-making, and whether this is healthy in a parliamentary democracy.

All that the SPG and DPC would achieve is to further bureaucratise the national security decision-making and centralise all national security powers under the PMO. Top-heavy systems hardly work well unless supported by a well-oiled institutional mechanism. There is some hope that these committees would take a close, hard look at the state of modernisation and domestic defence industry in the country, both of which are in a sorry state. Under the present system, where the ratio of revenue to capital expenditure in defence is roughly 65 to 35, any serious attempt at modernisation would be impossible.

AGGRESSION THAT BACKFIRED—PAKISTAN

Relations with Pakistan, one way or another, is one of India's most crucial bilateral relationships. While acknowledging the fact that

Indo-Pak relations have never been great except for short periods, the NDA-II government's Pakistan policy has been particularly directionless, lacked clarity, and has had little vision. As a result, the violence in Jammu and Kashmir and on the Line of Control (LoC) with Pakistan has increased exponentially since 2014.

In 2018, the violence in the Jammu and Kashmir stretch of the India–Pakistan border reached a new high: more than 2,140 Ceasefire Violations (CFVs) by Pakistan were reported by New Delhi, which claimed the lives of 30 civilians and 29 soldiers. Many more have been injured and several civilian habitats along the border destroyed. Until the first week of March 2018, Pakistan reported 2,350 CFVs by India, which had claimed 36 civilian lives (there is no data on Pakistani military casualties). Since 2014, terror attacks on India have increased and infiltration across the Indo-Pak border in Jammu and Kashmir has also gone up.

The 2016 surgical strikes have added fuel to this violent mix. The India–Pakistan escalation ladder has become far more precarious today than it has ever been in the past one-and-a-half decades, that is, since the ceasefire was agreed to in 2003. The recurrent, and almost daily occurrence of border battles between the two militaries in Jammu and Kashmir today have a worrying potential for escalation to higher levels. As is evident from the data from the past 15 years, the border stand-offs often lead to military, political, and diplomatic escalation, as well as contribute to heightening an ongoing crisis.

While this was common even prior to the surgical strikes, the September 2016 operation has made CFVs more worrisome in at least two ways: first, Pakistan has been retaliating ever since the surgical strikes by increasing the pressure on the frontlines; and second, surgical strikes have reduced the critical (psychological) distance between CFVs and conventional military escalation below the nuclear redline. The potentially widening space for conventional aggression is bad news for regional stability.

Despite the rise in violence, the NDA-II government has been unwilling to heed to calls from Pakistan to engage in a dialogue process, clearly with an electoral purpose in mind. There is no doubt that we have a Pakistan problem, but the question is, how do we deal with it—with aggression or with diplomacy and negotiations? Clearly, the former has not worked, and the BJP government has little interest in the latter, as is evidenced by its reluctance to respond to repeated Pakistani calls for talks.

The 14 February terrorist attack in South Kashmir's Pulwama by Pakistan-based Jaish-e-Mohammed (JeM), which killed over 40 Indian CRPF personnel, has once again triggered fears of an India-Pakistan armed escalation. While the Pakistani State's refusal to take decisive action against JeM operating from its soil needs to be called out, it must also be noted that the BJP-led government's political failure in Kashmir has provided the broader context of violence in which terrorist attacks have become routine today.

DEALING WITH A RISING CHINA

Pressure from China is on the rise and the NDA-II government may have mismanaged its relationship with Beijing. While the government valiantly claims that the standoff at Doklam conveyed to China that India is no pushover, the reality is that the Chinese forces (by all accounts including a report of the Parliamentary Standing Committee on External Affairs) are back in the Doklam plateau with greater force. The report goes on to fault the government for 'continuing with its conventionally deferential foreign policy towards China'.[7] Clearly, the government has been unable to assess and manage a rising China in the neighbourhood.

The current Indian strategies to 'checkmate' China seem more zero-sum and less efficient. New Delhi has chosen to adopt an unequivocal US-centric strategy to deal with Beijing, most recently the Quadrilateral Security Dialogue (Quad).[8] There are several problems with this approach: the US is a quickly receding extra-regional power whose long-term commitment to the region is increasingly indeterminate and unsure; US–China relations are far more complex than we generally assume; and Australia is caught between the US and China. While India may have shed its traditional reticence about a strategic partnership with the US, it would still not, nor should it, be what Japan is to the US.

The second broad policy direction seems to be to compete with China for regional influence in South Asia. Let us be realistic: trying to match the powerful yuan, backed by vigorous political support from Beijing, with our humble rupee is a losing battle. Military preparedness to offset any potential Chinese aggression is something that India can and should invest in, but cannot address as the main concern. India's central concern has not really been Chinese military aggression, but a China-dominated region in which India is hemmed in and forced to play second fiddle.

Some have suggested that India should use its USD 70 billion-strong trading relationship with China as a bargaining chip to check Chinese behaviour. However, doing so would hurt both sides. While it is true that India–China bilateral trade is heavily skewed in favour of China, we should not forget that China's exports to India comprise under 3 per cent of its total exports (and India's exports to China constitutes 3.6 per cent of its total exports). Boycotting Chinese goods would also mean Indian consumers paying more to get them from elsewhere. Clearly, trade as a bargaining chip vis-à-vis China is just a popular urban myth.

So what, then, are our options? Adopting a straightforward balancing strategy (which is what States normally do when faced with a stronger neighbour) may become costly, counter-productive, and not deliver the desired results. Bandwagoning (jumping on board the wave of the future, in this case, China), on the other hand, may be both undesirable and insufficient for obvious reasons. Neither of these two mutually exclusive options are ideal for serving India's current and future interests vis-à-vis China. Hence, New Delhi would be better served by adopting a more nuanced balancing strategy, that is, a strategy of 'smart-balancing', towards Beijing— one that involves deep engagements and, at the same time, a carefully calibrated balancing.

India–China relations have been under great stress in recent years, especially since 2014. The 2017 military standoff at the

Doklam tri-junction and the war of words that followed vitiated a relationship that was already reeling under a great deal of pressure. The India–China Informal Summit at Wuhan, 2018 should be viewed in the context of this vitiated atmosphere and a strong desire for stability and rapprochement.

The summit's outcomes may have been limited, but are very valuable to stabilise the relationship. The most significant outcome pertains to the contested border. The two countries have realised that local military activities on the border and tactical factors can have strategic and political implications—and that not everything that happens on the India–China border between the two militaries is politically sanctioned. That border tensions, which often occur without the explicit directives of the central leaderships, can potentially derail the relationship is an important realisation, and the two sides should be credited for addressing it.

For sure, this is not a new realisation. In 2013, New Delhi and Beijing signed the Border Defence Cooperation Agreement, which aimed at maintaining peace along the Line of Actual Control (LAC). In 2015, during Modi's visit to China, the two countries agreed on further measures, many of which, however, have not yet been implemented, most notably, the hotline between the two military headquarters.

Notwithstanding the positive outcome of the Wuhan Summit, it must be asked whether the summit has come too late in Modi's term as prime minister to herald a new beginning between India and China, especially on the border question. China watchers argue that the broad contours of an India–China border agreement have been worked out during the 20 rounds of talks at the Special Representatives level. However, an agreement can only be reached at a higher political level. Given his hyper-nationalist credentials, Modi could not have taken that gamble.

The MEA's reactive diplomacy is unable to see the wood for the trees in its relations with Beijing. How does, for instance, designating Masood Azhar a terrorist become India's core interest vis-à-vis China?

Should we allow a terror-monger to determine our relationship with one of our biggest trading partners?

Unfriendly Neighbourhood

The BJP-led NDA-II government's neighbourhood policy, which began exceptionally well with Modi's glamorous tour of the region soon after his equally glamorous swearing-in, has not only managed to make more enemies than friends in the region in such a surprisingly short span of time, but has also gone, in letter and spirit, against the eloquent promises made by the party in its election manifesto:

> BJP believes that political stability, progress and peace in the region are essential for South Asia's growth and development. The Congress-led UPA [United Progressive Alliance] has failed to establish enduring friendly and cooperative relations with India's neighbours. India's relations with traditional allies have turned cold. India and its neighbours have drifted apart. The absence of statecraft has never been felt so acutely as today.[9]

Save for Bhutan and perhaps Bangladesh, much of South Asia has major grievances against New Delhi today. Clearly, then, there is something fundamentally wrong with the BJP-led government's neighbourhood diplomacy. While New Delhi's not-so-friendly relationship with Islamabad is unsurprising, what has provoked the other countries, some of which figured very high on Modi's bilateral priorities, to suddenly come out openly against India?

One of the major reasons for India's growing unpopularity in the regional capitals is its increasing tendency to interfere in the domestic affairs of its smaller neighbours, either citing security implications, or to offset the target country's unfriendly strategic choices. Take the case of Nepal, for instance. New Delhi was deeply upset with the Constitution passed by the Nepalese Constituent Assembly in September 2015. Its unhappiness resulted from the legitimate feeling among the people of Terai, especially the Madhesis and Tharus, living close to Uttar Pradesh and Bihar, that they have been short-changed by the country's new Constitution. But a substantive political argument was thwarted by poor diplomatic style.

The problematic part was twofold: the manner in which New Delhi publicly expressed its displeasure with Nepal's sovereign act of Constitution-drafting; and the manner in which India allegedly abetted the Madhesi blockade of essential supplies to Nepal. In response to the blockade, Kathmandu complained to the United Nations (UN), prompting its Secretary-General to highlight 'Nepal's right of free transit, as a landlocked nation as well as for humanitarian reasons'.[10] India's Nepal 'diplomacy' did not stop there: in late 2018, New Delhi is widely reported to have played a role in attempting to topple the K. P. Sharma Oli regime in Kathmandu.[11]

While the current Nepalese Constitution is far from perfect, it is for the various political factions in Nepal to debate and resolve their differences: it is certainly not for New Delhi to thrust good sense upon Kathmandu. Second, aiding the imposition of a blockade on Nepal, which had a large-scale humanitarian impact, is an unwarranted coercion on a friendly neighbour. Third, playing even a minor role to topple a democratically elected regime in Nepal is unmistakably reprehensible.

India's public statements about Nepal's Constitution have been neither smart nor diplomatic. The MEA's statement on Nepal, that 'We had repeatedly cautioned the political leadership of Nepal to take urgent steps to defuse the tension in these regions', was undoubtedly patronising and undiplomatic.[12] Because of our unimaginative diplomacy with Nepal, Kathmandu today has an ever-stronger bilateral partnership with China. Since then, regimes have changed in Nepal, but its journey towards Beijing continues unabated, to the detriment of India's national interests.

If New Delhi's Mission Kathmandu was both a failure and distasteful, its 'subtle interference' in Sri Lanka in the run-up to the island nation's elections in 2015 has set a dangerous precedent. New Delhi had proactively promoted the coalition led by Maithripala Sirisena to defeat the then Sri Lankan President Mahinda Rajapaksa, whose anti-Tamil record and pro-China tilt it resented. Several reports at the time claimed that Colombo had asked New Delhi to withdraw the RAW's station chief in Sri Lanka for allegedly working to ensure the victory of the anti-Rajapaksa coalition.[13]

While involving ourselves in regime changes in the neighbourhood is a bad idea in the long run, we must ask whether the regime change in Colombo has actually prompted it to declare itself pro-India. The new developments in Sri Lanka suggest that the Chinese tilt of Colombo is far from over.

The Maldives, yet another traditional ally of ours, has also been resentful of Indian reactions to its domestic political developments. New Delhi, being highly critical of how the former pro-India Maldivian President Mohamed Nasheed was jailed by the current regime under terrorism charges, publicly stated that 'We are concerned at recent developments in the Maldives, including the arrest and manhandling of former President Nasheed.' The Maldivian government responded by saying it hoped that India would 'adhere to the principle of Panchsheel and will not intervene in domestic politics of Maldives'.[14]

During Minister of External Affairs Sushma Swaraj's visit to the Maldives in October 2015, Maldivian President Abdulla Yameen's office issued a sharply worded statement that his 'government will not tolerate foreign parties interfering with the country's domestic issues'.[15] Furthermore, the Maldives also strengthened its engagement with China, which has gladly been offering economic and infrastructural assistance to Male. Things have taken a positive turn for New Delhi in Male, owing more to the domestic political processes in Male than to the NDA-II government's subtle diplomacy.

In June 2013, Home Minister Rajnath Singh, then in the Opposition, had argued that 'The UPA government's foreign policy is so weak that it is not only large countries like China, but even smaller countries like Maldives giving India a hard time.'[16] In its overenthusiasm to control small neighbours, the BJP-led government has only made India's relations with them worse than ever before.

The argument here is not that India has absolutely no stake in what happens in Nepal, Sri Lanka, or the Maldives. Indeed, the domestic politics and foreign relations of its neighbours do, and should, concern India. But does that mean that we have the right to bully them to toe our line? More importantly, is it in our own national interest to push them around the way we often do? Let us recall Minister of State for Information and Broadcasting Rajyavardhan Rathore's ill-advised tweet referring to the Indian Army's operations inside Myanmar: 'Indian Army strikes into the heart of militants. #56inchRocks', and Myanmar's furious response: 'Every country must respect the other country's sovereignty.'[17]

The BJP-led government, in complete disregard of its own earlier promises and in a manner that could hurt India's national interest in the long run, has also been reducing the already limited amount of aid and loans to the neighbouring states. A recent Parliamentary Standing Committee report on External Affairs noted with alarm:

> There has been a sizeable reduction in aid and loans to countries in our immediate neighbourhood such as Maldives, Bhutan, Sri Lanka, Afghanistan and Bangladesh. The Committee contend that the quantum of aid to a country under this head is viewed as a reflection of India's diplomatic engagements with its immediate and extended neighbourhood.[18]

New Delhi has done precious little to counter either the major geopolitical reshaping of the region, or propose a collective regional future. The South Asian Association for Regional Cooperation (SAARC), which should have been the central plank of India's 'neighbourhood first' policy, is in the doldrums today. Having jettisoned the SAARC and unwilling to promote other regional initiatives, institutional or issue-based, India continues to prefer unilateralism towards its neighbours. The shortcomings of bilateralism in a world hungry for institutions and structures should be evident to us.

Finally, I would like to make a point about the China–Pakistan Economic Corridor (CPEC). While it is true that the CPEC will pass through Pakistan-controlled territory that India has claimed, we should find a via media with China on the issue rather than publicly dismiss the initiative. Given that the One Belt One Road (OBOR) is a futuristic mega-project, its benefits as well as cross-national and inter-continental linkages, all of which would eventually bypass India, will only become clearer in the years to come. To base our analysis on current cost-benefit calculations in terms of immediate returns and short-term sustainability is missing the big picture. Moreover, our ability to create regional infrastructural arrangements, excluding China and Pakistan, remains limited. In short, then, a few decades down the line, India could end up far more isolated: the logical conclusion of an inward-looking political class. The NDA-II government has been unable to take a long-term view of these issues.

Conclusion

The above discussion highlights several problems in India's foreign and security policy under the present government. First of all, there has been a tendency to project the country's foreign policy around the personality of Prime Minister Modi without drawing on India's past foreign policy practices and traditions. At the heart of the personality-driven foreign policy was a desire to achieve quick foreign policy results, which could be brought to bear on domestic political purposes. This was combined with a tendency to saffronise the country's foreign policy practices. While the first tendency continued throughout the tenure of the government, the second tended to dissipate towards later years, perhaps due to a realisation among the country's foreign policy managers that the cultural nationalists' agenda would deeply damage the pursuit of foreign policy goals.

The third issue has been an attempt to compete for space with China in the Southern Asian region, while at the same time trying to control political outcomes in those very countries where New Delhi was trying to hold on to its traditional influence. These competing objectives of New Delhi clashed with each other, thereby creating a situation where India ended up ceding more influence to China in the region, and simultaneously alienated its traditional friends in the regional capitals.

Finally, the NDA-II government was singularly unable to manage its relationships vis-à-vis the great powers. This was partly due to the haste that it seemed to be in while pursuing foreign policy goals, presumably for electoral purposes, and partly due to a clear lack of vision which, in turn, was a result of the monopolisation of foreign and security policy making in the PMO in New Delhi.

Notes and References

1. 'Modi Visit: UAE to Allot Land for First Temple in Abu Dhabi', *Hindustan Times*, 17 August 2015. Available at https://www.hindustantimes.com/india/modi-visit-uae-to-allot-land-for-first-temple-in-abu-dhabi/story-kvWukbBgfGWSNZkGbxwesL.html (accessed February 2019).

2. Krishnadas Rajagopal, 'Don't Want India to Become the Refugee Capital of the World, Govt. Tells SC', *The Hindu*, 31 January 2018. Available at https://www.thehindu.com/news/national/dont-want-india-to-become-the-refugee-capital-of-the-world-govt-to-sc/article22608096.ece (accessed February 2019).

3. BJP Election Manifesto 2014, 40. Available at https://www.bjp.org/images/pdf_2014/full_manifesto_english_07.04.2014.pdf (accessed February 2019).

4. India's projects in Iran's Chabahar port have been widely viewed in New Delhi as a crucial plank of its Iran–Afghanistan–Central Asia strategy. With US sanctions again tightening around Tehran, New Delhi has found it hard to continue with this project.

Note: This chapter uses some of the author's previously published op-eds in *The Hindu*, some of which are: 'Lessons from Doklam', *The Hindu*, 30 August 2017; 'Paint the United Colours of India', *The Hindu*, 12 July 2017; 'Lonely and Disinterested', *The Hindu*, 19 April 2017; 'Losing the Neighbourhood', *The Hindu*, 18 May 2016; 'Our National Security Mismanagement', *The Hindu*, 16 March 2016.

5. Shyam Saran, 'India's Nuclear Weapons Not for National Pride', *The Tribune*, 9 May 2013.

6. BJP Election Manifesto 2014, 38. Available at https://www.bjp.org/images/pdf_2014/full_manifesto_english_07.04.2014.pdf (accessed February 2019).

7. Anirudh Kanisetti, 'Parliamentary Committee Report on Doklam Can't See China's Game is Just Beginning', *The Print*, 10 October 2018. Available at https://theprint.in/opinion/parliamentary-committee-report-on-doklam-cant-see-chinas-game-is-just-beginning/128487/ (accessed February 2019).

8. The Quadrilateral Security Dialogue, or the Quad, is an informal consultative mechanism among the US, Australia, Japan, and India in the Indo-Pacific region.

9. BJP Election Manifesto 2014, 39. Available at https://www.bjp.org/images/pdf_2014/full_manifesto_english_07.04.2014.pdf (accessed February 2019).

10. 'UN Chief Calls for Lifting of Blockade on Indo-Nepal Border', *Hindustan Times*, 12 November 2015. Available at https://www.hindustantimes.com/world/un-chief-calls-for-lifting-of-blockade-on-indo-nepal-border/story-HLZss7xZyRLpccNmv4lnqI.html (accessed February 2019).

11. 'India has Nothing to do with Nepal Crisis, Say Government Sources', *NDTV*, 9 May 2016. Available at https://www.ndtv.com/india-news/india-has-nothing-to-do-with-nepal-crisis-say-government-sources-1404539 (accessed February 2019).

12. 'India Summons Home Envoy to Nepal as New Charter Sours Ties', *Reuters*, 22 September 2015. Available at https://in.reuters.com/article/nepal-india-constitution/india-summons-home-envoy-to-nepal-as-new-charter-sours-ties-idINKCN0RM0P920150922 (accessed February 2019).

13. 'India spy's role alleged in Sri Lankan President's poll defeat: Report', *Reuters*, 18 January 2015. Available at https://www.indiatoday.in/world/neighbours/story/indian-spys-role-alleged-in-sri-lankan-presidents-election-defeat-236217-2015-01-18 (accessed February 2019).

14. Suhasini Haidar, 'India Expresses Concern over "Manhandling" of Nasheed', *The Hindu*, 23 February 2015. Available at https://www.thehindu.com/news/national/india-expresses-concern-over-developments-in-maldives/article6925722.ece (accessed February 2019).

15. 'Government Will Not Tolerate Foreign Parties Interfering with the Country's Domestic Issues', *DNA*, 12 October 2015. Available at https://www.dnaindia.com/india/report-will-not-tolerate-foreign-interference-in-domestic-affairs-maldives-president-tells-sushma-swaraj-2133901 (accessed February 2019).

16. Happymon Jacob, 'Losing the Neighbourhood', *The Hindu*, 18 May 2016. Available at https://www.thehindu.com/opinion/lead/Losing-the-neighbourhood/article14324718.ece (accessed February 2019).

17. Suhasini Haidar and Josy Joseph, 'Army Chief Rawat going into detail on Myanmar surgical strike leave govt. red-faced', *The Hindu*, 3 December 2017. Available at https://www.thehindu.com/news/national/army-chief-rawats-remarks-on-myanmar-raid-leaves-centre-red-faced/article21255413.ece (accessed February 2019).

18. Press Release, Lok Sabha Secretariat, Parliament House, New Delhi, 'Report on Demands for Grants of the Ministry of External Affairs for the Year 2016–17', 2 May 2016. Available at http://164.100.47.193/lsscommittee/External%20Affairs/pr_files/Press%20Release-pdf.pdf (accessed February 2019).

fourteen

Damaging the Public Sphere
A Toxic Legacy of the NDA-II Regime

Srinivasan Ramani

On 1 April 2017, Pehlu Khan, a 55-year-old dairy farmer from Mewat, Haryana, was returning with his two sons, along with a dozen or so people, after buying cows and calves at Jaipur, having come this far as the prices for the cattle here were lower. He and his sons were mercilessly beaten up in Alwar by a mob numbering close to 200, who called themselves '*gau rakhsaks*' or 'cow vigilantes'.

Khan tried to show documents to prove that the cows had been bought for milk, but to no avail as the mob was in no mood to listen, and they beat him to death. In his dying declaration to the police, Khan named and identified six men as his attackers. Immediately after Khan's lynching to death, the Home Minister of Rajasthan, Gulab Chand, reportedly claimed that 'both parties'—those who were beaten up and the vigilantes, whom he termed 'cow-worshippers'—were guilty. The district's Police Superintendent also named Khan, his sons, and the other travellers with him as 'cow smugglers'.

Five months later, the Rajasthan police said that the six men named by Khan were not involved, and later, went on to file chargesheets against the other young men, Azmat and Rafeeq, who had been attacked along with Pehlu Khan, saying that they were 'cow smugglers'. One of those six men who were let out on bail later admitted to the lynching in an NDTV investigation. The trial is still on, but there seems to be no sign of justice for Khan and his sons.

Khan's killing was not an isolated incident. The lynching of Mohammad Akhlaq and his son in Dadri, Uttar Pradesh (UP) in September 2015 for allegedly consuming beef, the beating up of Dalits in Una, Gujarat in July 2016 for skinning dead cows, and the conflagration over cow carcasses in Bulandshahr, UP that resulted in the killing of a police inspector in December 2018 were three prominent incidents featuring the same aspect of vigilantism.

The data journalism website IndiaSpend tabulated 97 incidents of violence, which featured the deaths of 39 people and were related to cow vigilantism across India since May 2014—the month when the Bharatiya Janata Party (BJP) assumed power after winning the Lok Sabha Elections in an emphatic manner. UP, where the BJP and its allies won 73 of the 80 Lok Sabha seats, and 325 of the 403 Assembly constituencies in the 2017 State Elections, topped the list of states with 16 such incidents and nine deaths (Figure 14.1).

The spurt in such incidents is no surprise. These incidents and the increasing fervour with which vigilantism was used by those associated with the allied organisations of the Rashtriya Swayamsevak Sangh (RSS, or the Sangh Parivar), such as the Bajrang Dal, coincided with express steps taken by several BJP governments to expand upon cow slaughter laws. These had little to do with animal preservation and more with appeasing narrow communal impulses. When the BJP government led by Yogi Adityanath, a former leader of the militant Hindutva outfit Hindu Yuva Vahini, came to power in Uttar Pradesh, it launched a crackdown on 'illegal abattoirs', a thinly veiled manoeuvre to attack meat establishments largely owned by members of the Muslim community. In June 2017, the Gujarat government passed an amendment Bill in the State Assembly, without the presence of the entire Opposition, that made cow slaughter punishable with a life-term imprisonment.

In 2005, the Supreme Court had justified the total ban on cattle slaughter through an expansive interpretation of the Directive Principles of State Policy, and by relying on Article 48, 48A, and

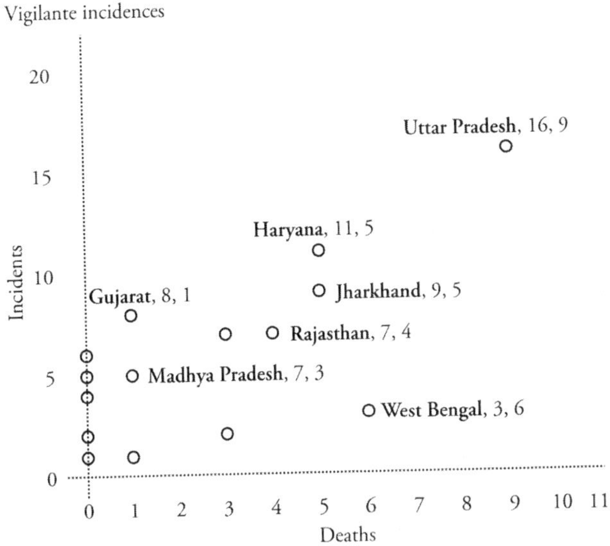

FIGURE 14.1: Deaths Due to Vigilantism Across India

Note: Reports of vigilantism came from 19 states, with UP registering the highest in terms of both deaths and incidents of violence. This scatterplot looks at incidents and deaths due to vigilante violence in all states (only the states with the highest incidents are marked).

Source: Base data available at https://docs.google.com/spreadsheets/d/1_mfkcYLFyW8eUNs6OrH_jIhP7ZWAbpABse-S2tY1zkE/edit#gid=0.

Article 51(A) of the Constitution that seeks to preserve breeds engaged in agriculture and animal husbandry, explicitly prohibiting the slaughter of cows and calves, and other milch and draught cattle, besides seeking to promote compassion towards animals. This has been utilised by state governments, largely led by the BJP, to come up with stringent laws on cow slaughter. The judgment overturned an earlier one in 1958, which limited the ban only to 'useful' cattle that are still engaged in agriculture and husbandry. This has led to the stigmatisation of communities, primarily dalits and Muslims, for their dietary habits, and many whose livelihoods are dependent upon cattle products. This has also emboldened vigilantes to attack them even if they acquire beef or cow hides through legal means (such as from dead cows) or are merely transporting cattle, as was the case in Alwar.

Despite a rise in such hate crimes, an eerie silence was maintained by Prime Minister Narendra Modi. Only once did he come up with a comprehensive response in July 2017, after protesters took to the streets in several cities asking for a halt to cow vigilantism. In a speech to mark the centenary of the Sabarmati Ashram, Modi said, '(K)illing people in the name of "*gau bhakti*" is not acceptable. This is not something Mahatma Gandhi would approve.'[1]

Considering that neither the NDA-II government nor other BJP-led state governments have done much to halt this menace of vigilantism, this was an empty rhetorical statement by a political leader who had made his bones for years with the RSS and was at the helm of the state of Gujarat during the horrific pogroms in 2002 that killed more than 1,000 people, according to official figures. Dozens of people, including high-profile ministers of the Gujarat government, have been convicted in riot cases and a few are still being heard. Modi has never apologised for his government's laxity during the riot incidents. His party has repeatedly used the riots and their aftermath to articulate a communal vision of Indian society, and it is no surprise that the cow vigilantism episodes have targeted people of the Muslim faith the most since 2014. A total of 118 of the 216 people who were injured or died in the violence due to cow vigilantism were Muslims (according to IndiaSpend). Dalits, with 23 people, came next in the number of people whose communities could be identified in the news reports tracked by IndiaSpend— which is also not a surprising revelation.

Changing the Polity

While commentators have argued that the NDA-II government came to power in 2014 on a plank of *vikas* (development) because the Congress-led United Progressive Alliance (UPA) government had been unable to deliver on this, progressives have been concerned about the rise of the Modi-led party to power. After all, the decisive win in 2014, especially in UP, was shaped by his trusted lieutenant Amit Shah, who was deputed to win the state for the BJP. One of the key reasons for the emphatic victory was the high margin of electoral support in western UP, where a communal conflagration in Muzaffarnagar and adjoining districts had helped to polarise voters according to religious identity. This had helped the BJP to garner significant support as voters in the area—many of whom had traditionally supported peasant leader-dominated parties such as the Rashtriya Lok Dal (RLD)—chose to register their mandate as 'Hindu voters' favouring the 'Hindutva' party. The BJP had aggressively used communal slogans and fielded candidates who were accused of engaging in rioting and spreading religious hatred in Muzaffarnagar.[2]

Besides the incidents of vigilantism and communal violence, the insistence on treating long-settled immigrants as infiltrators in Assam and the muddying of the National Register of Citizens (NRC) process into a communal issue, the vocal challenge to the special status of Jammu and Kashmir, the strident branding of any dissidence as 'anti-national', and the labelling of social workers and civil society activists as 'Urban Naxals'—all of these flow from the emphasis on rewriting the rules of engagement between the Indian State and the citizenry. We will look at each of these issues in further detail below.

The Communal Project

The fears of a communal project have been realised with the high incidents of 'cow vigilantism' and other cases that targeted members of the Muslim community in BJP-ruled states. People engaging in mob violence and lynching were further emboldened by a series of victories for the BJP in more than a few Assembly elections since 2014, especially the emphatic win in UP in 2017.

The Sangh Parivar has pursued its project of a *Hindu rashtra* (Hindu nation) by seeking to subvert the Indian Constitution by any means. The government has provided it the best conjuncture to push the envelope on this project. It has not yet succeeded in this because of India's inherent diversity and the irrelevance of the Sangh Parivar in several parts of India, especially the south. The Sangh's aim of building a Ram temple at the site of the demolished Babri Masjid in Ayodhya has been curtailed by judicial orders preventing this from happening so far. But the BJP's presence at the Centre, riding a wave of populism, has given it a key opportunity to further the Hindutva agenda in other ways.

As political scientist Suhas Palshikar[3] puts it:

> ... there is a very happy and convenient situation for the BJP, which is keen to construct its dominance politically and ideologically. *The party has ready-made apparatus of voluntary organisations, which supplies manpower and generates support for the regime, but, at the same time, also raises issues that the party may not formally want to be seen as raising.*

He further says:

> The formal electoral battle will be fought by the party .... *but the real battle is ideological and, for that, the network is all the more important to expand and complicate the agenda, and thus overcome the limits of the party.* (emphasis mine)

In other words, the Central government has used a disingenuous narrative with regard to 'mainstream elements versus the fringe' to conceal the intentions of the ruling party, while its allied organisations in the Sangh Parivar have carried forward the ideological battle of Hindutva. The persistence of cow vigilantism, despite a token disavowal from the Central government, can be explained by this. There is also anecdotal evidence to show that the footsoldiers of the Sangh Parivar and its militant organisations such as the Bajrang Dal include many youth who are unemployed and who have given in easily to the communal rhetoric. The unemployed tend to be swayed by ideas that demonise the 'other'—minorities among similar poorer sections—when they are mobilised by the Sangh.

The ideological battle waged by the Hindutva-*vadi* regime is to decisively change the character of the Indian State and its linkages with society, informed by the Constitution. The very idea of a composite Indian nationhood, built on a regime of rights enshrined in a liberal Constitution that guarantees equality and various freedoms, is under threat.

The Kashmir Quagmire

Having a regime that espouses hardline Hindutva at the Centre has had consequences for India's internal security and an impact on crucial issues such as the continuing public unrest in Jammu and Kashmir and the Maoist insurgency. In Jammu and Kashmir, the BJP formed a coalition government with the People's Democratic Party (PDP)—an unlikely arrangement, considering the wide disagreement over important issues such as Article 370 and the status of Jammu and Kashmir. The alliance was a marriage of convenience between disparate partners, and this affected governance in the state.

Unlike the previous Central government, the National Democratic Alliance (NDA) government refused to engage in a meaningful dialogue with various political actors in Kashmir and to take forward steps begun by the previous regimes, including the Vajpayee-led NDA government. This allowed the situation in the Valley to fester after the killing of a 23-year-old militant leader, Burhan Wani, of the terrorist organisation Hizbul Mujahideen, in a miltary operation. By then, anger against the presence of security forces and the denial of substantial freedoms, besides unresolved issues related to the Public Safety Act and the Armed Forces Special Powers Act had already peaked.

The eruption of stone pelting incidents and protests in 2016 and the responses by the Indian security forces to use crowd control measures such as pellet guns only added to public anger in the Valley. The hardline approach was clearly to satisfy the supporters of this regime in the rest of India, for whom Kashmir is a hotbed of terrorism and Islamism. This is an ill-informed and reductive understanding of the conflict in the Valley.

This approach was best exemplified in the way an innocent bystander and a Kashmiri voter, Farooq Dar, was (by many reported accounts) tied to an army jeep to deter protesters on voting day in Srinagar on 9 April 2017. The Army Chief, the Central government, and the ruling party chief went on to justify this action.

Meanwhile, this hardline approach has yielded few dividends in the Valley; students boycotted schools for a long period in 2016, and disaffection peaked with the lack of participation in the formal aspects of the Indian electoral democracy.

The Kashmir valley had erupted in periodic outbursts of protest against the Indian government and the armed forces on various occasions during the UPA-II government's tenure as well. However, over the last three decades, in spite of varying degrees of conflict, more people turned up in various rounds of elections to the local body, civic polls, and by-elections to the Assembly and parliamentary constituencies. This is best illustrated in the voting patterns in the conflict-driven Srinagar constituency (Figure 14.2).

Voting in the Kashmir valley in urban local body polls in October 2018, however, showed that less than 5 per cent of the voters turned out—a clear indication of the disaffection in the Valley with various aspects of governance and the absence of a political process to ease the conflict.

Incidents of militant attacks and violence have also peaked following a long lull in the early 2010s and after the BJP government took power (Figure 14.3).

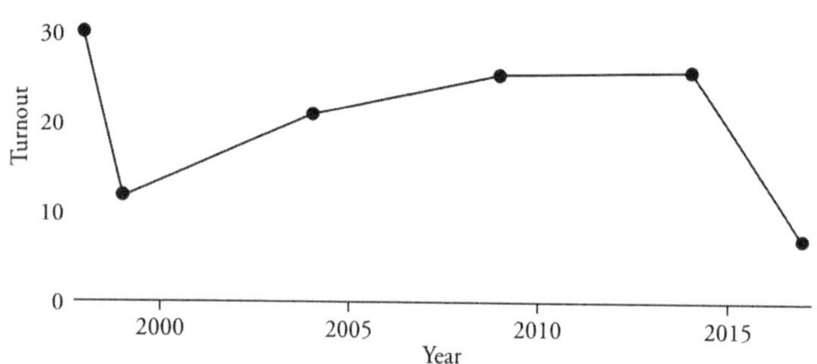

FIGURE 14.2: When Voters Did Not Come Out: Srinagar's Voter Turnout is its Lowest Ever in Lok Sabha Polls

Source: Election Commission of India.

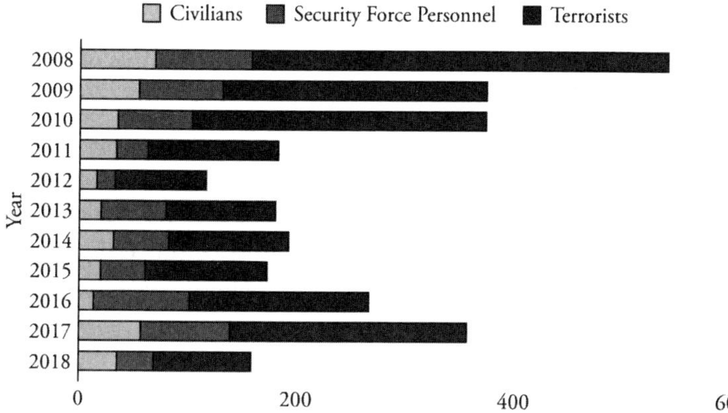

FIGURE 14.3: Deaths Due to Violence in the Valley

Source: South Asia Terrorism Portal.

The withdrawal of support by the BJP to the PDP in June 2018 led to the imposition of Governor's rule in the state and the eventual dissolution of the Assembly in November 2018, despite the possibility of the formation of a government with the rivals PDP, the National Conference, and the Congress together in coalition.

The current situation in Kashmir is akin to a crisis, reminding one of the days leading up to the full-blown military conflict in the 1990s; and it signifies substantial regression due to the approach of the Central government.

Muddying the Waters in Assam

The BJP and the Sangh Parivar's emphasis on rewriting the engagement between the Indian State and the citizenry by redefining the idea of a citizen, where people of other faiths and beliefs are reduced to second-class citizens, has been widely criticised.

But this has not stopped the BJP from trying to communalise other controversial issues, for example, the as yet unresolved issue of immigration in Assam. The Assam Peace Accord of 1985 had mandated the need to 'detect and deport' illegal Bangladeshi immigrants, following a Supreme Court order to create the National

Register of Citizens (NRC), the draft of which left out over 40 lakh of 3.29 crore applicants. This was a huge number of people on whom the onus was placed to prove their citizenship as on 24 March 1971 using various identity records. The NRC process is problematic and complicated, but it has received broad public approval and political consensus in the state. Even as it was stressed that this list was not final and applicants would be given more time to prove the origins of their identity, the BJP termed all those whose names were not registered as 'infiltrators'.

This was compounded by the BJP putting forth a Citizenship (Amendment) Bill that communalised the idea of Indian citizenship by seeking to label only Muslim immigrants as 'illegal immigrants' for whom the relevant rules under the Foreigners Act, 1946 would apply. Ostensibly drafted to provide a path to citizenship to people of minority religions being persecuted in neighbouring Muslim-dominant countries, the Bill conflated the idea of migrants—people who shift locations voluntarily—with that of refugees, who are forced to do so under stress.

This communal emphasis on migration clearly discriminates against other refugees such as the Rohingyas—the target of persecution by the Myanmar State and those fleeing the violence in Rakhine state in Myanmar—who have been treated as hostile infiltrators by the Indian government. This is in sharp contrast to the BJP's treatment of non-Muslim migrants from neighbouring countries, such as Hindus from Pakistan and Bangladesh.

Clearly, the BJP government and its ideological fellow travellers have been signalling the idea that Indian citizenship is limited to select faiths and communities, with others not being treated on par. This explains its policies and pronouncements in Kashmir and Assam and its controversial Bills on migration.

Brooking No Dissidence

Another front of the ideological battle led by the Hindu nationalist forces has been its branding of dissent and critique of government policies to be akin to a critique of the Indian nation and, therefore, 'anti-national'. This rhetoric about any form of dissent has been amplified by the allied organisations of the Sangh Parivar in various civil society forums, in the loud television media, and by a legion of activists on social media who use troll accounts to castigate members of the media, opposition leaders, and other activists opposed to the regime.

This use of Hindu nationalist rhetoric through the pliant news media in both the English and vernacular channels has contributed to a diminished public discourse that seeks to ignore several critical issues of public interest, such as farmer distress, economic problems, tribal discontent, among others. Civil society activists who have taken up such causes have been quickly branded as anti-nationals, while the more radical among them have been arrested, based on questionable and controversial evidence.

This has been most profoundly done in university campuses against student activists—seen in the sedition cases against student leaders in Jawaharlal Nehru University and in the measures taken to expel those seen as radical activists in Hyderabad Central University, a move that led to the suicide of dalit activist Rohith Vemula in 2016. Soon, the target was civil society activists (espousing dalit and other human rights causes) from Chhattisgarh and Maharashtra, most of whom turned up at an otherwise peaceful protest event in Bhima Koregaon in January 2018. These protesters were subject to violent attacks by Hindu Right-wing groups, but the investigation of the cases placed the onus on the protesters for the violence and alleged links with Maoists. The result was a crackdown on human rights activists across various states and their arrests and detention using draconian anti-terrorism laws. The cases continue to be heard in various courts.

Meanwhile, extremist Hindu fundamentalist groups have targeted progressives and rationalists through assassinations, such as those of leftist leader Govind Pansare in Maharashtra in February 2015, litterateur M. M. Kalburgi in August 2015, and Kannada journalist Gauri Lankesh in September 2017. In all these cases, besides the assassination of anti-superstition activist and rationalist Narendra Dabholkar in 2013, credible evidence has emerged about the involvement of the Hindu radical group Sanatan Sanstha and its allied organisations.

These individuals sought to take on the Hindu Right-wing project by mobilising people through campaigns and literary work (largely in the vernacular languages) emphasising rationalism, a scientific temper, and secularism. This made them irritants to the Hindu nationalist project and a target of organisations such as the Sanstha. The RSS and its affiliates have claimed distance from these outfits, stating that they have no relations with them. But these outfits have been emboldened by a Hindu nationalist government at the Centre and have been beneficiaries of a silent patronage by some state governments.[4]

In sum and in substance, the presence of a Hindu Right-wing government at the Centre has justified fears of a regime that will lead an assault on the values of secularism, and on the equality of citizenship enshrined in the Constitution. How does the government fare on its promise of development that catapulted it to power in 2014?

A Quantum Leap in the Wrong Direction

The success of the BJP's populist platform needs to be understood to explain its resonance, which has enabled it to become the single largest political force in India by displacing the Indian National Congress from that position. The BJP pitchforked itself into power by adopting a right-of-centre political positioning that appealed to various sections in various ways. Palshikar (2015)[5] argues:

> ... the BJP became a party of different meanings for different sections. To its core constituency, it continued to be a party of Hindutva; to the OBCs [Other Backward Classes], it represented a vehicle of political power, a vehicle articulating and absorbing their democratic upsurge; for power seekers, it was a convenient platform offering the possibility of tactical use of the Hindutva weapon when required; for devout Hindus,

it represented the religious assertion of the Hindu religion; to the new and upwardly-mobile lower-middle sections, the party represented new possibilities of economic benefit.

Indeed, Modi's campaign slogan, '*sabka saath, sabka vikas*' ('collective effort, inclusive growth'), was tailored to expand his party's constituency beyond the core Hindutva supporters. But, as argued extensively in the previous chapters, when the *vikas purush* (the man of development) could not deliver on development, the Hindutva champion came to the fore. In fact, the BJP's diminished returns in vote shares in by-elections held in 2017 and 2018, as compared to the steady increase in the previous three years, tell a story of the political fallout of the sluggishness in the economy (Table 14.1). By late 2018, the BJP had also lost to the Congress in the Assembly elections in three states in the Hindi heartland—Madhya Pradesh, Rajasthan, and Chhattisgarh. In these three states, the party had won 62 of the 65 Lok Sabha constituencies in the 2014 elections.

TABLE 14.1: Data for Parliamentary By-elections Held in Two Time Periods: 2014–16 and 2017–18

Period	Total Seats	Won	Lost	Retained	Opposition Retained	Net Loss/ Gain	BJP Voteshare (VS)	Original BJP VS	Swing
2014–16	8	2	6	2	5	−1	31.8%	30.9%	0.9%
2017–18	14	2	12	2	5	−8	36.6%	41.5%	−4.8%

Source: Election Commission of India.

In the campaigns during the run-up to these elections, the BJP went back to raising Hindutva slogans more strongly and the old slogans about development were lost in the communal rhetoric. Hardline Hindutva leader Yogi Adityanath was a star campaigner for the party, using his polarising rhetoric to little avail in the polls. After exhausting slogans about growth and sensing that the government had little by way of claiming success in bringing about the development it had promised, the BJP has sought to return to its roots and its central plank—Hindutva. The diminished returns despite the campaign using Hindu Right-wing rhetoric in the Hindi heartland suggests that the electorate is privileging economic concerns over cultural tropes as the government heads towards the Lok Sabha polls in 2019.

This is in sharp contrast to 2014, when, riding a wave of anti-incumbency, the highly personalised campaign of the party, centred around Narendra Modi, helped to create a powerful prime minister unencumbered by coalitional pressures—a bugbear often associated with the previous governments in India.

A BJP government at the Centre spelt danger to the secular fabric of the country, and the hard-earned successes in creating a liberal constitutional order that brought unity in diversity in India. There were also concerns about how the BJP's politics would play itself out in addressing trickier issues related to India's nationhood—the Kashmir conflict and the long-pending ethnic issues in border states such as Assam. Fears were also expressed for the civic spaces in India's public sphere—in universities, in civil services, and the army—due to the BJP and the RSS' emphasis on narrow nationalism.

Unfortunately, these fears have been realised. Further, people belonging to the minority community have come under threat in various parts of the country; dissidents among India's civil society who have questioned the Indian State's failings have been branded as seditious; fragile equations in border states have been strained as Kashmir has been on the boil, and the issue of citizenship in Assam has taken a communal turn. These are among some of the regressive changes that have been witnessed.

Issues that dominate public discourse today are cow vigilantism, communalism, and religious mobilisation, thus diverting attention away from issues such as unemployment, climate change, renewable energy, etc., thereby vitiating the public sphere.

It is this vitiation of the public sphere and the inability to take forward an agenda of sustainable development during the past five years of the NDA-II government's tenure that has perhaps led economist and philosopher Amartya Sen to argue that India has taken a 'quantum leap in the wrong direction'.

Notes and References

1. Twitter Account, Office of the Prime Minister of India, 29 June 2017. Available at https://twitter.com/PMOIndia/status/880330845495500800 (accessed February 2019).

2. 'Political Parties in Uttar Pradesh field five Muzaffarnagar riots accused in Lok Sabha polls', *NDTV*, 27 March 2014. Available at https://www.ndtv.com/elections-news/political-parties-in-uttar-pradesh-field-five-muzaffarnagar-riots-accused-in-lok-sabha-polls-555318 (accessed February 2019).

3. Suhas Palshikar, 'What makes BJP Really Different', *Economic and Political Weekly* 52 (19), 2017, 12–13.

4. Devika Sequiera, 'How Political Patronage Has Kept the Sanatan Sanstha Afloat in Goa', *The Wire,* 14 September 2017. Available at https://thewire.in/politics/political-patronage-kept-sanatan-sanstha-afloat-goa (accessed February 2019).

5. Suhas Palshikar, 'The BJP and Hindu Nationalism: Centrist Politics and Majoritarian Impulses', *South Asia: Journal of South Asian Studies* 38 (4), 2015, 724.

Notes on the Contributors

ISHAN ANAND is an Assistant Professor (visiting) at the School of Liberal Studies, Ambedkar University Delhi.

ROHIT AZAD teaches at Jawaharlal Nehru University, New Delhi.

ARINDAM BANERJEE is an Associate Professor at the School of Liberal Studies, Ambedkar University Delhi.

KIRAN BHATTY is Senior Fellow at Centre for Policy Research (CPR), Delhi.

PRASENJIT BOSE is an economist and activist.

SHOUVIK CHAKRABORTY is a researcher at the Political Economy Research Institute, UMASS, Amherst.

SUBHANIL CHOWDHURY is an Assistant Professor at the Institute of Development Studies, Kolkata, and editor of the Bengali journal *Arekrakam*.

ZICO DASGUPTA is a post-doctoral consultant at Azim Premji University.

HAPPYMON JACOB is Associate Professor of Disarmament Studies at Jawaharlal Nehru University, New Delhi.

AYESHA KIDWAI is a Professor of Linguistics at Jawaharlal Nehru University, New Delhi.

ROSHAN KISHORE is the Data and Political Economy Editor and an author at *Hindustan Times*.

Sona Mitra is Principal Economist, Initiative for What Works to Advance Women and Girls in the Economy (IWWAGE), at IFMR-LEAD.

Indranil Mukhopadhyay is Associate Professor at the School of Government and Public Policy, OP Jindal University, Haryana, and is with the Jan Swasthya Abhiyan, Delhi.

Srinivasan Ramani is Associate Editor, *The Hindu*, where he contributes to opinion, data, and value adds sections.

Dipa Sinha teaches at the School of Liberal Studies, Ambedkar University Delhi.

Anmol Somanchi is an independent researcher and is currently associated with IDinsight in Delhi.

Amit Thorat teaches economics at Jawaharlal Nehru University, New Delhi.